P9-AQJ-679

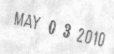

MAY 0 3 2010

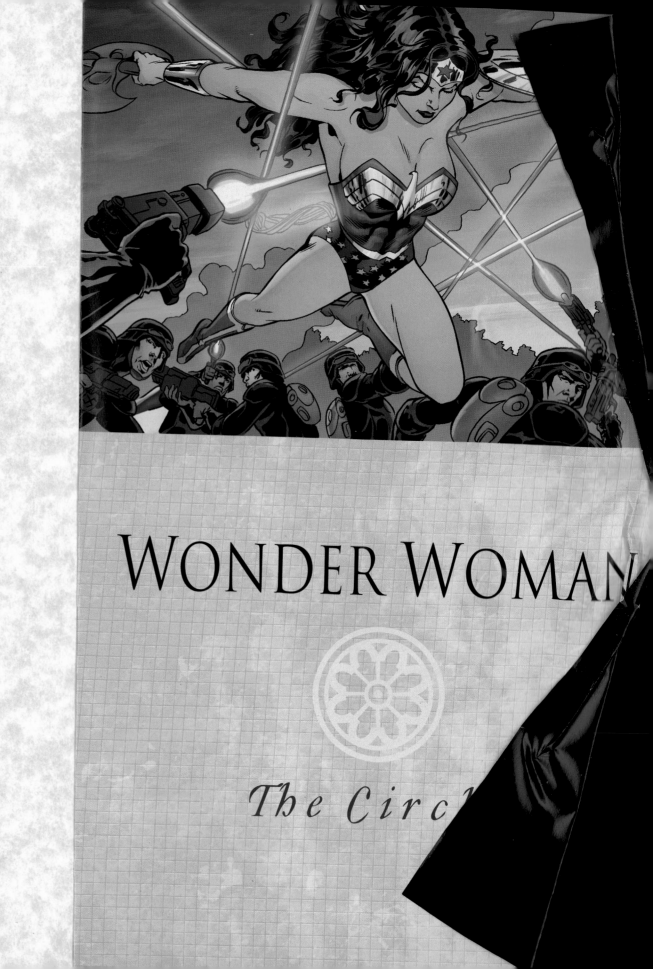

WONDER WOMAN

The Circle

WONDER WOMAN

The Circle

Gail Simone
Writer

Terry Dodson
Bernard Chang
Ron Randall
Pencillers

Rachel Dodson
Bernard Chang
Ron Randall
Jon Holdridge
Inkers

Alex Sinclair
I.L.L.
Lee Loughridge
Pete Pantazis
Colorists

Rob Leigh
Travis Lanham
John J. Hill
Letterers

Wonder Woman created by William Moulton Marston

Dan DiDio
Senior VP-Executive Editor

Matt Idelson
Editor-original series

Nachie Castro
Associate Editor-original series

Anton Kawasaki
Editor-collected edition

Robbin Brosterman
Senior Art Director

Paul Levitz
President & Publisher

Georg Brewer
VP-Design & DC Direct Creative

Richard Bruning
Senior VP-Creative Director

Patrick Caldon
Executive VP-Finance & Operations

Chris Caramalis
VP-Finance

John Cunningham
VP-Marketing

Terri Cunningham
VP-Managing Editor

Alison Gill
VP-Manufacturing

David Hyde
VP-Publicity

Hank Kanalz
VP-General Manager, WildStorm

Jim Lee
Editorial Director-WildStorm

Paula Lowitt
Senior VP-Business & Legal Affairs

MaryEllen McLaughlin
VP-Advertising & Custom Publishing

John Nee
Senior VP-Business Development

Gregory Noveck
Senior VP-Creative Affairs

Sue Pohja
VP-Book Trade Sales

Steve Rotterdam
Senior VP-Sales & Marketing

Cheryl Rubin
Senior VP-Brand Management

Jeff Trojan
VP-Business Development, DC Direct

Bob Wayne
VP-Sales

Cover by Terry Dodson &
Rachel Dodson with Alex Sinclair
Logo design by Nancy Ogami

WONDER WOMAN: THE CIRCLE

DC Comics, 1700 Broadway, New York,
NY 10019
A Warner Bros. Entertainment Company
Printed in USA. First Printing.

HC ISBN: 978-1-4012-1932-1
SC ISBN: 978-1-4012-2011-2

Mercedes Lackey

i n t r o d u c t i o n

THE (RE)MAKING OF A GODDESS

I have a confession to make. For most of my life I've found Wonder Woman kind of an embarrassment.

I should have liked her. The comics writers certainly intended for her to be the girls' version of Superman. Here she was, Amazon Princess, strong, powerful and independent, the very icon of Woman, right?

Yeah, right. The very icon of Woman, who was relegated to being secretary of the JLA at its founding. Who ran around simpering after Steve Trevor like Betty after Archie...

Gah.

Now, don't get me wrong. The other Big Icons could be just as bad, if not worse, as the SuperDickery website abundantly demonstrates. But there were lots of superheroes; super women were kind of scarce on the ground, and that made the Amazon Princess's lapses and lacks all the more obvious.

Nevertheless, I kept trying to like her. And there were some great moments, and good writing in Diana's life. But not enough of them to grab and hold me.

Until now.

Because what you hold in your hands is the essence of everything I always wanted Wonder Woman to be, and more. The Amazon Princess. Warrior, Diplomat, Protector, Healer.

And Goddess.

Writers and storytellers have had a love/hate relationship with the Amazons ever since misogynistic Greeks created them out of hearsay stories that were probably about Scythian and Sarmatian female warriors as a lesson to their own females on the perils of getting Uppity. In the case of the Greeks, it was hate, because a Woman's Place in most of Grecian society was locked behind walls for the purposes of procreation. And for the Greeks, it was also love, because after denying their wives and daughters freedom and education, the learned men of Greece wondered why they were so dull and imagined something wilder, and imbued it with everything they wanted and feared at the same time.

For modern writers the problem has been much the same. On the one hand, the Powerful Woman is powerfully attractive. On the other hand she is scary. And writers have, as a consequence, tended to do things to weaken Diana — from removing her supernatural powers altogether, to making her into a sidekick to a superhero, to relegating her to the job of secretary. Not all writers have done this, of course, but enough have that it's discouraged those of us who had all but given up on the character.

The result has been an incoherent mishmash of backstory that anyone coming into the writer's seat would probably be tempted to throw up her hands and decide to just ignore whole chunks of it.

Not Gail Simone.

Now, if you aren't familiar with these issues, I am going to try not to throw any spoilers your way. But as I read through them, I was filled with admiration. Here is Wonder Woman, coherent. Wonder Woman as literally *everything* she could be. Wonder Woman as the kind of Warrior that Sun Tzu would recognize as the supreme example of the kind.

Wonder Woman reimagined as Goddess.

Even the Dark Years when Diana became merely Diana Prince, martial artist, have a coherent explanation, for a Goddess can choose to limit herself, to lock herself into the merely human form, in order to try to comprehend the human condition from the inside.

Here is the Supreme Warrior, who is fully aware that war is the failure of diplomacy, and that the goal of making war is to *end conflict*. Here is the Warrior who understands strategy at the bone-deep level, who chooses her ground, who prepares the field, who even when fighting within severe limitations knows how to use every advantage she has. Here is the Warrior who knows that negotiation and compromise are tools fit for a warrior's use, and who never loses sight of the goal of *ending the conflict*.

Here is the Goddess who never loses compassion, not even for an enemy, and who can see all sides to a question.

I believe it is Gail herself who said, "When you need to stop an asteroid, you get Superman. When you need to solve a mystery, you call in Batman. But when you need to end a war, you get Wonder Woman."

Make no mistake about it: as a novelist, I am in awe of what Gail has done here. Not only in taking all of that backstory and integrating it logically and methodically, but in going where no writer has dared to go before, to the moment of Diana's creation. It's a brilliant solution to the very dubious problem of did-Hippolyta-break-her-vows-and-do-it-with-a-man-or-not. No dancing around avoiding it; Gail has gone right to the target and hit a bull's-eye.

I am also in awe of *how* Gail is portraying Diana-as-Goddess. There is no more difficult proposition for a human writer than to show the un-human viewpoint, especially one with the sheer level of power that Diana has. I don't think that even the writers of Superman have had to achieve quite that level of alien-ness; Supes at heart has probably always thought of himself as human, because he was raised as human. That's the root of his essential loneliness; he *thinks* of himself as one of us, and yet, he never can be.

But Diana was raised as a Goddess. Her peers and allies — and she treats them as such — are the gods of the Greco-Roman and other pantheons. She is utterly, completely, alien. No matter that she has *tried* to limit herself to human form to understand humanity better; at heart, she will always be Other.

Far too many times in comics, gods have been portrayed as being, well…silly. Inflated humans, not unlike a Macy's Thanksgiving Day balloon. In some cases that's justified mythologically; some gods really are just exaggerated humans. But all too often, all it is, unfortunately, is the writer's lack of imagination. Gail Simone has given us a true Goddess; there is no lack of imagination here.

It's not just in concept that Gail has succeeded. That "more than human" aspect is incredibly difficult for a writer to get across. Gail does it brilliantly. From little thought-balloon asides, to the nuance of gesture and phrase, I never once forgot that this charismatic, enchanting creature was not, and never had been, human.

Even the "magic lasso," widely lampooned in comedy as "the lamest super-power ever" becomes one of the most frightening super-powers ever in Gail's hands. The lasso not only compels its captive to tell the truth; in Diana's hands, as the Avatar of Truth herself, it compels its captive to *see and confront the truth*. All the truth. Unvarnished and unhidden. Which of us, if forced to confront all the truth about ourselves, could stand up to that? Even the worst villains find themselves reduced to weeping incoherence. And then — the Compassionate Goddess forgives them.

Secondary characters get first rate treatment here too. No more Steve-cipher-Trevor, the "we have to give Diana a boyfriend because girls gotta have a boyfriend." Nemesis is nuanced, complex, and in a surprisingly few scenes, is convincing as someone in whom Diana sees a Truth that he cannot yet see for himself — truly someone worthy of her attention and affection.

And on behalf of every single overweight girl who has ever lived, I must personally thank Gail for turning Etta Candy from the bon-bon-devouring, fat, silly secretary into a tough, intelligent, funny, savvy warrior in her own right, from Watsonian comic relief to Sherlockian sleuth. I actually laughed to see Etta get right in Steel's face with her deductions of his substantial substance abuse — and I cried when she spoke to the Ichor's heart with truly human warmth and a compassion she had to have learned from being with Diana.

Now, don't let all this philosophizing put you off. There is plenty of action in here, from good old-fashioned Nazi Punching (and who *doesn't* like to punch Nazis?) to interplanetary warfare. There's a good leavening of humor too; Diana is too much of a Goddess to take herself too seriously, and Gail is too good a writer to let the chance for a great one-liner slip past.

In short, this is it, the Real Deal, the Good Stuff. And finally after all these years of disappointment, I can say it.

I *love* Wonder Woman.

Mercedes Lackey
Oklahoma, June 2008

Mercedes Lackey is a science fiction and fantasy author with over 80 books in print, either solo or in collaboration. She is the author of the long-running Heralds of Valdemar series (DAW Books), with James Mallory, the New York Times best-selling Obsidian Mountain trilogy (TOR/St Martin), the romantic fantasy Five Hundred Kingdoms series (Harlequin/Luna), and many more, from Edwardian to urban fantasy. She and her cowriter husband, artist Larry Dixon, share their home in Oklahoma with a dozen parrots. It is never quiet.

WONDER WOMAN #14 Cover by Terry & Rachel Dodson with Alex Sinclair

Art this issue by Terry Dodson & Rachel Dodson

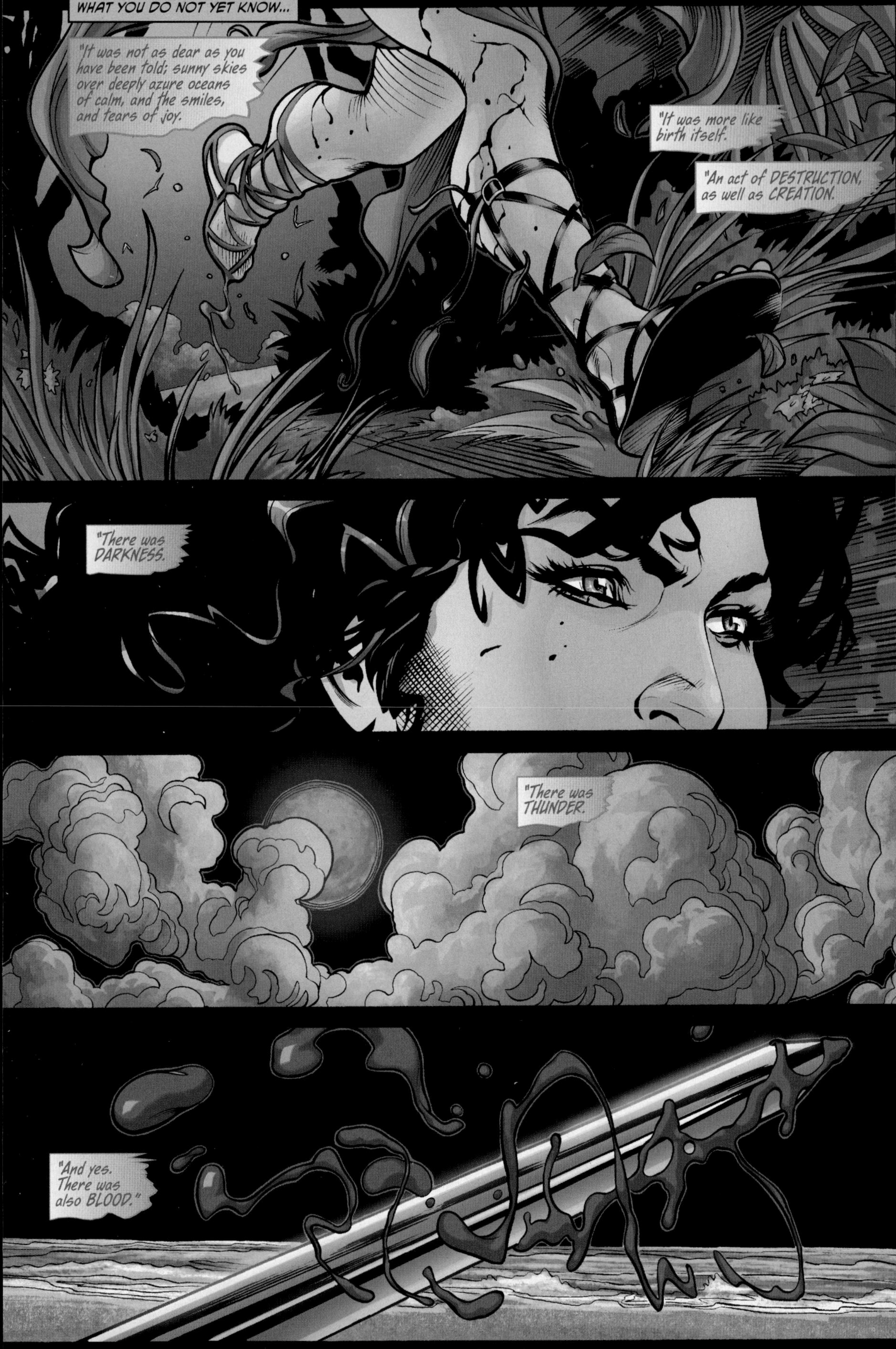
WHAT YOU DO NOT YET KNOW...
"It was not as dear as you have been told; sunny skies over deeply azure oceans of calm, and the smiles, and tears of joy.
"It was more like birth itself.
"An act of DESTRUCTION, as well as CREATION.
"There was DARKNESS.
"There was THUNDER.
"And yes. There was also BLOOD."

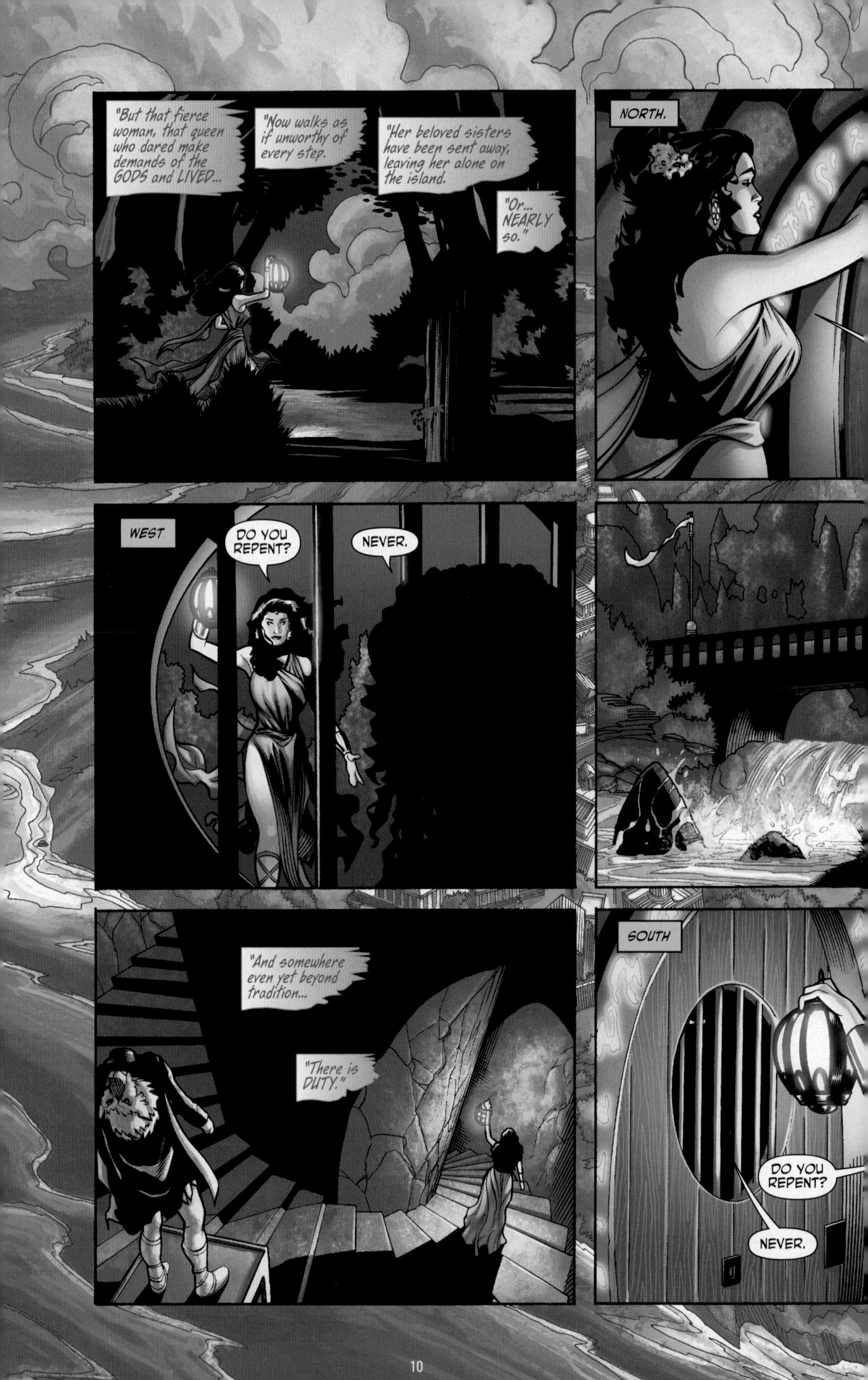

"But that fierce woman, that queen who dared make demands of the GODS and LIVED...
"Now walks as if unworthy of every step.
"Her beloved sisters have been sent away, leaving her alone on the island.
"Or... NEARLY so."
NORTH.
WEST
DO YOU REPENT?
NEVER.
"And somewhere even yet beyond tradition...
"There is DUTY."
SOUTH
DO YOU REPENT?
NEVER.

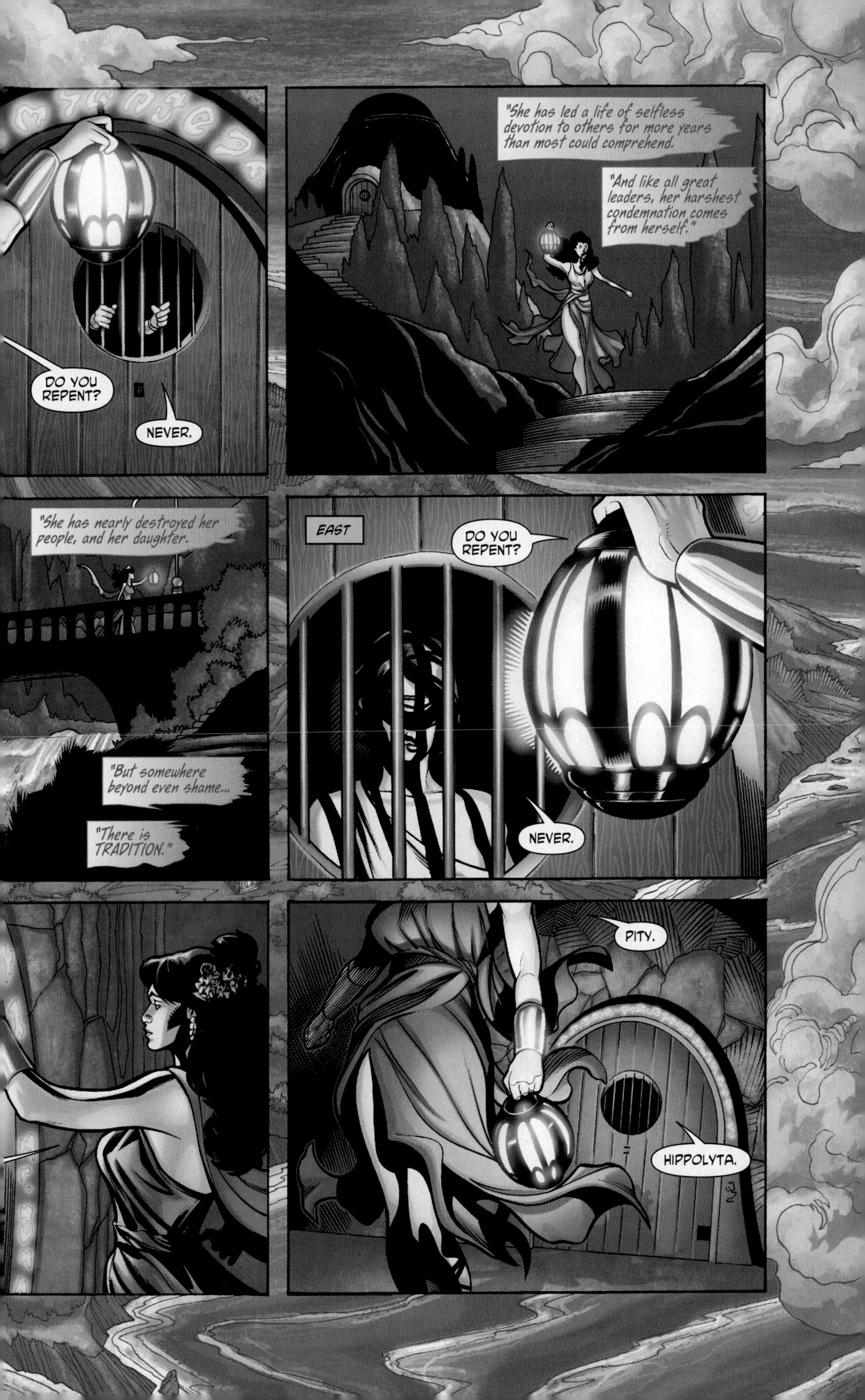

DO YOU REPENT?
NEVER.
"She has led a life of selfless devotion to others for more years than most could comprehend.
"And like all great leaders, her harshest condemnation comes from herself."
"She has nearly destroyed her people, and her daughter.
"But somewhere beyond even shame...
"There is TRADITION."
EAST
DO YOU REPENT?
NEVER.
PITY.
HIPPOLYTA.

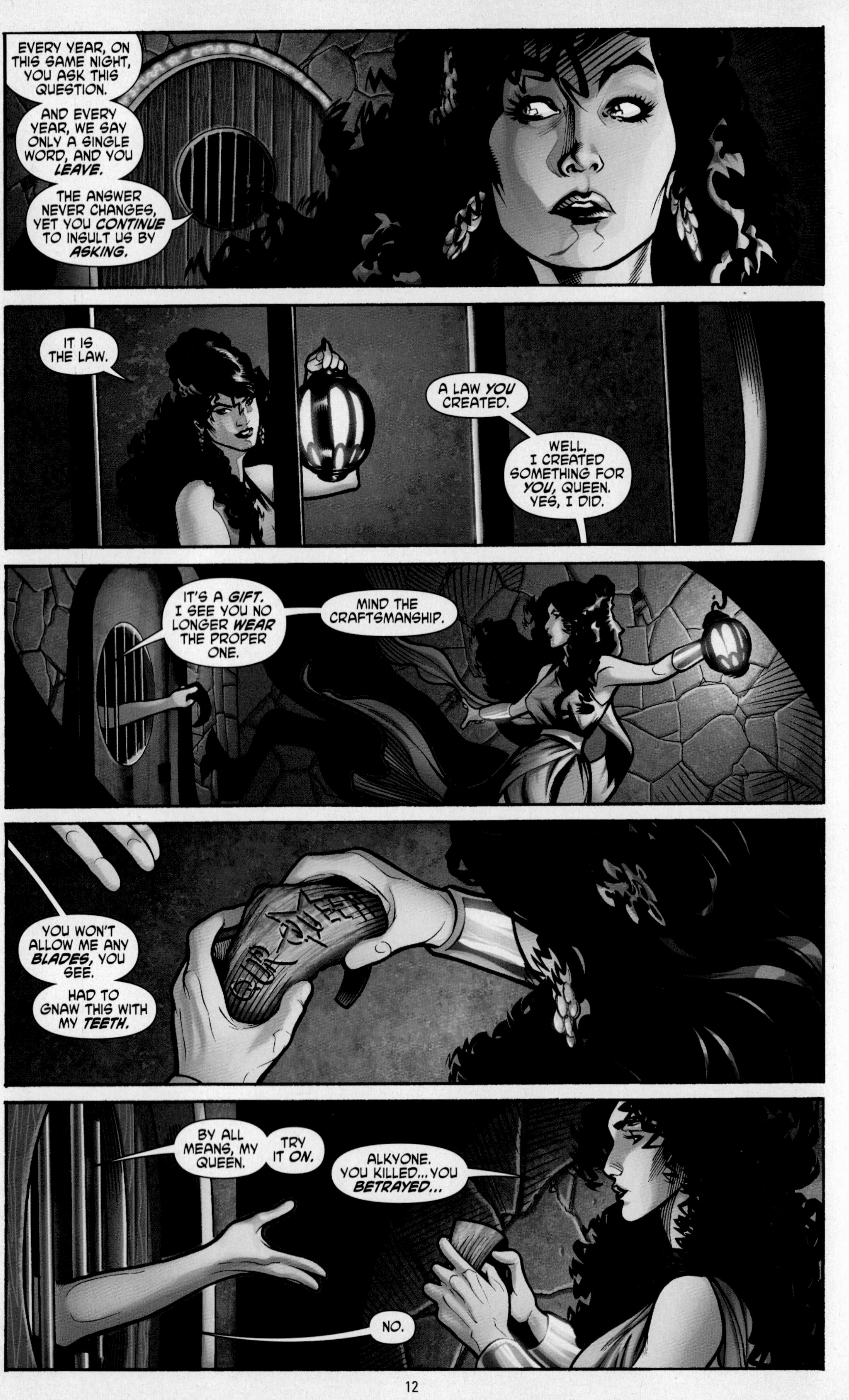
EVERY YEAR, ON THIS SAME NIGHT, YOU ASK THIS QUESTION.
AND EVERY YEAR, WE SAY ONLY A SINGLE WORD, AND YOU *LEAVE.*
THE ANSWER NEVER CHANGES, YET YOU *CONTINUE* TO INSULT US BY *ASKING.*
IT IS THE LAW.
A LAW *YOU* CREATED.
WELL, I CREATED SOMETHING FOR *YOU,* QUEEN. YES, I DID.
IT'S A *GIFT.* I SEE YOU NO LONGER *WEAR* THE PROPER ONE.
MIND THE CRAFTSMANSHIP.
YOU WON'T ALLOW ME ANY *BLADES,* YOU SEE.
HAD TO GNAW THIS WITH MY *TEETH.*
BY ALL MEANS, MY QUEEN.
TRY IT *ON.*
ALKYONE. YOU KILLED... YOU *BETRAYED...*
NO.

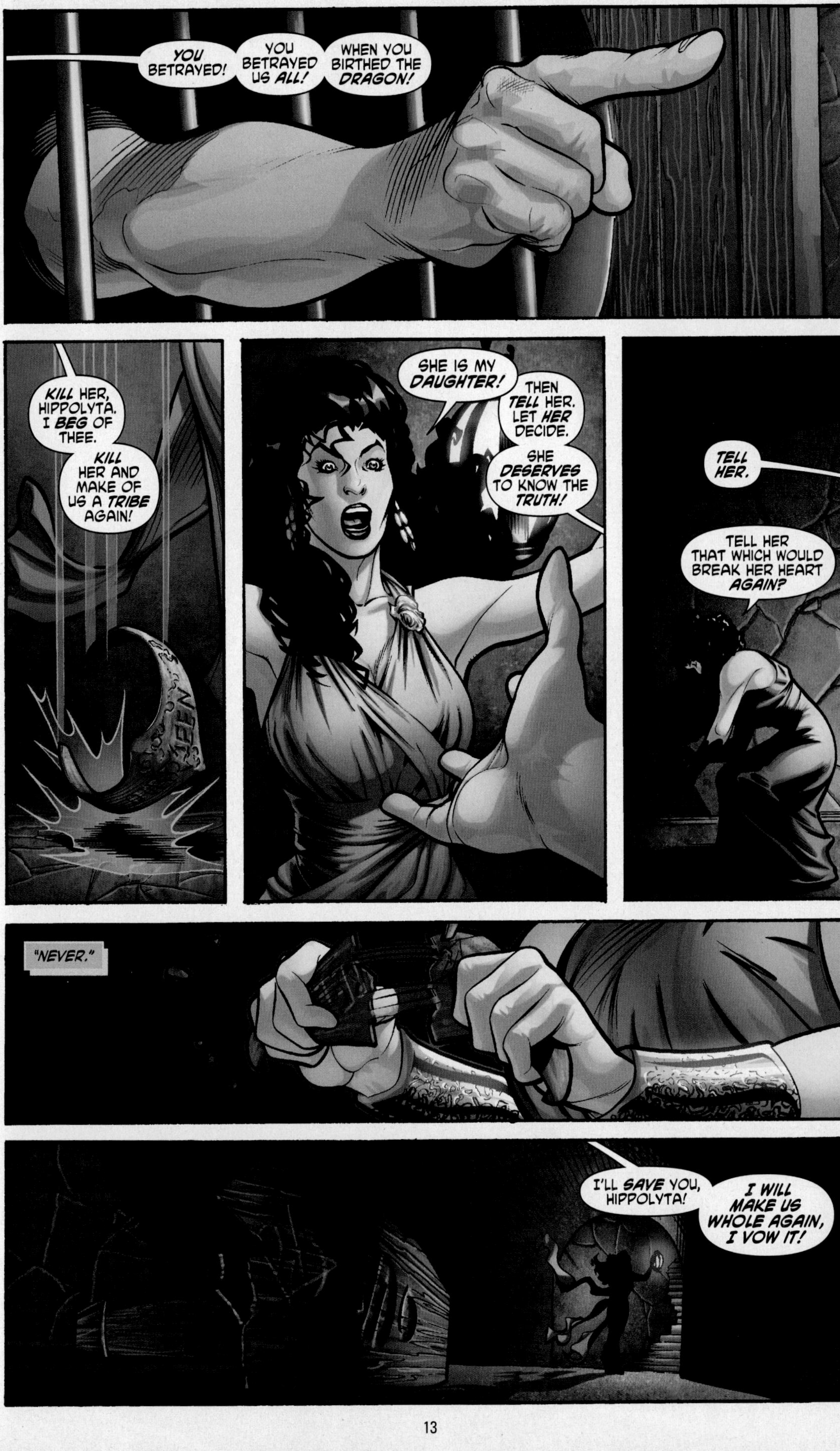

YOU BETRAYED!
YOU BETRAYED US ALL!
WHEN YOU BIRTHED THE DRAGON!
KILL HER, HIPPOLYTA. I BEG OF THEE.
KILL HER AND MAKE OF US A TRIBE AGAIN!
SHE IS MY DAUGHTER!
THEN TELL HER. LET HER DECIDE.
SHE DESERVES TO KNOW THE TRUTH!
TELL HER.
TELL HER THAT WHICH WOULD BREAK HER HEART AGAIN?
"NEVER."
I'LL SAVE YOU, HIPPOLYTA!
I WILL MAKE US WHOLE AGAIN, I VOW IT!

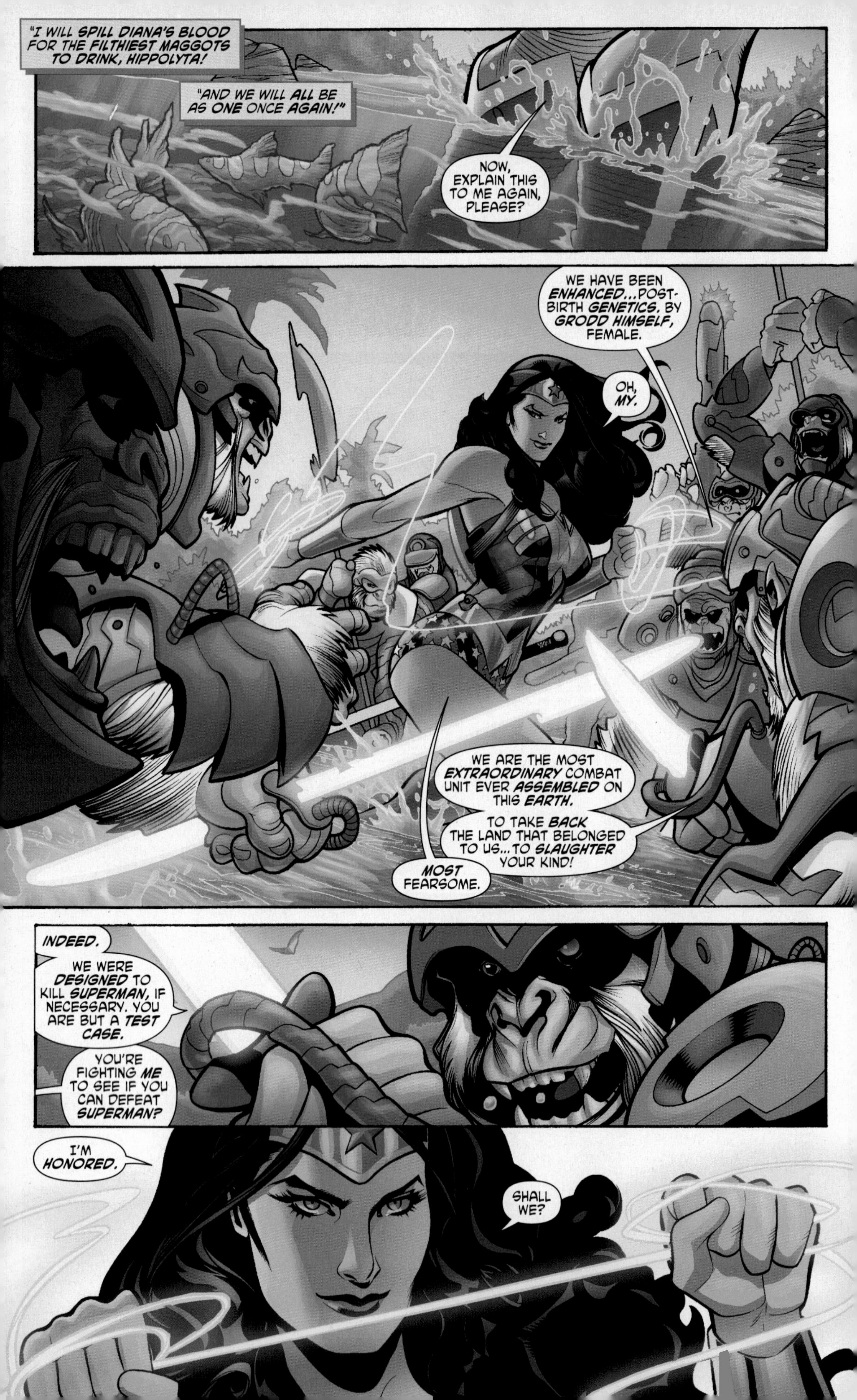
"I WILL SPILL DIANA'S BLOOD FOR THE FILTHIEST MAGGOTS TO DRINK, HIPPOLYTA!
"AND WE WILL ALL BE AS ONE ONCE AGAIN!"
NOW, EXPLAIN THIS TO ME AGAIN, PLEASE?
WE HAVE BEEN ENHANCED...POST-BIRTH GENETICS. BY GRODD HIMSELF, FEMALE.
OH, MY.
WE ARE THE MOST EXTRAORDINARY COMBAT UNIT EVER ASSEMBLED ON THIS EARTH.
TO TAKE BACK THE LAND THAT BELONGED TO US...TO SLAUGHTER YOUR KIND!
MOST FEARSOME.
INDEED.
WE WERE DESIGNED TO KILL SUPERMAN, IF NECESSARY. YOU ARE BUT A TEST CASE.
YOU'RE FIGHTING ME TO SEE IF YOU CAN DEFEAT SUPERMAN?
I'M HONORED.
SHALL WE?

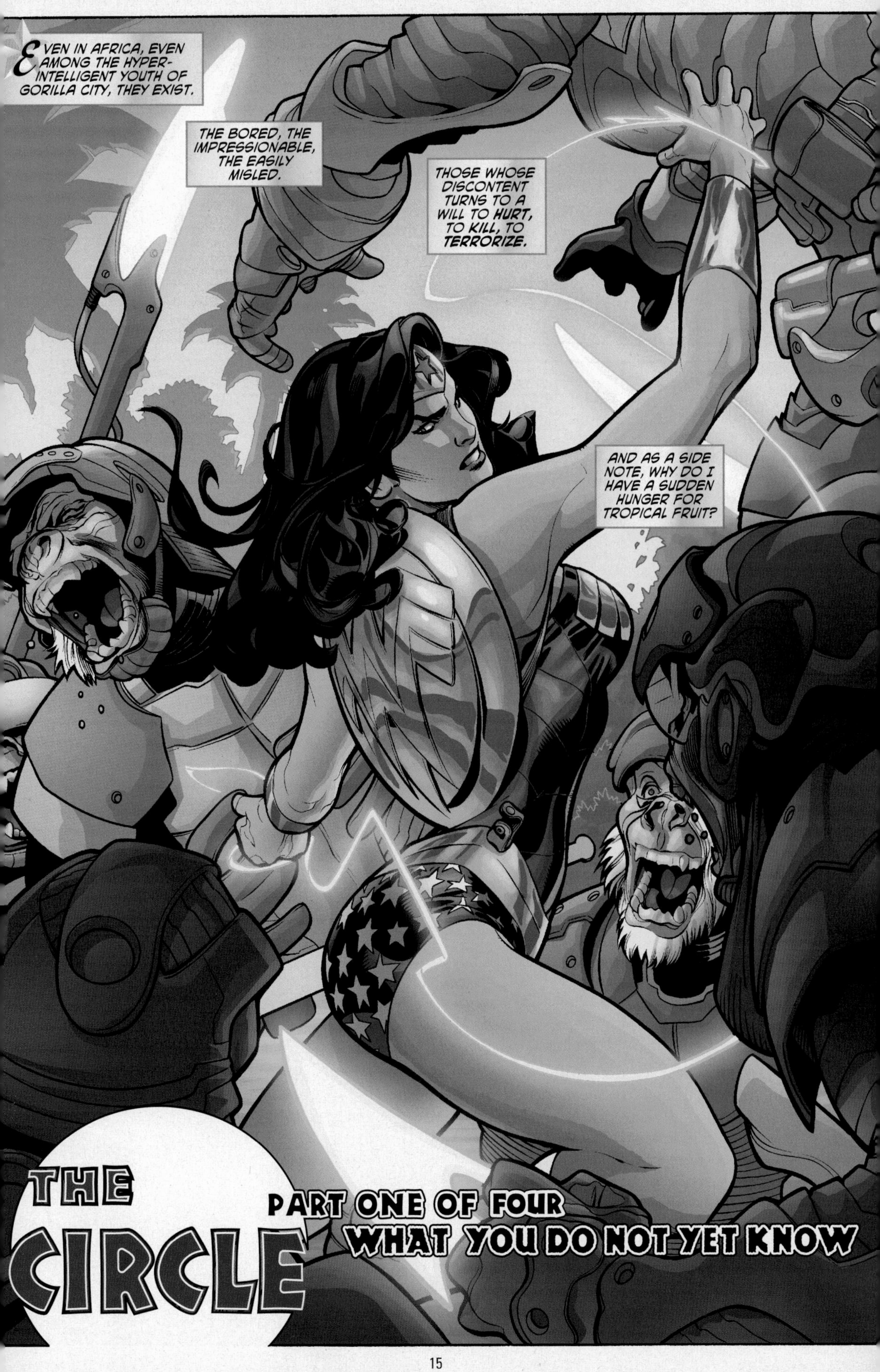
EVEN IN AFRICA, EVEN AMONG THE HYPER-INTELLIGENT YOUTH OF GORILLA CITY, THEY EXIST.
THE BORED, THE IMPRESSIONABLE, THE EASILY MISLED.
THOSE WHOSE DISCONTENT TURNS TO A WILL TO HURT, TO KILL, TO TERRORIZE.
AND AS A SIDE NOTE, WHY DO I HAVE A SUDDEN HUNGER FOR TROPICAL FRUIT?
THE CIRCLE
PART ONE OF FOUR
WHAT YOU DO NOT YET KNOW

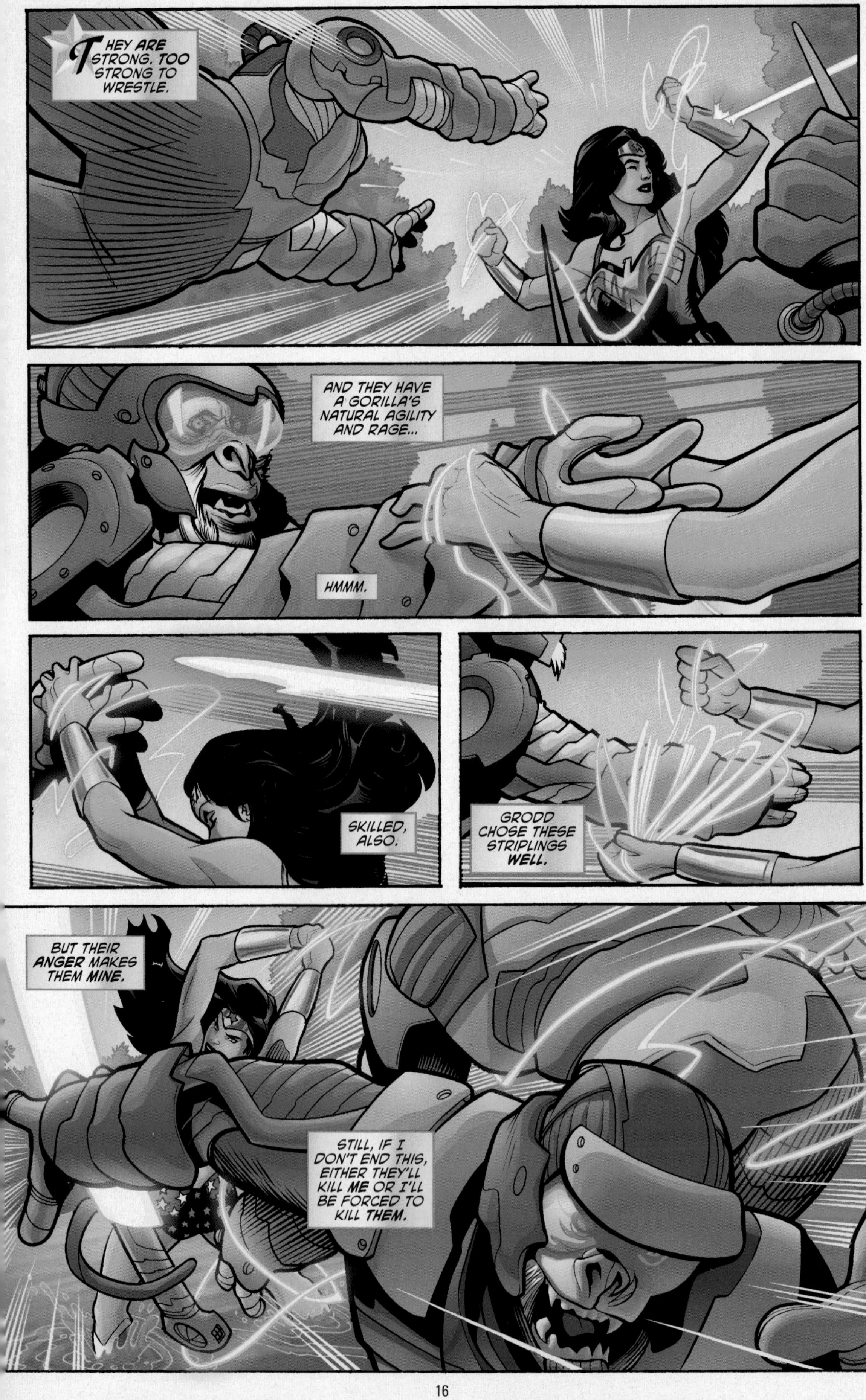
THEY ARE STRONG. TOO STRONG TO WRESTLE.
AND THEY HAVE A GORILLA'S NATURAL AGILITY AND RAGE...
HMMM.
SKILLED, ALSO.
GRODD CHOSE THESE STRIPLINGS WELL.
BUT THEIR ANGER MAKES THEM MINE.
STILL, IF I DON'T END THIS, EITHER THEY'LL KILL ME OR I'LL BE FORCED TO KILL THEM.

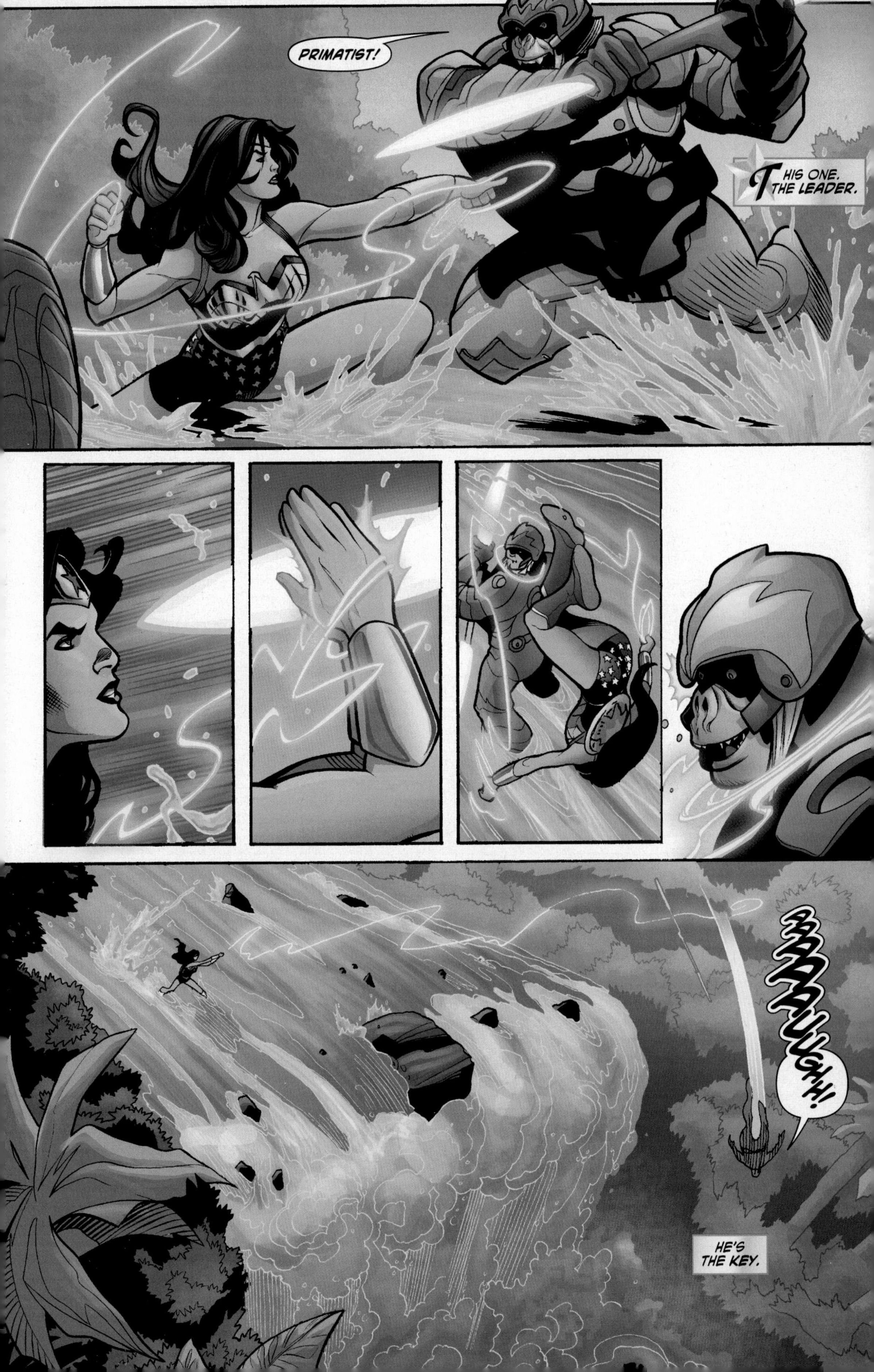
PRIMATIST!
THIS ONE. THE LEADER.
AAAAAUUGHH!
HE'S THE KEY.

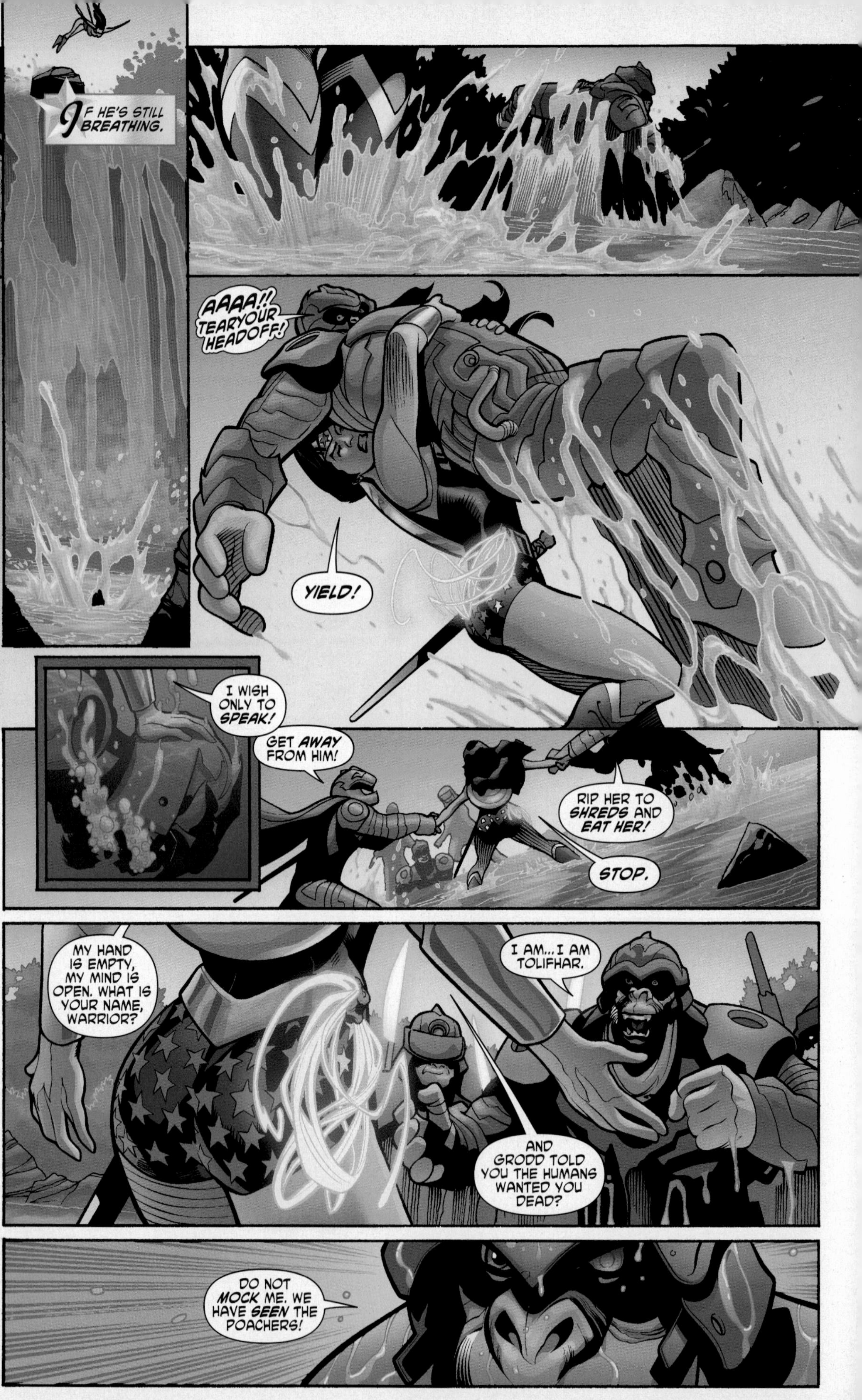
IF HE'S STILL BREATHING.
AAAA!! TEARYOUR HEADOFF!
YIELD!
I WISH ONLY TO SPEAK!
GET AWAY FROM HIM!
RIP HER TO SHREDS AND EAT HER!
STOP.
MY HAND IS EMPTY, MY MIND IS OPEN. WHAT IS YOUR NAME, WARRIOR?
I AM...I AM TOLIFHAR.
AND GRODD TOLD YOU THE HUMANS WANTED YOU DEAD?
DO NOT MOCK ME. WE HAVE SEEN THE POACHERS!

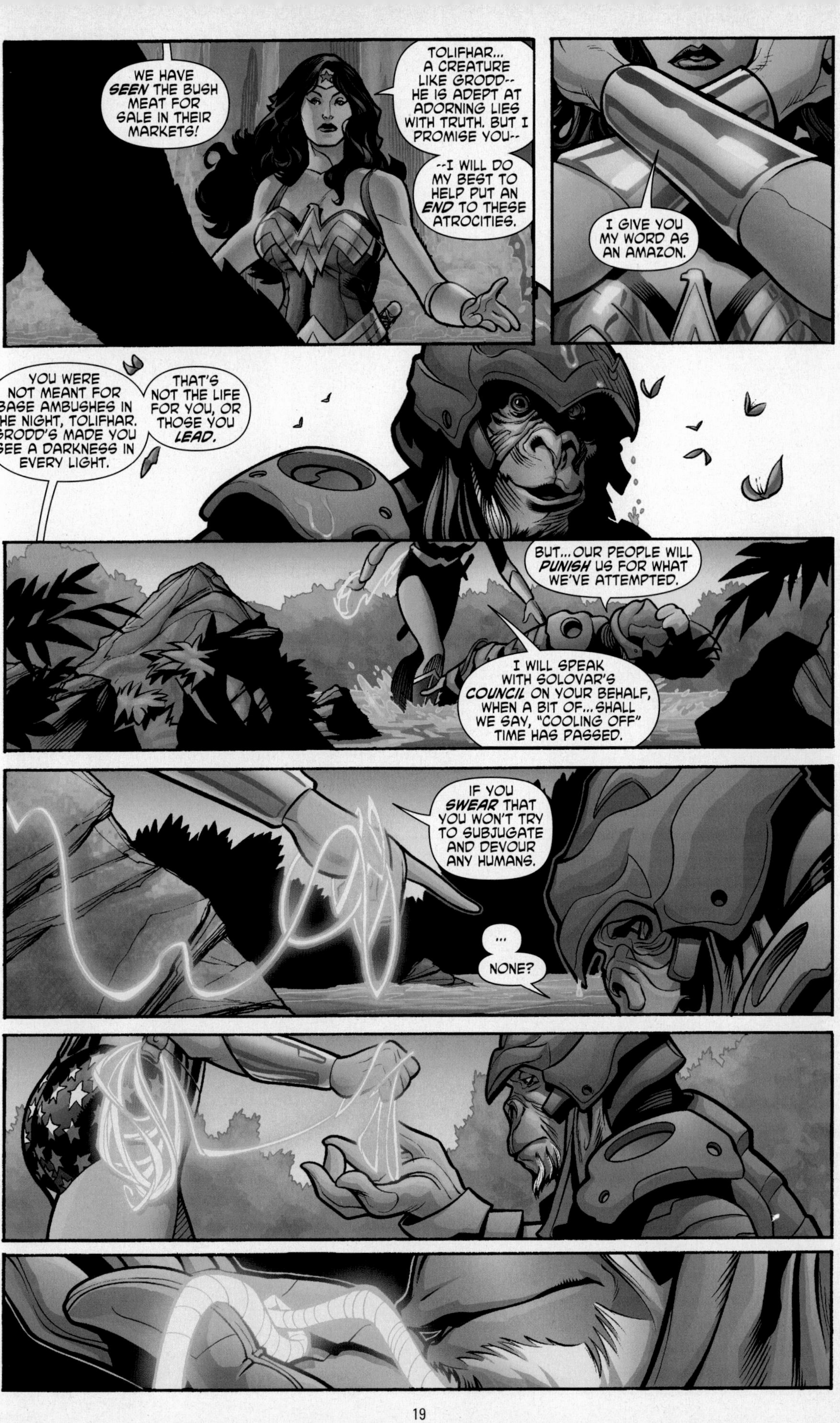

WE HAVE SEEN THE BUSH MEAT FOR SALE IN THEIR MARKETS!
TOLIFHAR... A CREATURE LIKE GRODD-- HE IS ADEPT AT ADORNING LIES WITH TRUTH. BUT I PROMISE YOU--
--I WILL DO MY BEST TO HELP PUT AN END TO THESE ATROCITIES.
I GIVE YOU MY WORD AS AN AMAZON.
YOU WERE NOT MEANT FOR BASE AMBUSHES IN THE NIGHT, TOLIFHAR. GRODD'S MADE YOU SEE A DARKNESS IN EVERY LIGHT.
THAT'S NOT THE LIFE FOR YOU, OR THOSE YOU LEAD.
BUT...OUR PEOPLE WILL PUNISH US FOR WHAT WE'VE ATTEMPTED.
I WILL SPEAK WITH SOLOVAR'S COUNCIL ON YOUR BEHALF, WHEN A BIT OF...SHALL WE SAY, "COOLING OFF" TIME HAS PASSED.
IF YOU SWEAR THAT YOU WON'T TRY TO SUBJUGATE AND DEVOUR ANY HUMANS.
...
NONE?

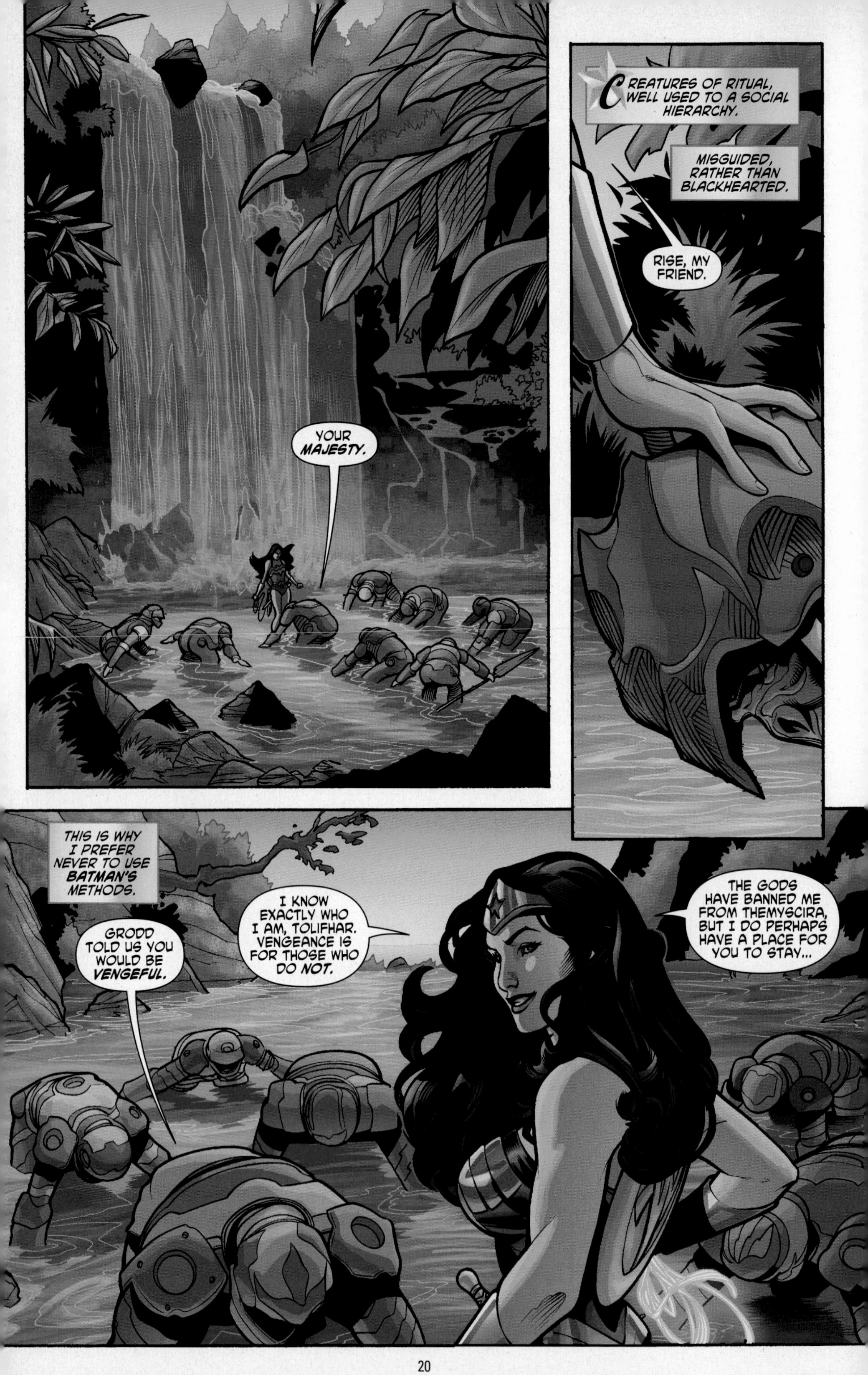
YOUR MAJESTY.
CREATURES OF RITUAL, WELL USED TO A SOCIAL HIERARCHY.
MISGUIDED, RATHER THAN BLACKHEARTED.
RISE, MY FRIEND.
THIS IS WHY I PREFER NEVER TO USE BATMAN'S METHODS.
GRODD TOLD US YOU WOULD BE VENGEFUL.
I KNOW EXACTLY WHO I AM, TOLIFHAR. VENGEANCE IS FOR THOSE WHO DO NOT.
THE GODS HAVE BANNED ME FROM THEMYSCIRA, BUT I DO PERHAPS HAVE A PLACE FOR YOU TO STAY...

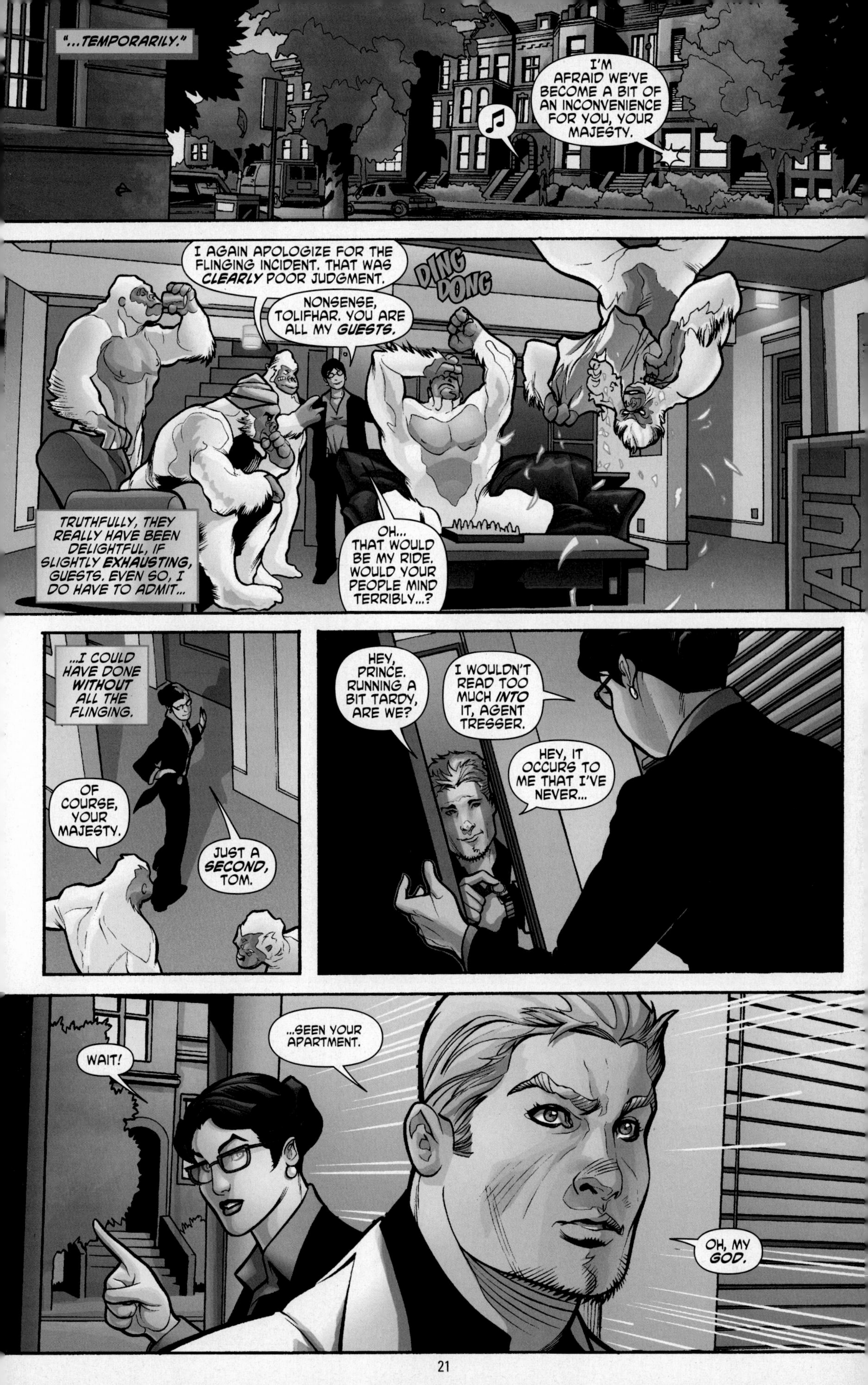
"...TEMPORARILY."
I'M AFRAID WE'VE BECOME A BIT OF AN INCONVENIENCE FOR YOU, YOUR MAJESTY.
♫
I AGAIN APOLOGIZE FOR THE FLINGING INCIDENT. THAT WAS CLEARLY POOR JUDGMENT.
NONSENSE, TOLIFHAR. YOU ARE ALL MY GUESTS.
DING DONG
TRUTHFULLY, THEY REALLY HAVE BEEN DELIGHTFUL, IF SLIGHTLY EXHAUSTING, GUESTS. EVEN SO, I DO HAVE TO ADMIT...
OH... THAT WOULD BE MY RIDE. WOULD YOUR PEOPLE MIND TERRIBLY...?
...I COULD HAVE DONE WITHOUT ALL THE FLINGING.
OF COURSE, YOUR MAJESTY.
JUST A SECOND, TOM.
HEY, PRINCE. RUNNING A BIT TARDY, ARE WE?
I WOULDN'T READ TOO MUCH INTO IT, AGENT TRESSER.
HEY, IT OCCURS TO ME THAT I'VE NEVER...
...SEEN YOUR APARTMENT.
WAIT!
OH, MY GOD.

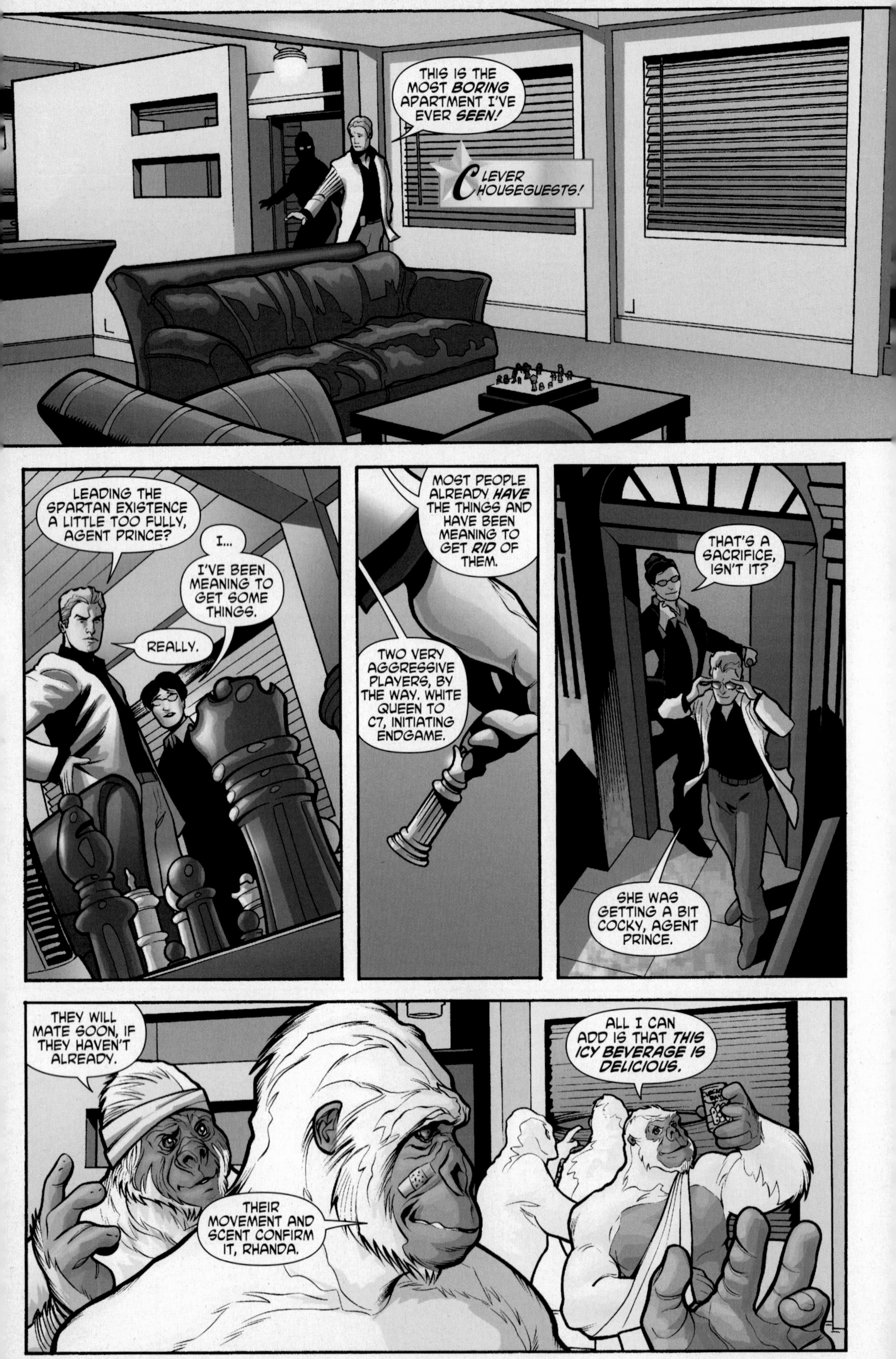
THIS IS THE MOST BORING APARTMENT I'VE EVER SEEN!
CLEVER HOUSEGUESTS!
LEADING THE SPARTAN EXISTENCE A LITTLE TOO FULLY, AGENT PRINCE?
I...
I'VE BEEN MEANING TO GET SOME THINGS.
REALLY.
MOST PEOPLE ALREADY HAVE THE THINGS AND HAVE BEEN MEANING TO GET RID OF THEM.
TWO VERY AGGRESSIVE PLAYERS, BY THE WAY. WHITE QUEEN TO C7, INITIATING ENDGAME.
THAT'S A SACRIFICE, ISN'T IT?
SHE WAS GETTING A BIT COCKY, AGENT PRINCE.
THEY WILL MATE SOON, IF THEY HAVEN'T ALREADY.
THEIR MOVEMENT AND SCENT CONFIRM IT, RHANDA.
ALL I CAN ADD IS THAT THIS ICY BEVERAGE IS DELICIOUS.

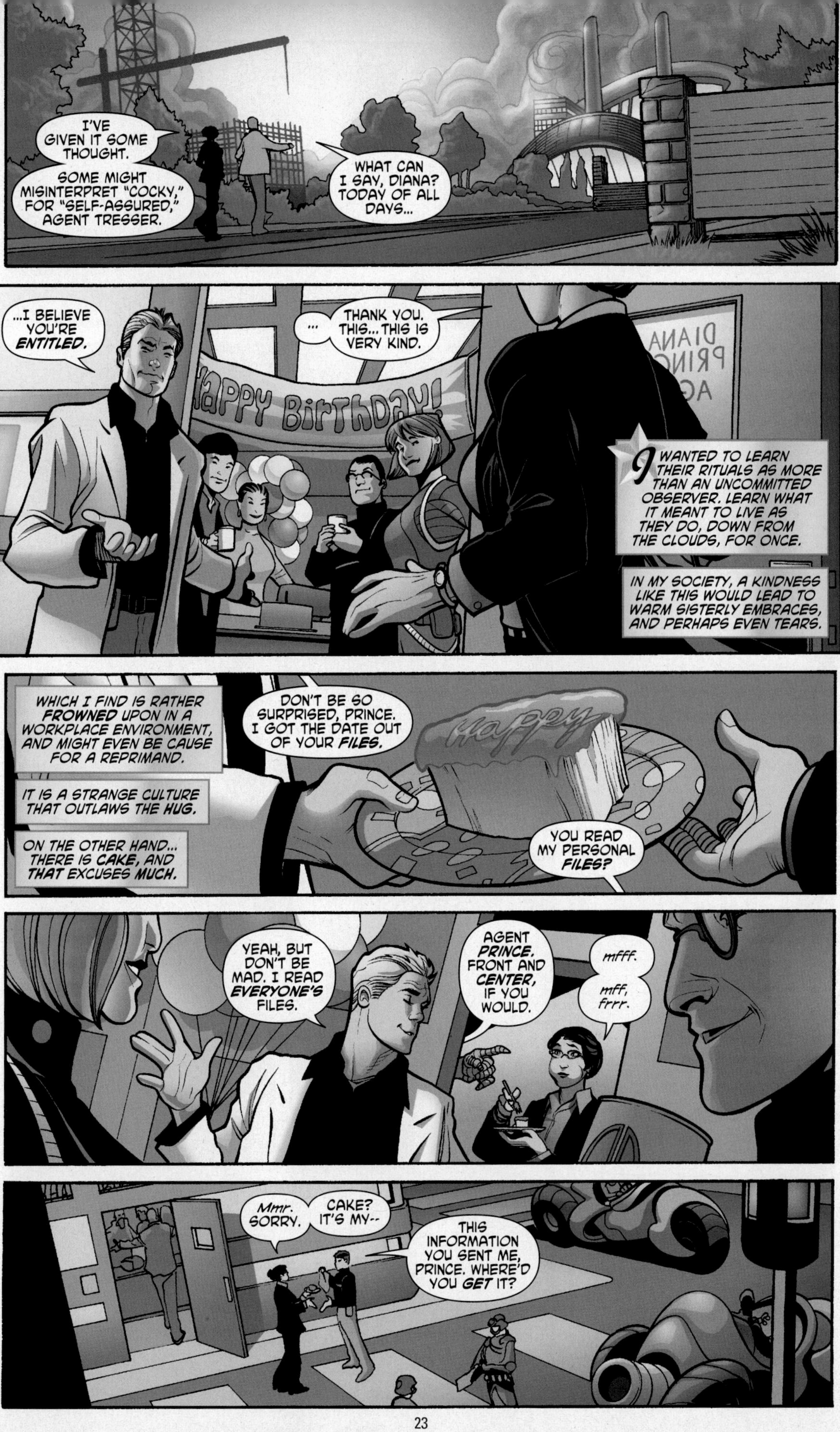
I'VE GIVEN IT SOME THOUGHT.
SOME MIGHT MISINTERPRET "COCKY," FOR "SELF-ASSURED," AGENT TRESSER.
WHAT CAN I SAY, DIANA? TODAY OF ALL DAYS...
...I BELIEVE YOU'RE ENTITLED.
...
THANK YOU. THIS... THIS IS VERY KIND.
HAPPY BIRTHDAY!
DIANA PRINC AG
I WANTED TO LEARN THEIR RITUALS AS MORE THAN AN UNCOMMITTED OBSERVER. LEARN WHAT IT MEANT TO LIVE AS THEY DO, DOWN FROM THE CLOUDS, FOR ONCE.
IN MY SOCIETY, A KINDNESS LIKE THIS WOULD LEAD TO WARM SISTERLY EMBRACES, AND PERHAPS EVEN TEARS.
WHICH I FIND IS RATHER FROWNED UPON IN A WORKPLACE ENVIRONMENT, AND MIGHT EVEN BE CAUSE FOR A REPRIMAND.
IT IS A STRANGE CULTURE THAT OUTLAWS THE HUG.
ON THE OTHER HAND... THERE IS CAKE, AND THAT EXCUSES MUCH.
DON'T BE SO SURPRISED, PRINCE. I GOT THE DATE OUT OF YOUR FILES.
Happy
YOU READ MY PERSONAL FILES?
YEAH, BUT DON'T BE MAD. I READ EVERYONE'S FILES.
AGENT PRINCE. FRONT AND CENTER, IF YOU WOULD.
mfff.
mff, frrr.
Mmr. SORRY.
CAKE? IT'S MY--
THIS INFORMATION YOU SENT ME, PRINCE. WHERE'D YOU GET IT?

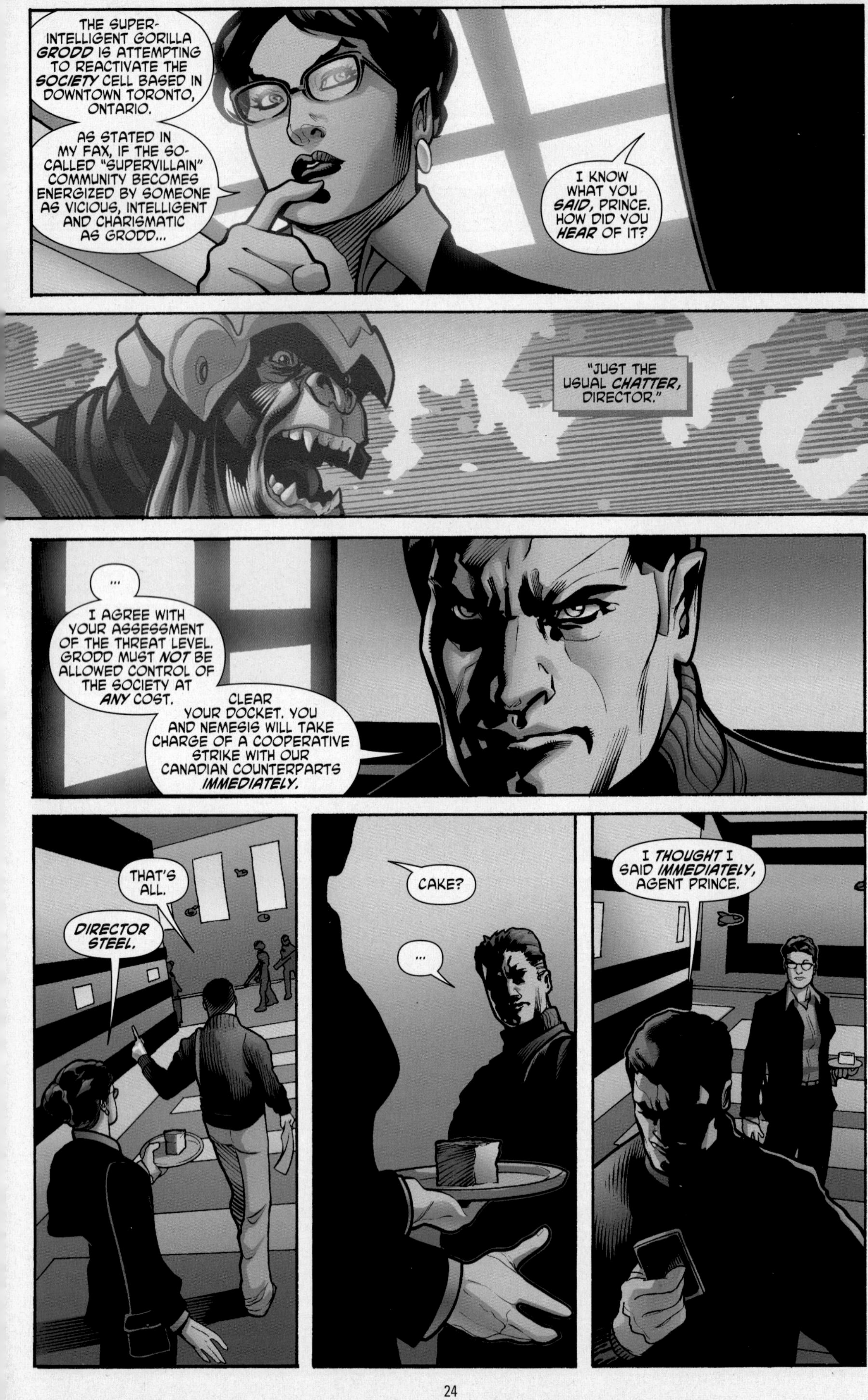
THE SUPER-INTELLIGENT GORILLA GRODD IS ATTEMPTING TO REACTIVATE THE SOCIETY CELL BASED IN DOWNTOWN TORONTO, ONTARIO.
AS STATED IN MY FAX, IF THE SO-CALLED "SUPERVILLAIN" COMMUNITY BECOMES ENERGIZED BY SOMEONE AS VICIOUS, INTELLIGENT AND CHARISMATIC AS GRODD...
I KNOW WHAT YOU SAID, PRINCE. HOW DID YOU HEAR OF IT?
"JUST THE USUAL CHATTER, DIRECTOR."
...
I AGREE WITH YOUR ASSESSMENT OF THE THREAT LEVEL. GRODD MUST NOT BE ALLOWED CONTROL OF THE SOCIETY AT ANY COST.
CLEAR YOUR DOCKET. YOU AND NEMESIS WILL TAKE CHARGE OF A COOPERATIVE STRIKE WITH OUR CANADIAN COUNTERPARTS IMMEDIATELY.
THAT'S ALL.
DIRECTOR STEEL.
CAKE?
...
I THOUGHT I SAID IMMEDIATELY, AGENT PRINCE.

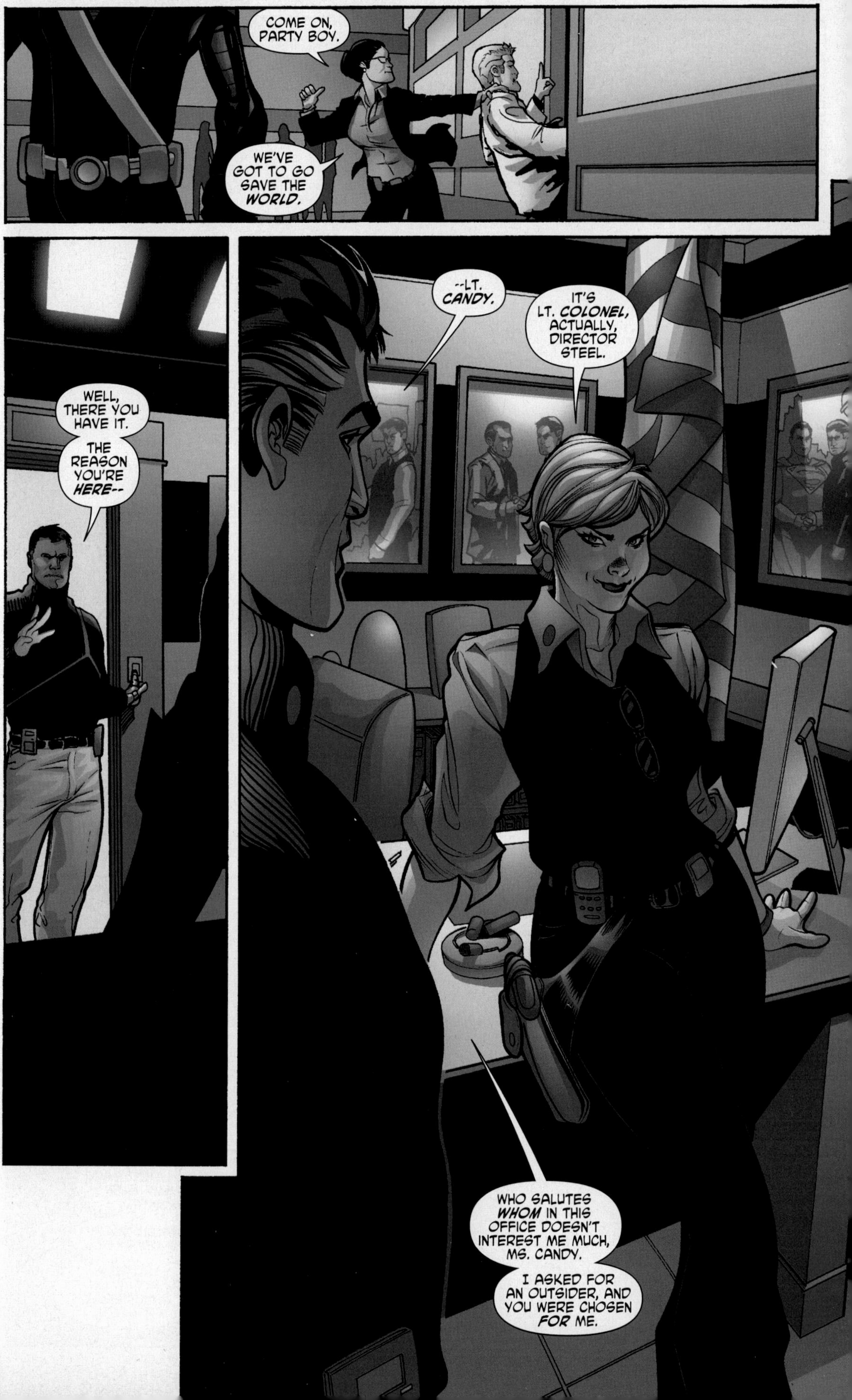
COME ON, PARTY BOY.
WE'VE GOT TO GO SAVE THE *WORLD.*
WELL, THERE YOU HAVE IT.
THE REASON YOU'RE *HERE--*
--LT. *CANDY.*
IT'S LT. *COLONEL,* ACTUALLY, DIRECTOR STEEL.
WHO SALUTES *WHOM* IN THIS OFFICE DOESN'T INTEREST ME MUCH, MS. CANDY.
I ASKED FOR AN OUTSIDER, AND YOU WERE CHOSEN *FOR* ME.

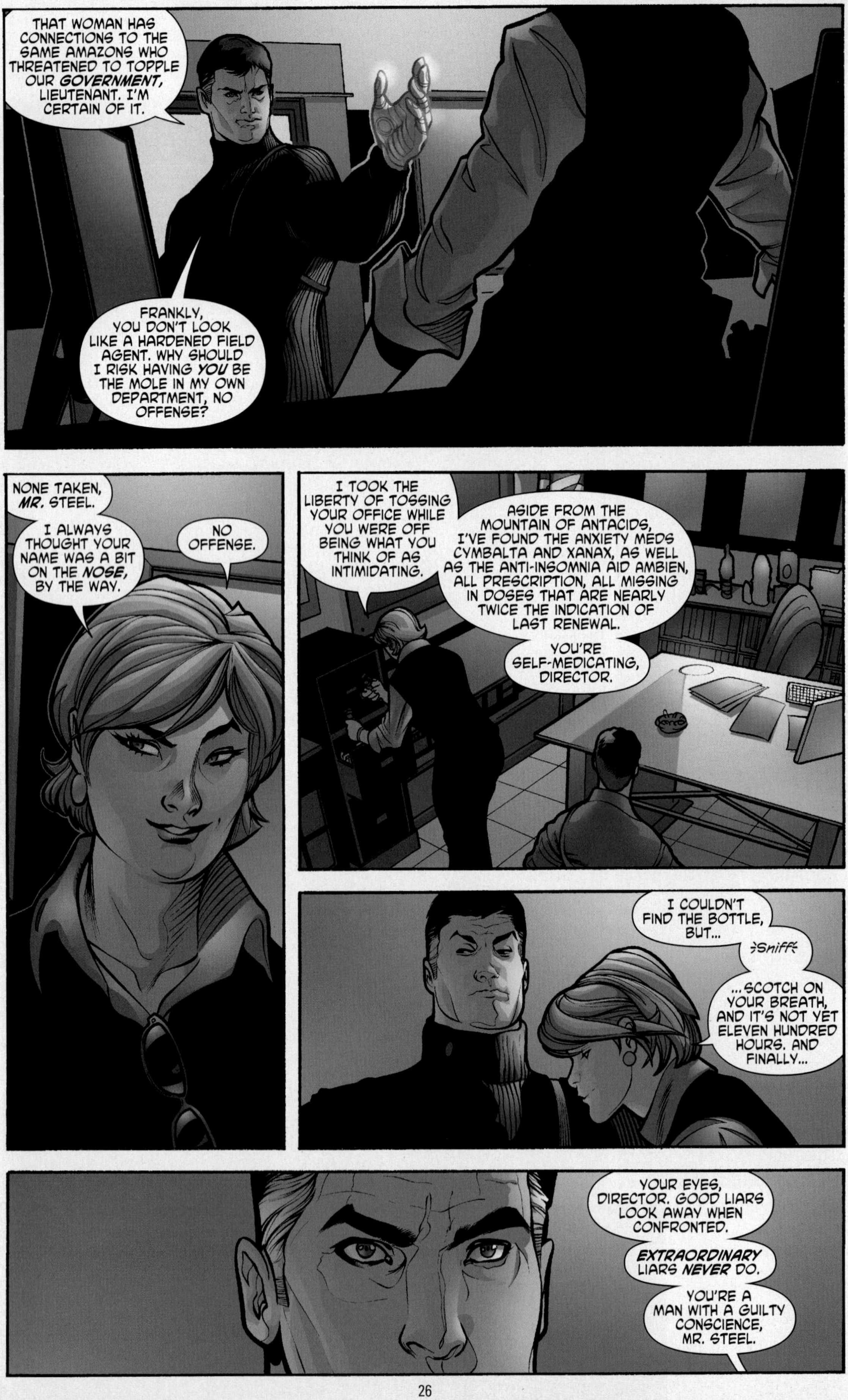
THAT WOMAN HAS CONNECTIONS TO THE SAME AMAZONS WHO THREATENED TO TOPPLE OUR **GOVERNMENT,** LIEUTENANT. I'M CERTAIN OF IT.
FRANKLY, YOU DON'T LOOK LIKE A HARDENED FIELD AGENT. WHY SHOULD I RISK HAVING **YOU** BE THE MOLE IN MY OWN DEPARTMENT, NO OFFENSE?
NONE TAKEN, **MR.** STEEL.
I ALWAYS THOUGHT YOUR NAME WAS A BIT ON THE **NOSE,** BY THE WAY.
NO OFFENSE.
I TOOK THE LIBERTY OF TOSSING YOUR OFFICE WHILE YOU WERE OFF BEING WHAT YOU THINK OF AS INTIMIDATING.
ASIDE FROM THE MOUNTAIN OF ANTACIDS, I'VE FOUND THE ANXIETY MEDS CYMBALTA AND XANAX, AS WELL AS THE ANTI-INSOMNIA AID AMBIEN, ALL PRESCRIPTION, ALL MISSING IN DOSES THAT ARE NEARLY TWICE THE INDICATION OF LAST RENEWAL.
YOU'RE SELF-MEDICATING, DIRECTOR.
I COULDN'T FIND THE BOTTLE, BUT...
Sniff
...SCOTCH ON YOUR BREATH, AND IT'S NOT YET ELEVEN HUNDRED HOURS. AND FINALLY...
YOUR EYES, DIRECTOR. GOOD LIARS LOOK AWAY WHEN CONFRONTED.
EXTRAORDINARY LIARS **NEVER** DO.
YOU'RE A MAN WITH A GUILTY CONSCIENCE, MR. STEEL.

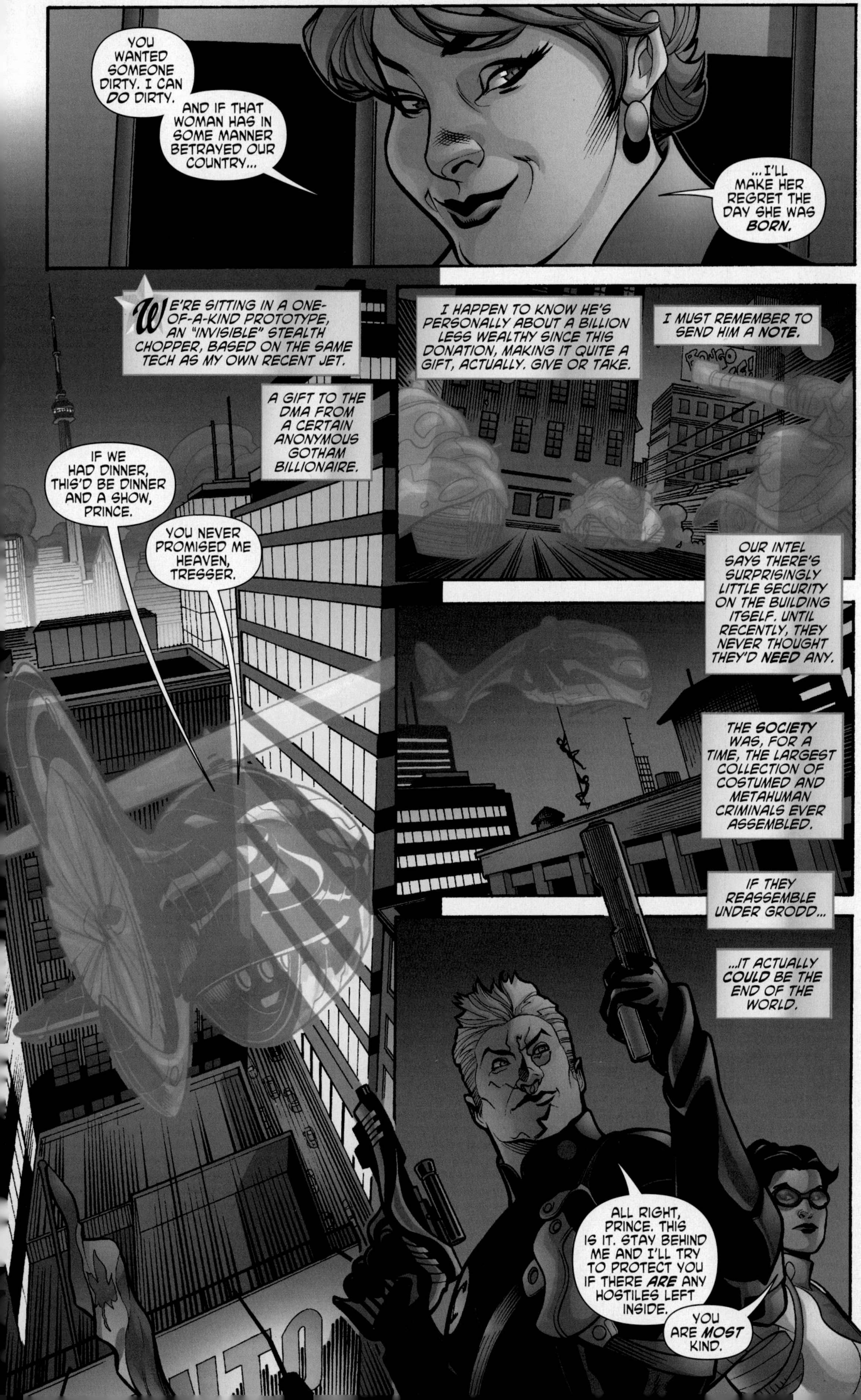
YOU WANTED SOMEONE DIRTY. I CAN DO DIRTY.
AND IF THAT WOMAN HAS IN SOME MANNER BETRAYED OUR COUNTRY...
...I'LL MAKE HER REGRET THE DAY SHE WAS BORN.
WE'RE SITTING IN A ONE-OF-A-KIND PROTOTYPE, AN "INVISIBLE" STEALTH CHOPPER, BASED ON THE SAME TECH AS MY OWN RECENT JET.
A GIFT TO THE DMA FROM A CERTAIN ANONYMOUS GOTHAM BILLIONAIRE.
IF WE HAD DINNER, THIS'D BE DINNER AND A SHOW, PRINCE.
YOU NEVER PROMISED ME HEAVEN, TRESSER.
I HAPPEN TO KNOW HE'S PERSONALLY ABOUT A BILLION LESS WEALTHY SINCE THIS DONATION, MAKING IT QUITE A GIFT, ACTUALLY. GIVE OR TAKE.
I MUST REMEMBER TO SEND HIM A NOTE.
OUR INTEL SAYS THERE'S SURPRISINGLY LITTLE SECURITY ON THE BUILDING ITSELF. UNTIL RECENTLY, THEY NEVER THOUGHT THEY'D NEED ANY.
THE SOCIETY WAS, FOR A TIME, THE LARGEST COLLECTION OF COSTUMED AND METAHUMAN CRIMINALS EVER ASSEMBLED.
IF THEY REASSEMBLE UNDER GRODD...
...IT ACTUALLY COULD BE THE END OF THE WORLD.
ALL RIGHT, PRINCE. THIS IS IT. STAY BEHIND ME AND I'LL TRY TO PROTECT YOU IF THERE ARE ANY HOSTILES LEFT INSIDE.
YOU ARE MOST KIND.

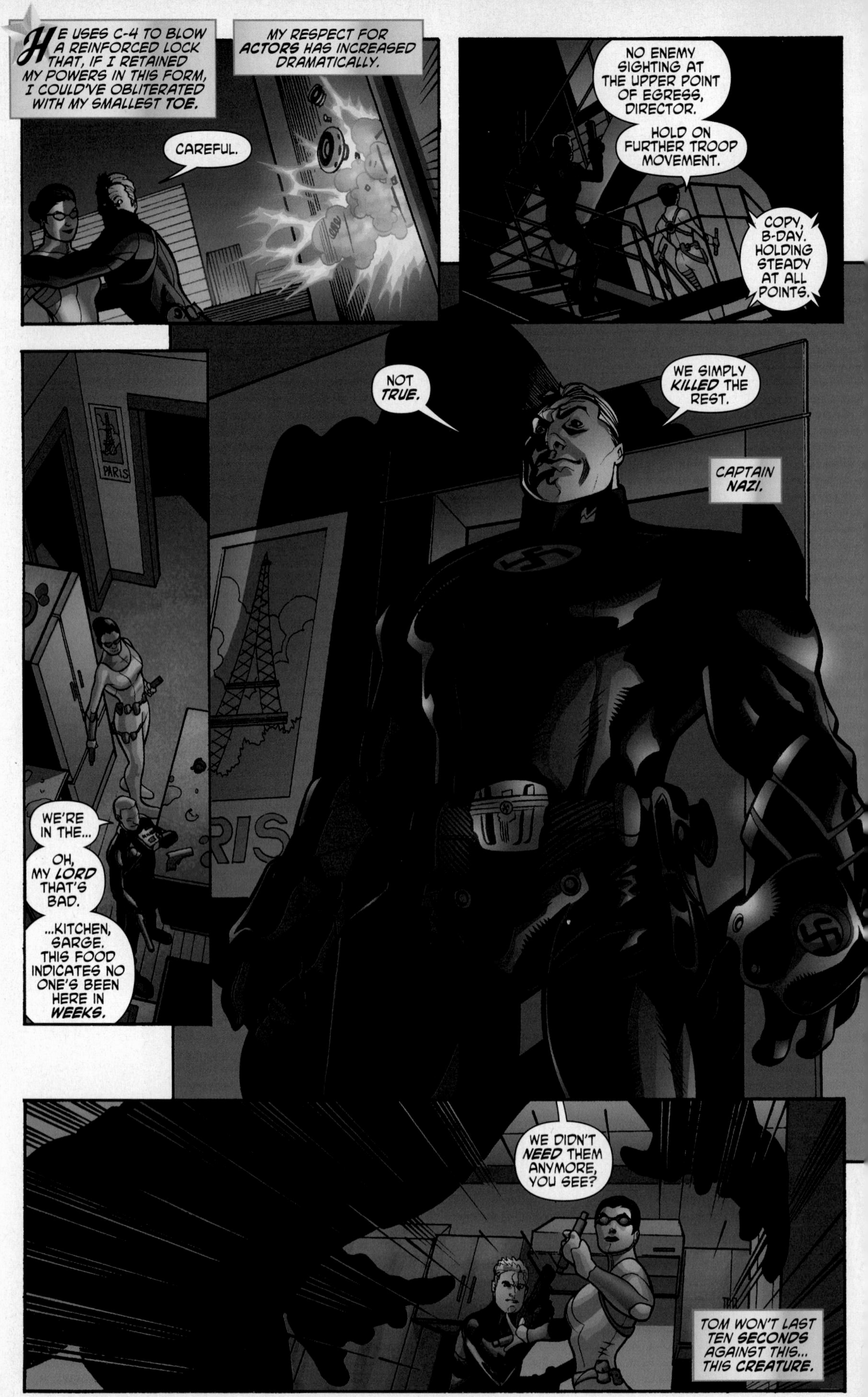
HE USES C-4 TO BLOW A REINFORCED LOCK THAT, IF I RETAINED MY POWERS IN THIS FORM, I COULD'VE OBLITERATED WITH MY SMALLEST TOE.
MY RESPECT FOR ACTORS HAS INCREASED DRAMATICALLY.
CAREFUL.
NO ENEMY SIGHTING AT THE UPPER POINT OF EGRESS, DIRECTOR.
HOLD ON FURTHER TROOP MOVEMENT.
COPY, B-DAY. HOLDING STEADY AT ALL POINTS.
PARIS
WE'RE IN THE...
OH, MY LORD THAT'S BAD.
...KITCHEN, SARGE. THIS FOOD INDICATES NO ONE'S BEEN HERE IN WEEKS.
NOT TRUE.
WE SIMPLY KILLED THE REST.
CAPTAIN NAZI.
WE DIDN'T NEED THEM ANYMORE, YOU SEE?
TOM WON'T LAST TEN SECONDS AGAINST THIS... THIS CREATURE.

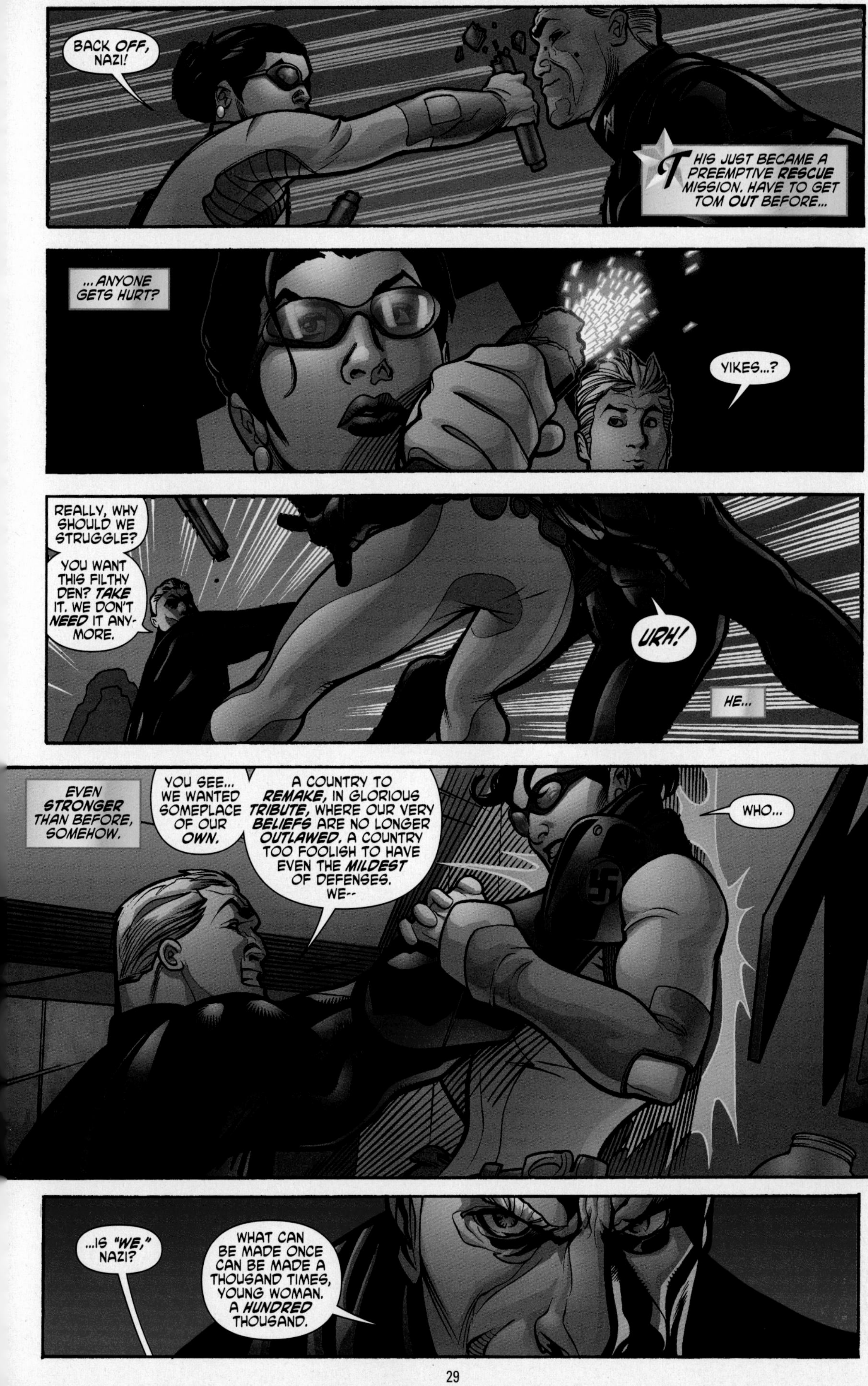
BACK OFF, NAZI!
THIS JUST BECAME A PREEMPTIVE RESCUE MISSION. HAVE TO GET TOM OUT BEFORE...
...ANYONE GETS HURT?
YIKES...?
REALLY, WHY SHOULD WE STRUGGLE?
YOU WANT THIS FILTHY DEN? TAKE IT. WE DON'T NEED IT ANYMORE.
URH!
HE...
EVEN STRONGER THAN BEFORE, SOMEHOW.
YOU SEE... WE WANTED SOMEPLACE OF OUR OWN.
A COUNTRY TO REMAKE, IN GLORIOUS TRIBUTE, WHERE OUR VERY BELIEFS ARE NO LONGER OUTLAWED. A COUNTRY TOO FOOLISH TO HAVE EVEN THE MILDEST OF DEFENSES. WE--
WHO...
...IS "WE," NAZI?
WHAT CAN BE MADE ONCE CAN BE MADE A THOUSAND TIMES, YOUNG WOMAN. A HUNDRED THOUSAND.

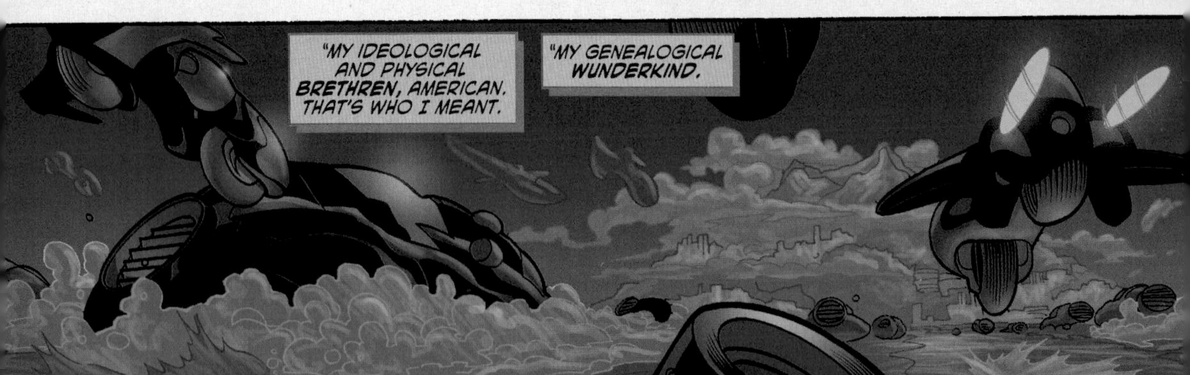
"MY IDEOLOGICAL AND PHYSICAL BRETHREN, AMERICAN. THAT'S WHO I MEANT.
"MY GENEALOGICAL WUNDERKIND.

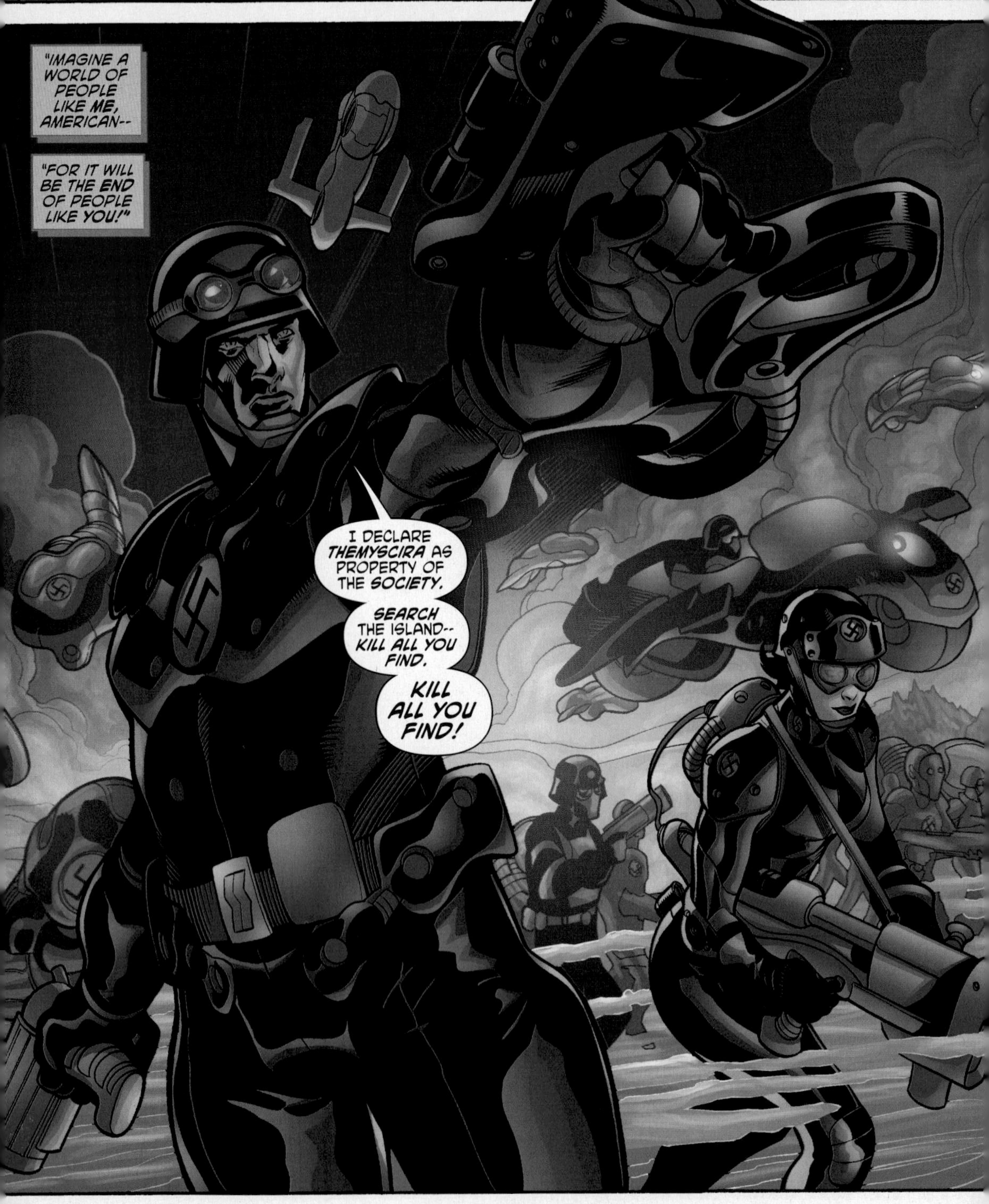
"IMAGINE A WORLD OF PEOPLE LIKE ME, AMERICAN--
"FOR IT WILL BE THE END OF PEOPLE LIKE YOU!"
I DECLARE THEMYSCIRA AS PROPERTY OF THE SOCIETY.
SEARCH THE ISLAND-- KILL ALL YOU FIND.
KILL ALL YOU FIND!

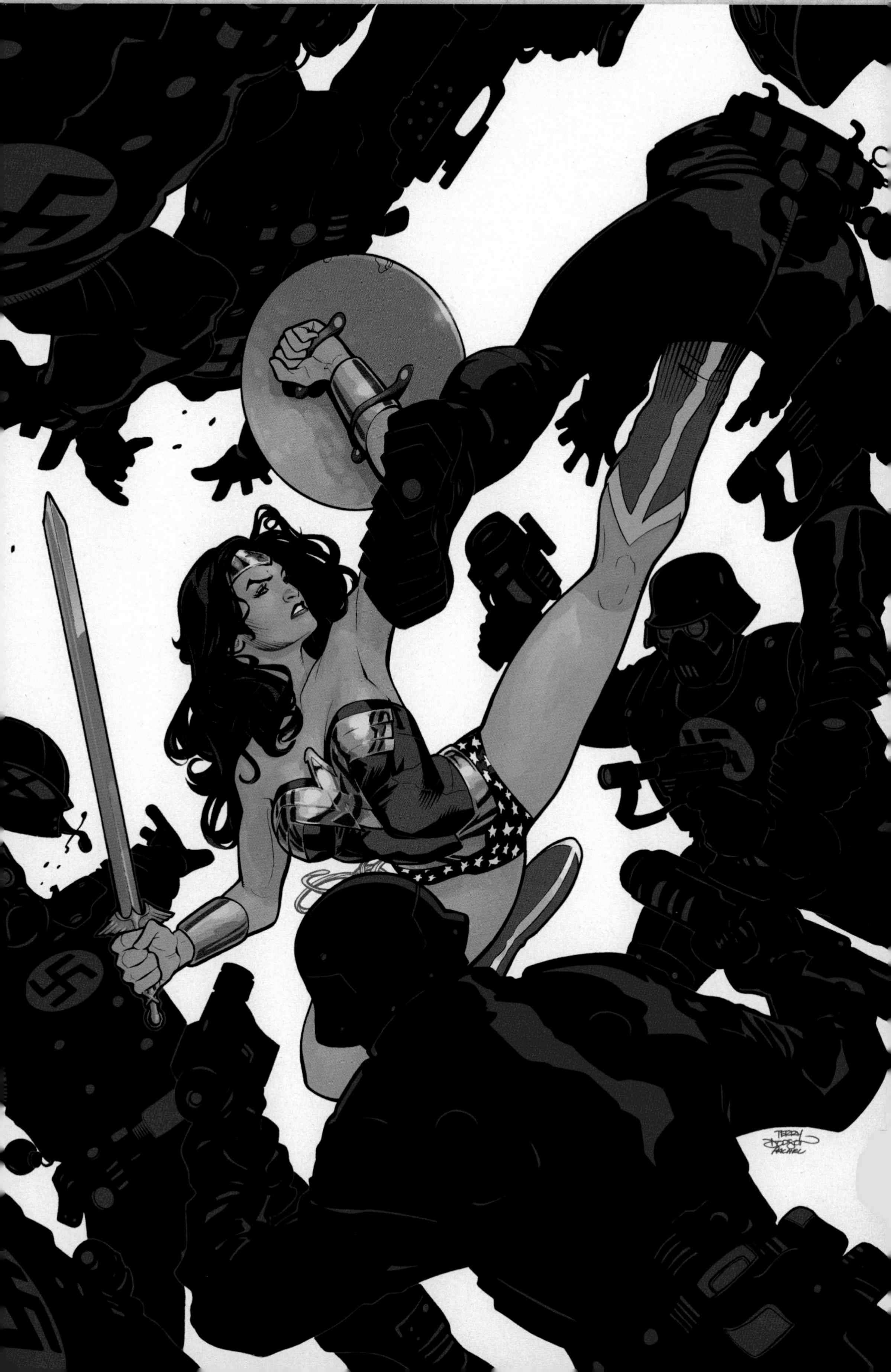
TERRY
DODSON
RACHEL

Art this issue by Terry Dodson & Rachel Dodson

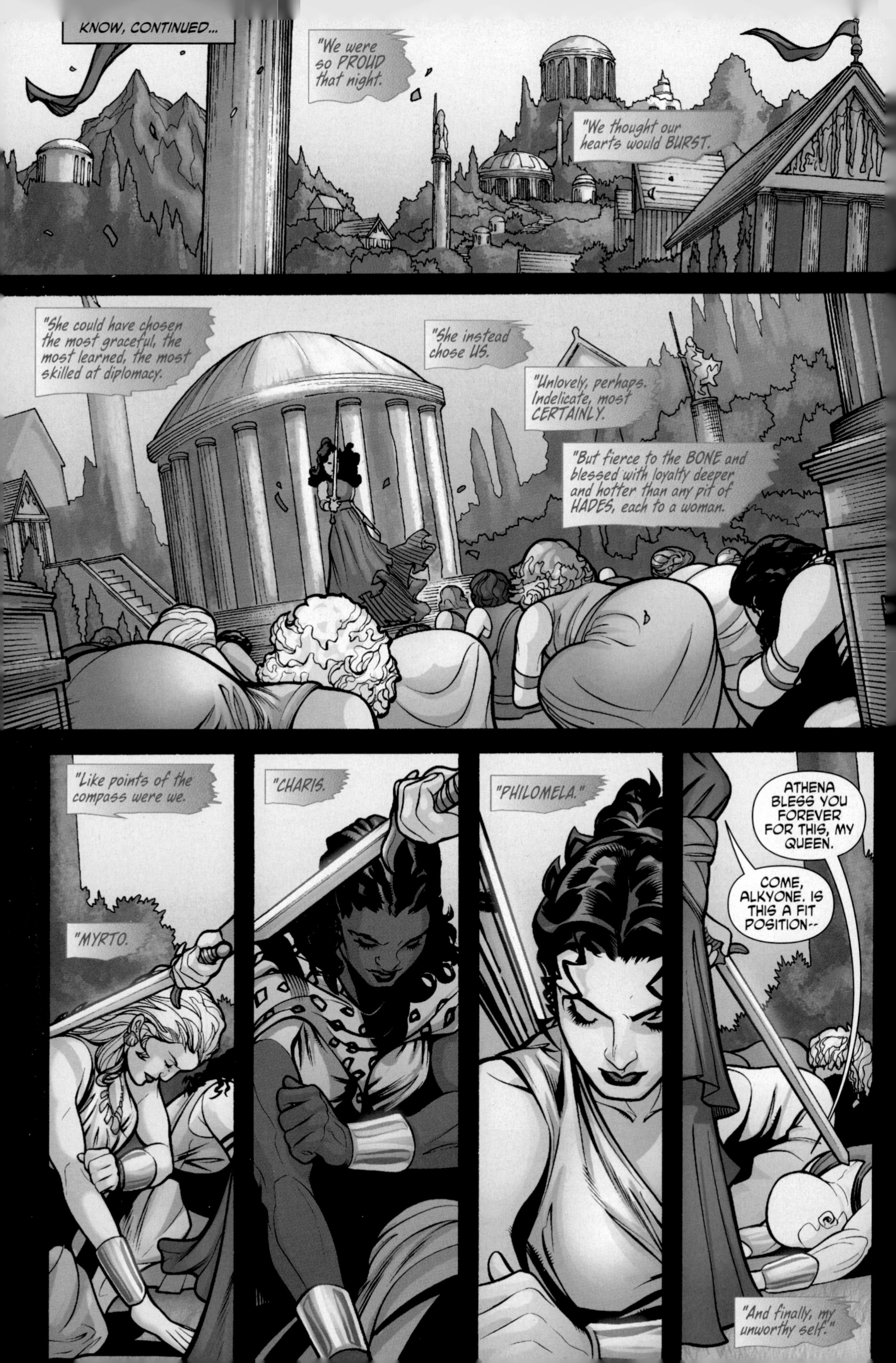
KNOW, CONTINUED...
"We were so PROUD that night.
"We thought our hearts would BURST.
"She could have chosen the most graceful, the most learned, the most skilled at diplomacy.
"She instead chose US.
"Unlovely, perhaps. Indelicate, most CERTAINLY.
"But fierce to the BONE and blessed with loyalty deeper and hotter than any pit of HADES, each to a woman.
"Like points of the compass were we.
"MYRTO.
"CHARIS.
"PHILOMELA."
ATHENA BLESS YOU FOREVER FOR THIS, MY QUEEN.
COME, ALKYONE. IS THIS A FIT POSITION--
"And finally, my unworthy self."

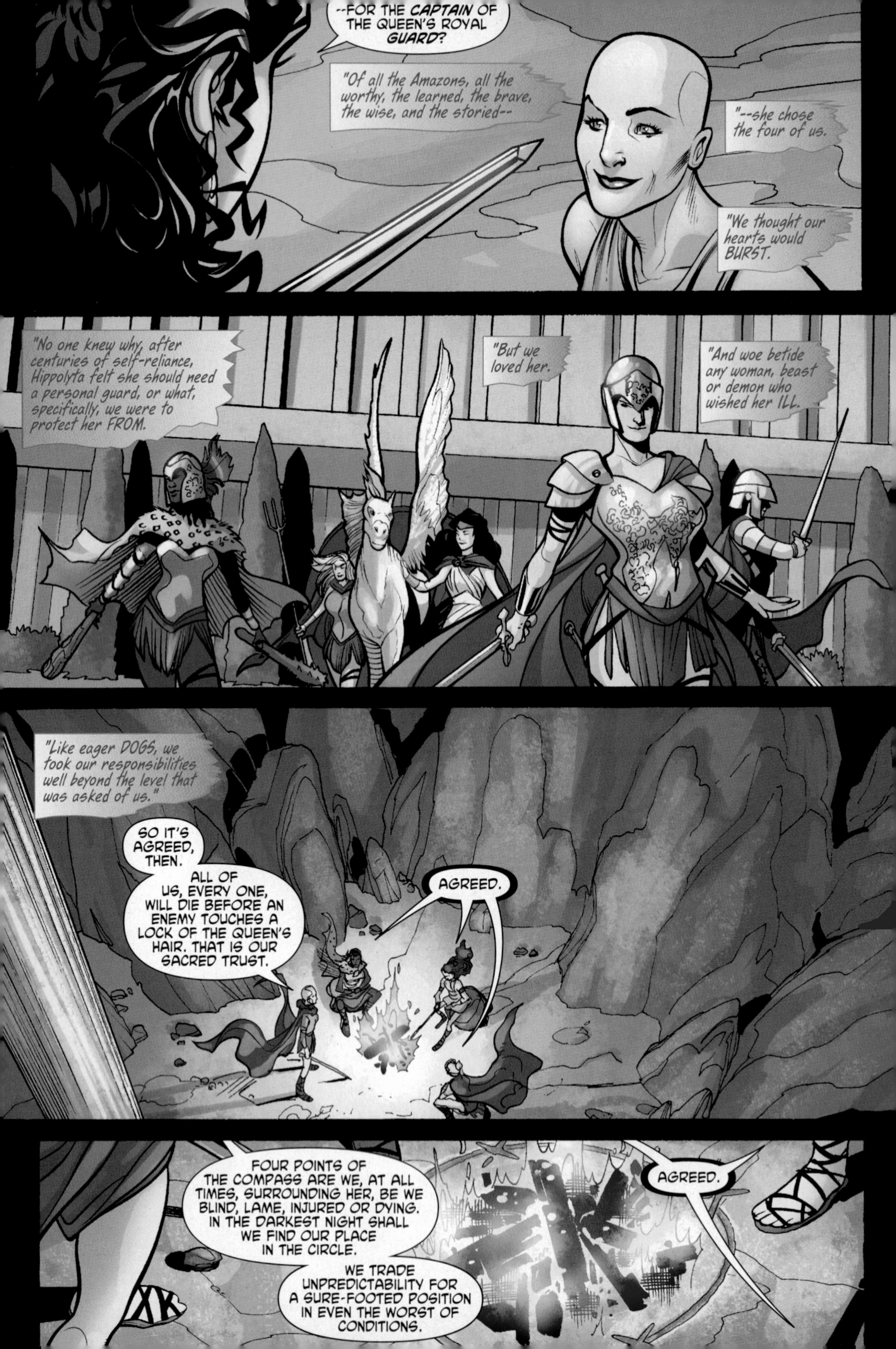
--FOR THE CAPTAIN OF THE QUEEN'S ROYAL GUARD?
"Of all the Amazons, all the worthy, the learned, the brave, the wise, and the storied--
"--she chose the four of us.
"We thought our hearts would BURST.
"No one knew why, after centuries of self-reliance, Hippolyta felt she should need a personal guard, or what, specifically, we were to protect her FROM.
"But we loved her.
"And woe betide any woman, beast or demon who wished her ILL.
"Like eager DOGS, we took our responsibilities well beyond the level that was asked of us."
SO IT'S AGREED, THEN.
ALL OF US, EVERY ONE, WILL DIE BEFORE AN ENEMY TOUCHES A LOCK OF THE QUEEN'S HAIR. THAT IS OUR SACRED TRUST.
AGREED.
FOUR POINTS OF THE COMPASS ARE WE, AT ALL TIMES, SURROUNDING HER, BE WE BLIND, LAME, INJURED OR DYING. IN THE DARKEST NIGHT SHALL WE FIND OUR PLACE IN THE CIRCLE.
WE TRADE UNPREDICTABILITY FOR A SURE-FOOTED POSITION IN EVEN THE WORST OF CONDITIONS.
AGREED.

"So we made a vow of woman's blood.

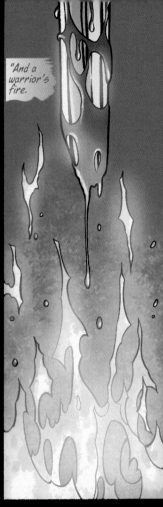

"And a warrior's fire.

"And danced a dance the likes of which my tongue cannot explain to any who did not witness it.

"Oh, we were not without our detractors.

"The captain of the GENERAL guard, Phillipus--

"--she warned the Queen that we were overzealous and brutal-minded.

...hich we WERE. ...e slept in four ...orless compart-...nts surrounding ...e Queen's ...ivate chambers. ...e at least ...ake at all ...es.

"When we dreamt, we prayed to Athena that we could guard our Queen in HER dreams, as well."

ALKYONE, THEY SAY THAT THE QUEEN, THAT SHE'S PLEADED WITH THE GODS...

SHE'S ASKING FOR A CHILD, CAPTAIN!

OUTRAGEOUS. IMPOSSIBLE!

SHE, THE QUEEN... SHE WOULD NEVER BE SO...

IT WOULD DESTROY US!

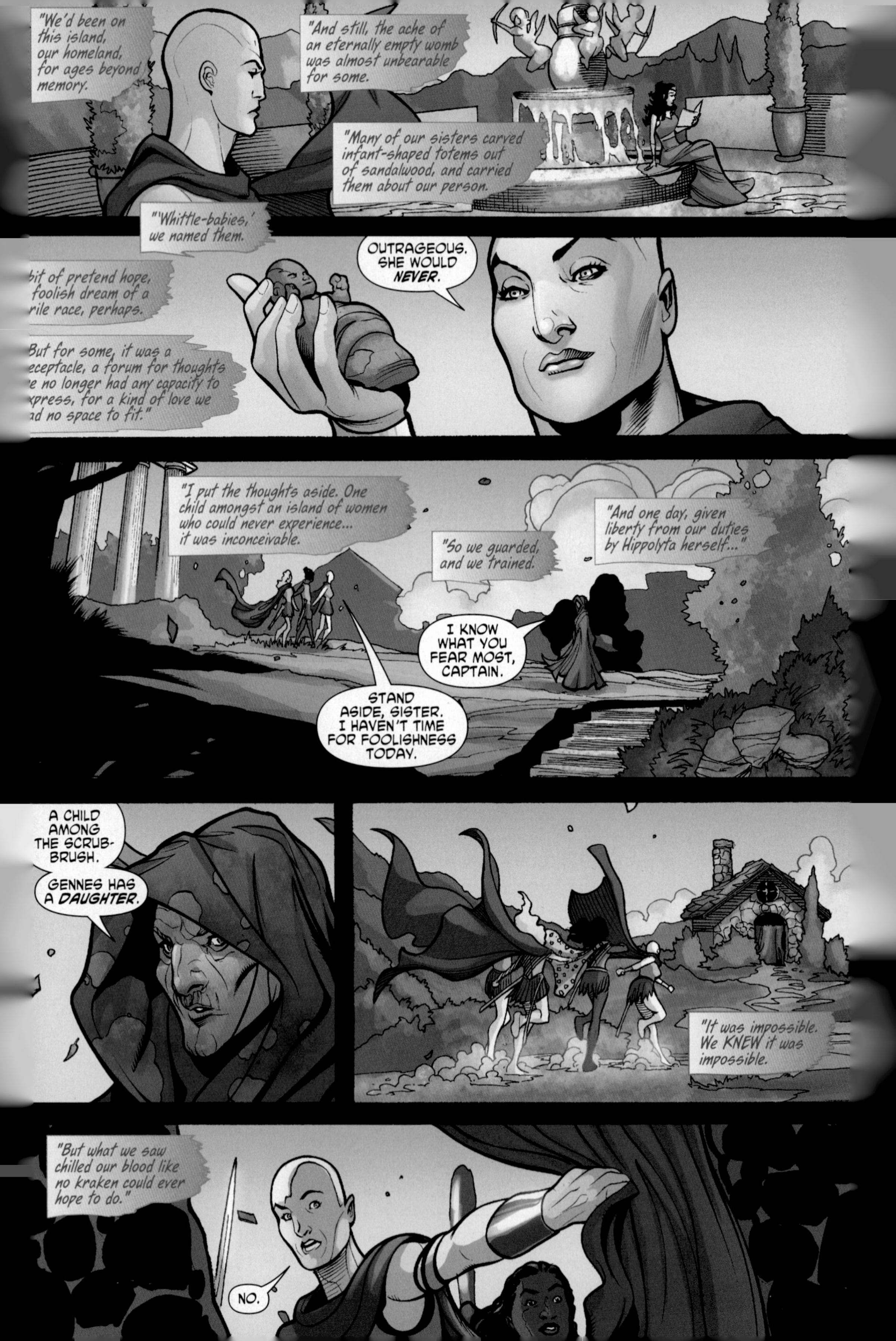
"We'd been on this island, our homeland, for ages beyond memory.
"And still, the ache of an eternally empty womb was almost unbearable for some.
"Many of our sisters carved infant-shaped totems out of sandalwood, and carried them about our person.
"'Whittle-babies,' we named them.
bit of pretend hope, foolish dream of a rile race, perhaps.
But for some, it was a eceptacle, a forum for thoughts e no longer had any capacity to xpress, for a kind of love we ad no space to fit."
OUTRAGEOUS. SHE WOULD NEVER.
"I put the thoughts aside. One child amongst an island of women who could never experience... it was inconceivable.
"So we guarded, and we trained.
"And one day, given liberty from our duties by Hippolyta herself..."
I KNOW WHAT YOU FEAR MOST, CAPTAIN.
STAND ASIDE, SISTER. I HAVEN'T TIME FOR FOOLISHNESS TODAY.
A CHILD AMONG THE SCRUB-BRUSH.
GENNES HAS A DAUGHTER.
"It was impossible. We KNEW it was impossible.
"But what we saw chilled our blood like no kraken could ever hope to do."
NO.

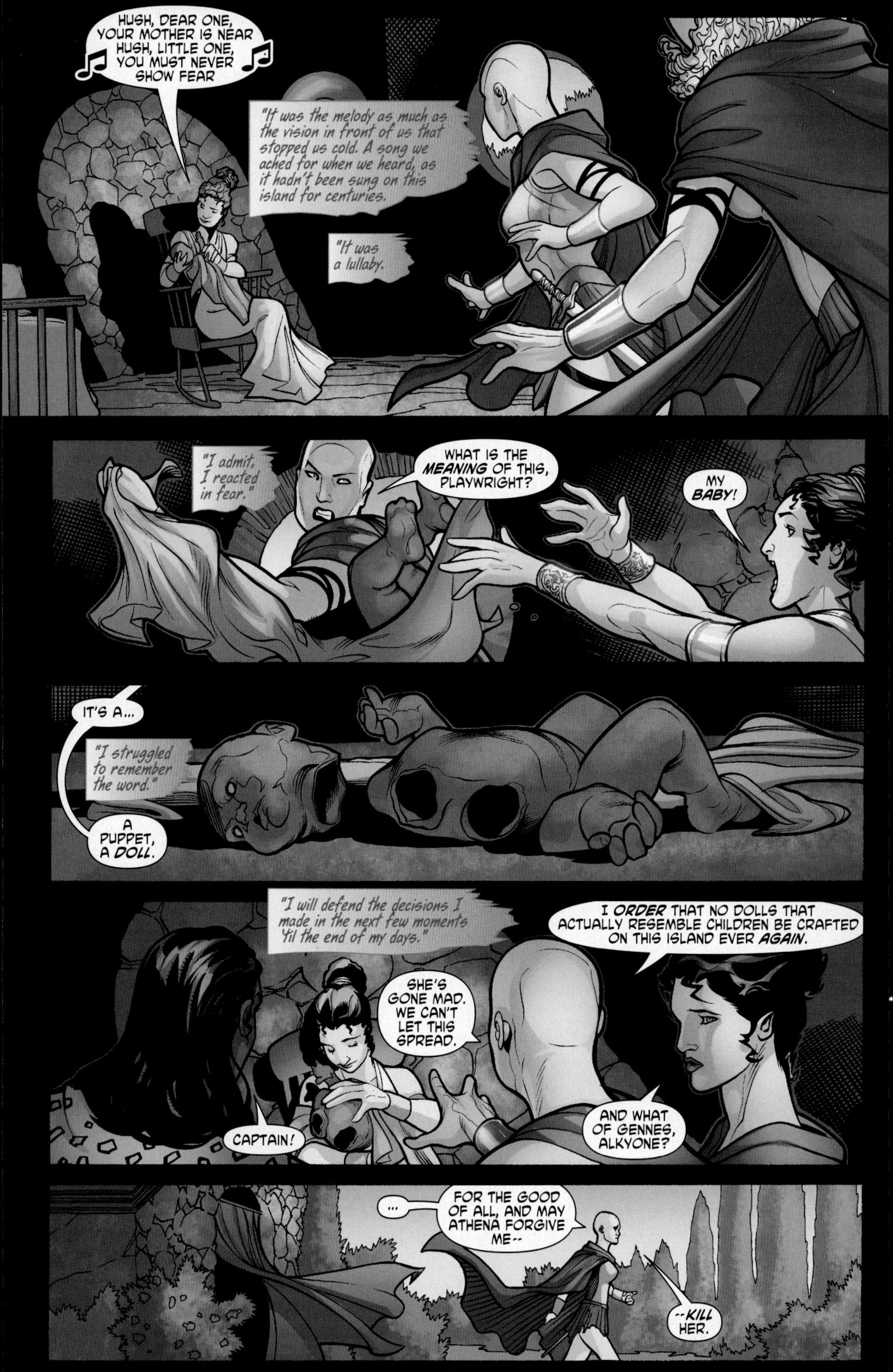
HUSH, DEAR ONE, YOUR MOTHER IS NEAR HUSH, LITTLE ONE, YOU MUST NEVER SHOW FEAR
"It was the melody as much as the vision in front of us that stopped us cold. A song we ached for when we heard, as it hadn't been sung on this island for centuries.
"It was a lullaby.
"I admit, I reacted in fear."
WHAT IS THE MEANING OF THIS, PLAYWRIGHT?
MY BABY!
IT'S A...
"I struggled to remember the word."
A PUPPET, A DOLL.
"I will defend the decisions I made in the next few moments 'til the end of my days."
I ORDER THAT NO DOLLS THAT ACTUALLY RESEMBLE CHILDREN BE CRAFTED ON THIS ISLAND EVER AGAIN.
SHE'S GONE MAD. WE CAN'T LET THIS SPREAD.
CAPTAIN!
AND WHAT OF GENNES, ALKYONE?
...
FOR THE GOOD OF ALL, AND MAY ATHENA FORGIVE ME--
--KILL HER.

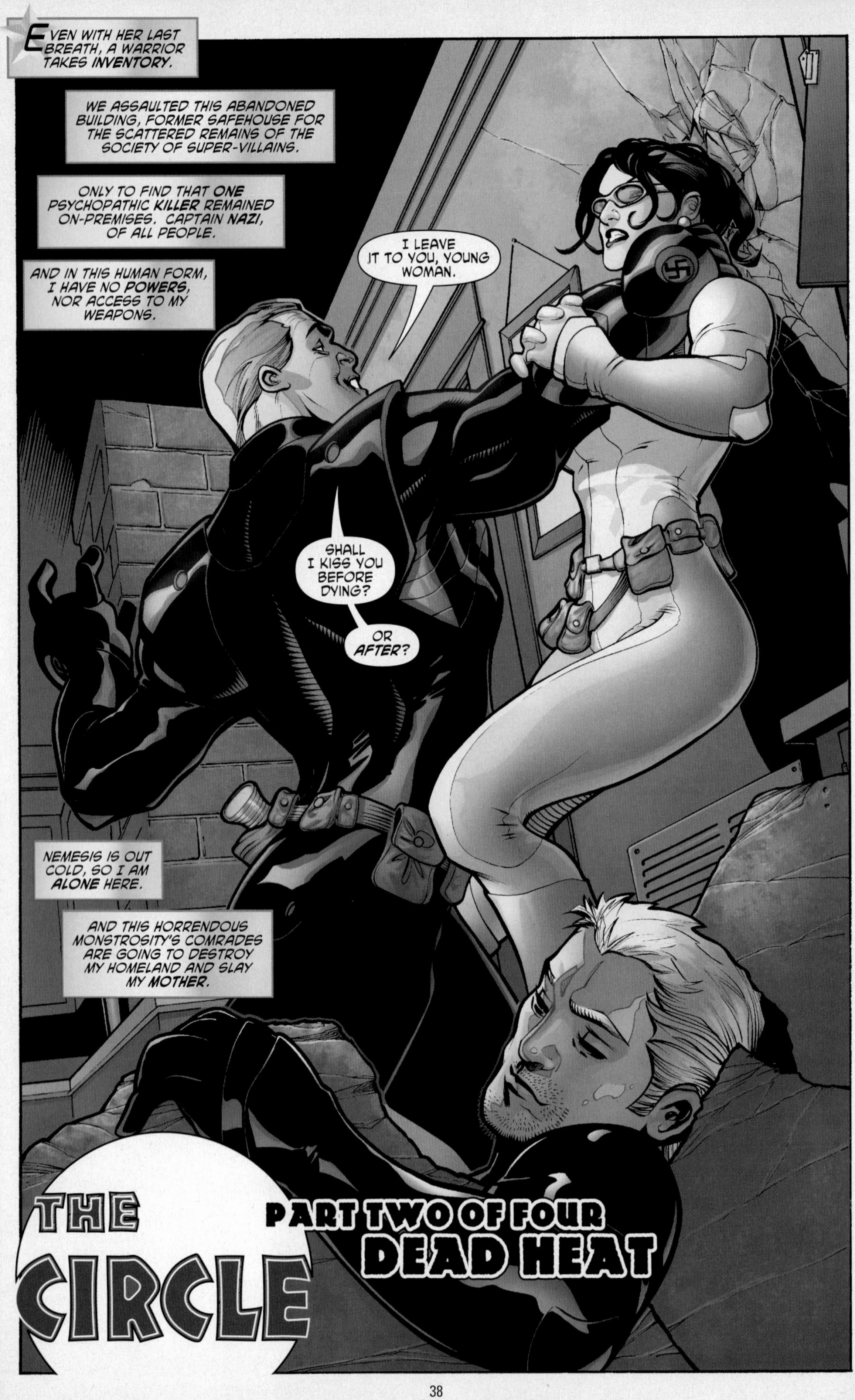

EVEN WITH HER LAST BREATH, A WARRIOR TAKES INVENTORY.
WE ASSAULTED THIS ABANDONED BUILDING, FORMER SAFEHOUSE FOR THE SCATTERED REMAINS OF THE SOCIETY OF SUPER-VILLAINS.
ONLY TO FIND THAT ONE PSYCHOPATHIC KILLER REMAINED ON-PREMISES. CAPTAIN NAZI, OF ALL PEOPLE.
AND IN THIS HUMAN FORM, I HAVE NO POWERS, NOR ACCESS TO MY WEAPONS.
I LEAVE IT TO YOU, YOUNG WOMAN.
SHALL I KISS YOU BEFORE DYING?
OR AFTER?
NEMESIS IS OUT COLD, SO I AM ALONE HERE.
AND THIS HORRENDOUS MONSTROSITY'S COMRADES ARE GOING TO DESTROY MY HOMELAND AND SLAY MY MOTHER.
THE CIRCLE
PART TWO OF FOUR
DEAD HEAT

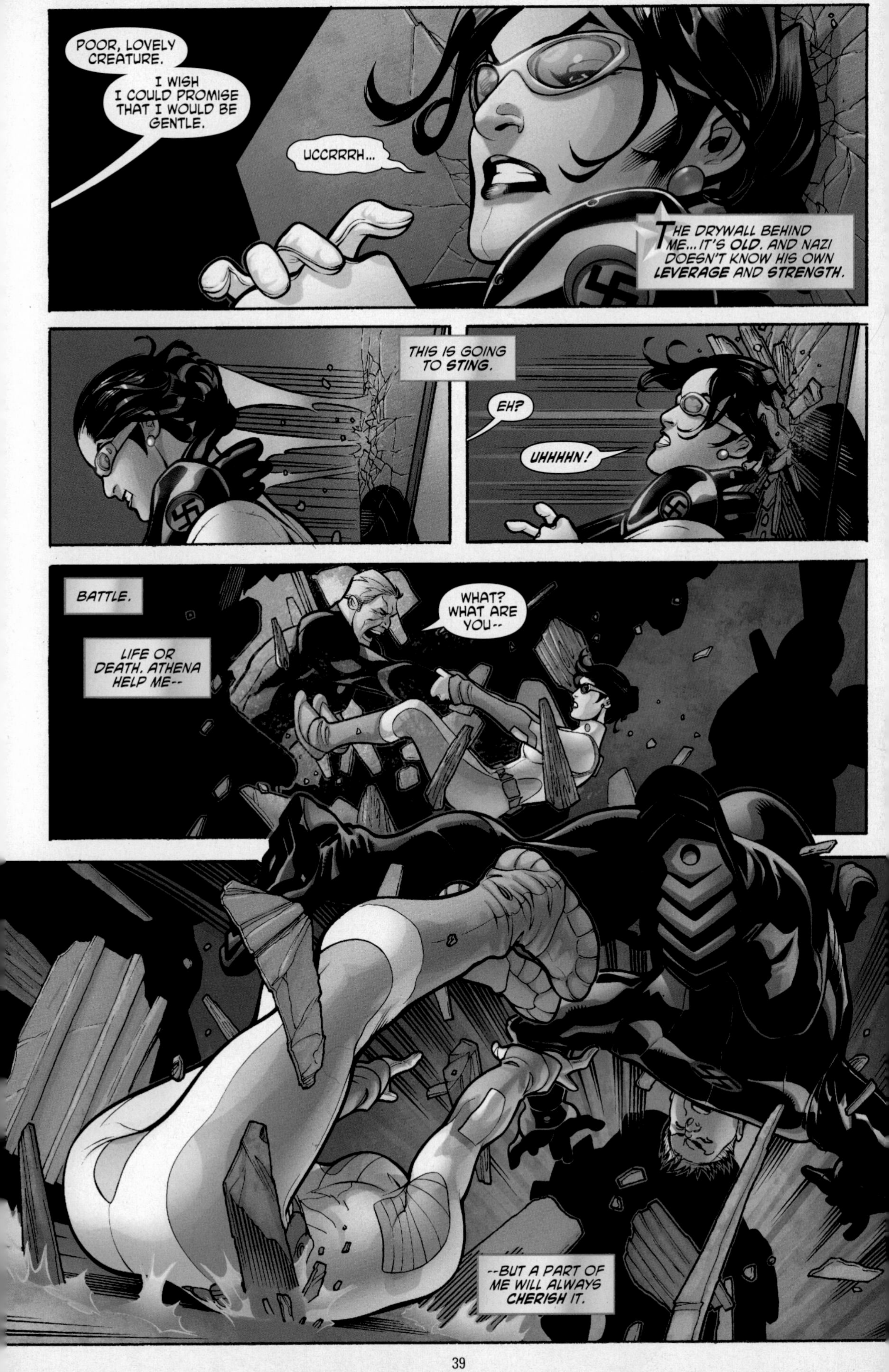
POOR, LOVELY CREATURE.
I WISH I COULD PROMISE THAT I WOULD BE GENTLE.
UCCRRRH...
THE DRYWALL BEHIND ME... IT'S OLD. AND NAZI DOESN'T KNOW HIS OWN LEVERAGE AND STRENGTH.
THIS IS GOING TO STING.
EH?
UHHHHN!
BATTLE.
LIFE OR DEATH. ATHENA HELP ME--
WHAT? WHAT ARE YOU--
--BUT A PART OF ME WILL ALWAYS CHERISH IT.

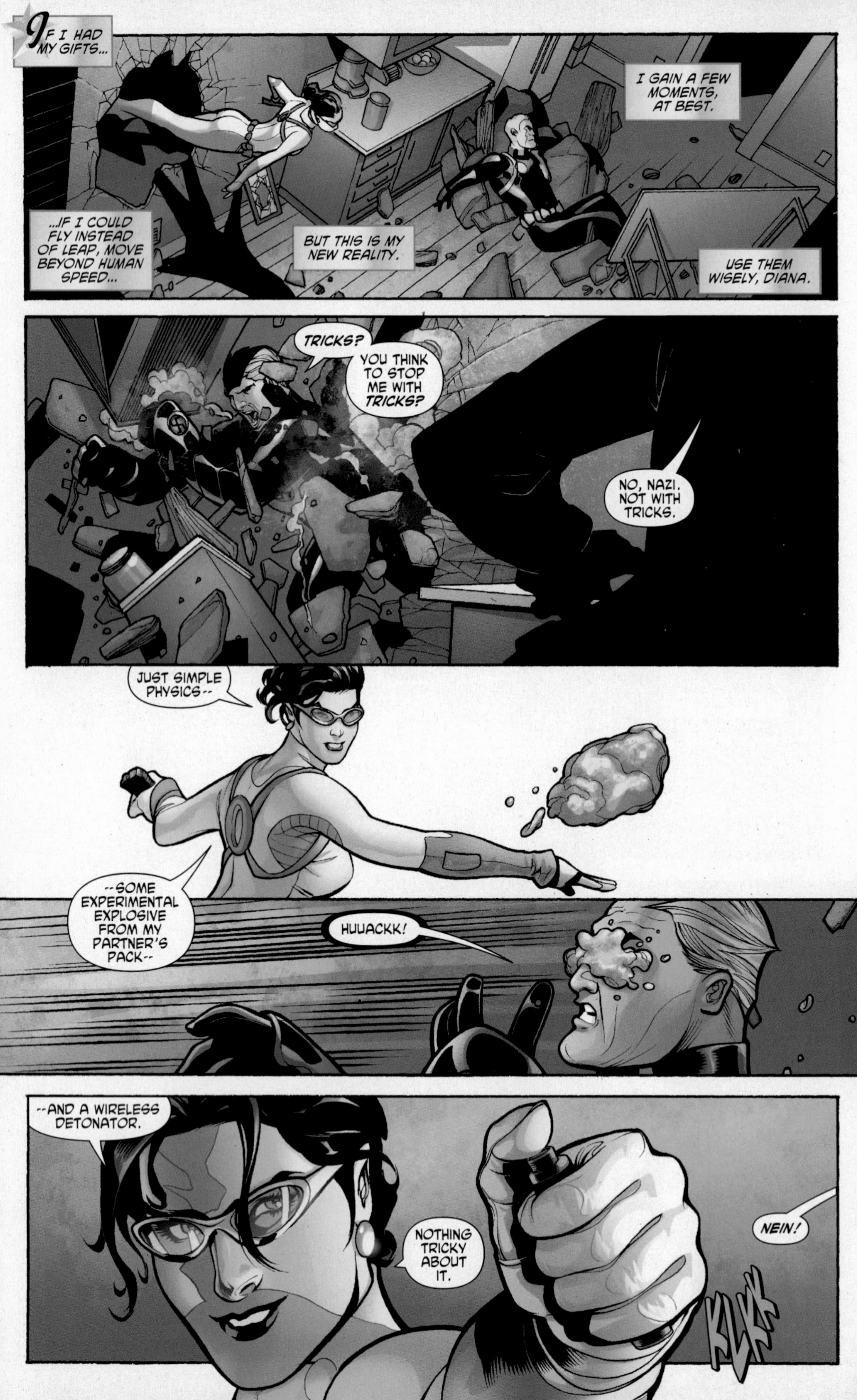
IF I HAD MY GIFTS...
I GAIN A FEW MOMENTS, AT BEST.
...IF I COULD FLY INSTEAD OF LEAP, MOVE BEYOND HUMAN SPEED...
BUT THIS IS MY NEW REALITY.
USE THEM WISELY, DIANA.
TRICKS?
YOU THINK TO STOP ME WITH TRICKS?
NO, NAZI. NOT WITH TRICKS.
JUST SIMPLE PHYSICS--
--SOME EXPERIMENTAL EXPLOSIVE FROM MY PARTNER'S PACK--
HUUACKK!
--AND A WIRELESS DETONATOR.
NOTHING TRICKY ABOUT IT.
NEIN!
KLIK

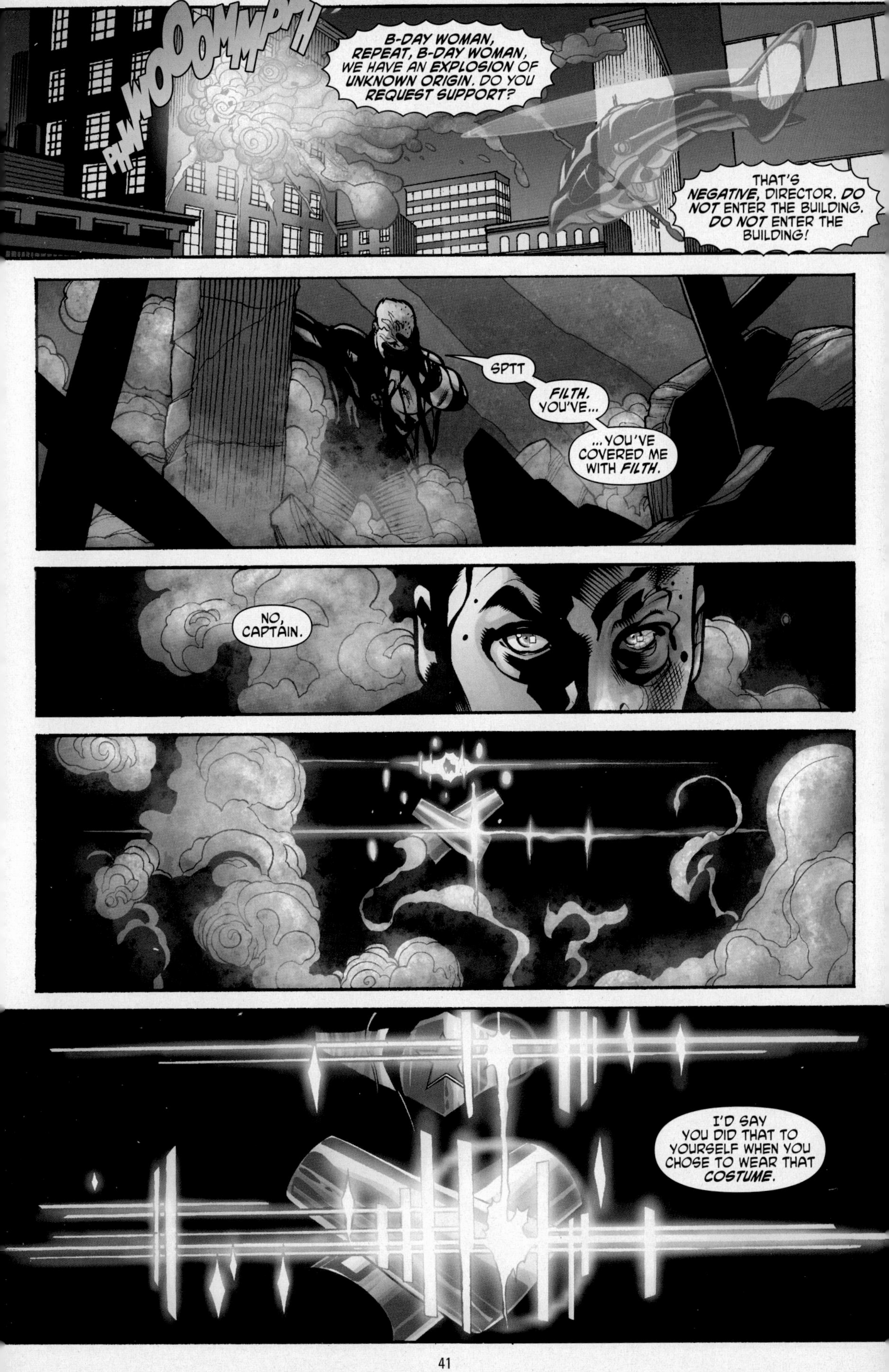
PHWOOOMMPH
B-DAY WOMAN, REPEAT, B-DAY WOMAN, WE HAVE AN EXPLOSION OF UNKNOWN ORIGIN. DO YOU REQUEST SUPPORT?
THAT'S NEGATIVE, DIRECTOR. DO NOT ENTER THE BUILDING. DO NOT ENTER THE BUILDING!
SPTT
FILTH. YOU'VE...
...YOU'VE COVERED ME WITH FILTH.
NO, CAPTAIN.
I'D SAY YOU DID THAT TO YOURSELF WHEN YOU CHOSE TO WEAR THAT COSTUME.

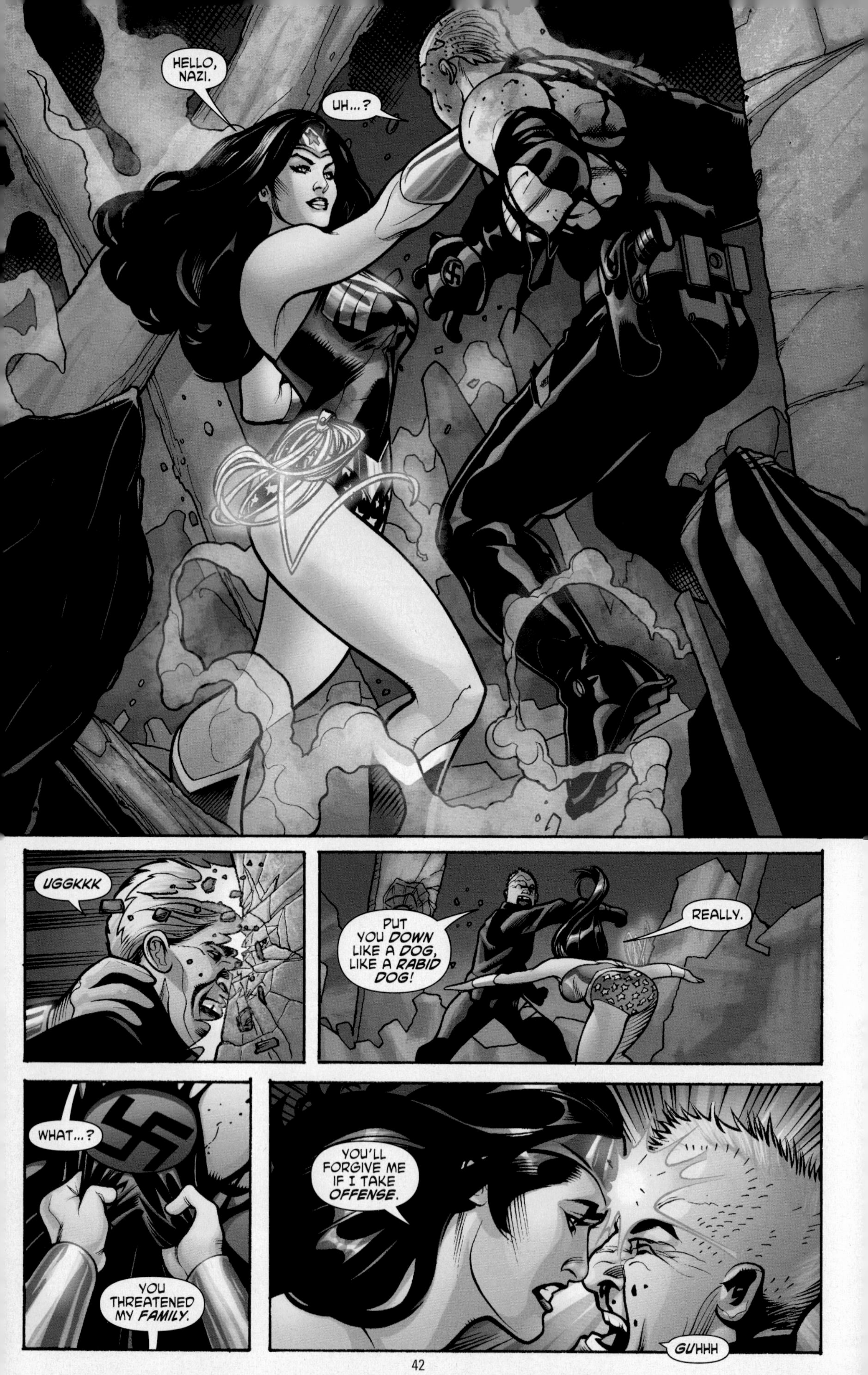

HELLO, NAZI.
UH...?
UGGKKK
PUT YOU *DOWN* LIKE A *DOG*, LIKE A *RABID* *DOG*!
REALLY.
WHAT...?
YOU THREATENED MY *FAMILY*.
YOU'LL FORGIVE ME IF I TAKE *OFFENSE*.
GUHHH

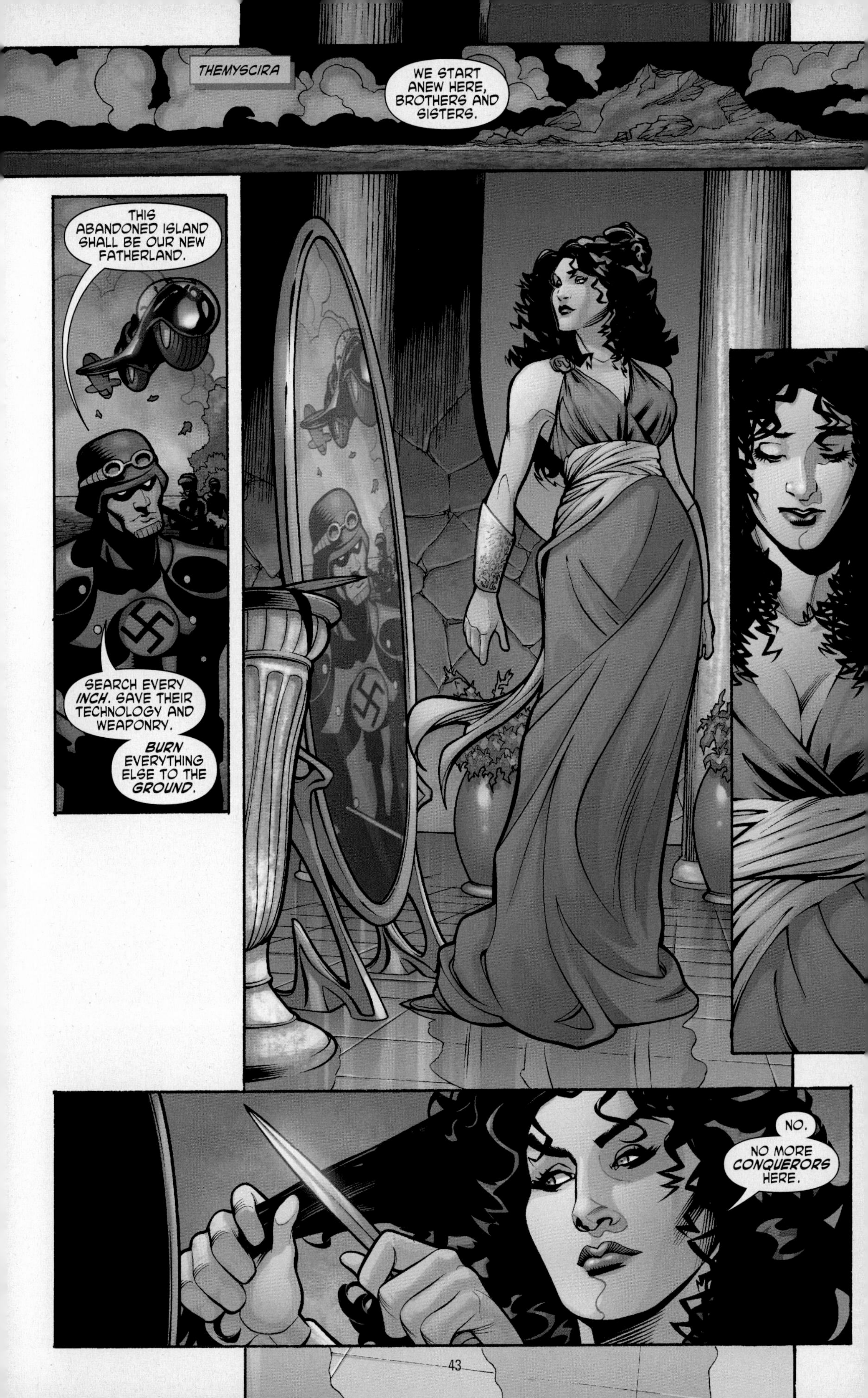
THEMYSCIRA
WE START ANEW HERE, BROTHERS AND SISTERS.
THIS ABANDONED ISLAND SHALL BE OUR NEW FATHERLAND.
SEARCH EVERY INCH. SAVE THEIR TECHNOLOGY AND WEAPONRY.
BURN EVERYTHING ELSE TO THE GROUND.
NO.
NO MORE CONQUERORS HERE.

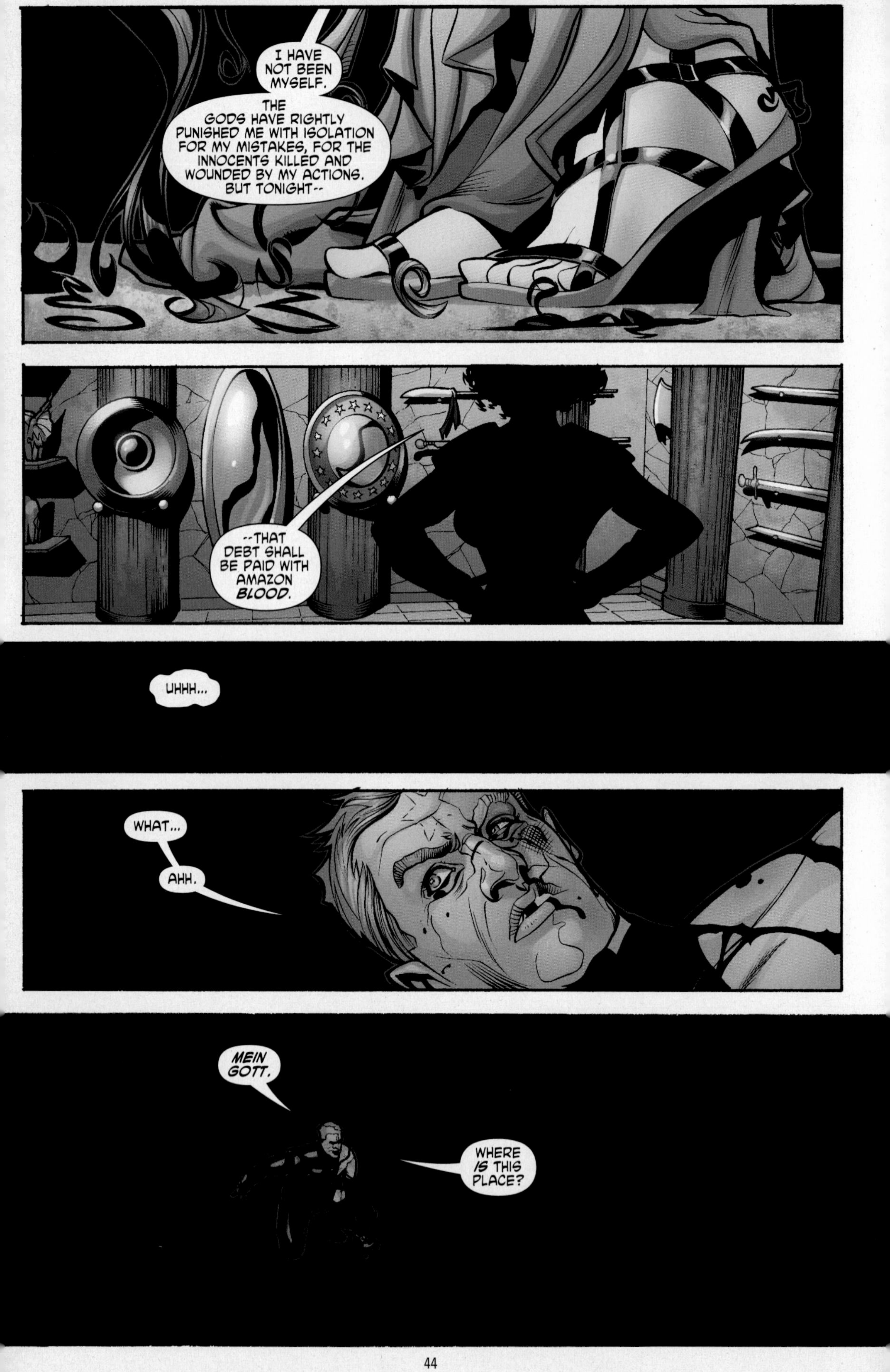
I HAVE NOT BEEN MYSELF.
THE GODS HAVE RIGHTLY PUNISHED ME WITH ISOLATION FOR MY MISTAKES, FOR THE INNOCENTS KILLED AND WOUNDED BY MY ACTIONS. BUT TONIGHT--
--THAT DEBT SHALL BE PAID WITH AMAZON *BLOOD*.
UHHH...
WHAT...
AHH.
MEIN GOTT.
WHERE *IS* THIS PLACE?

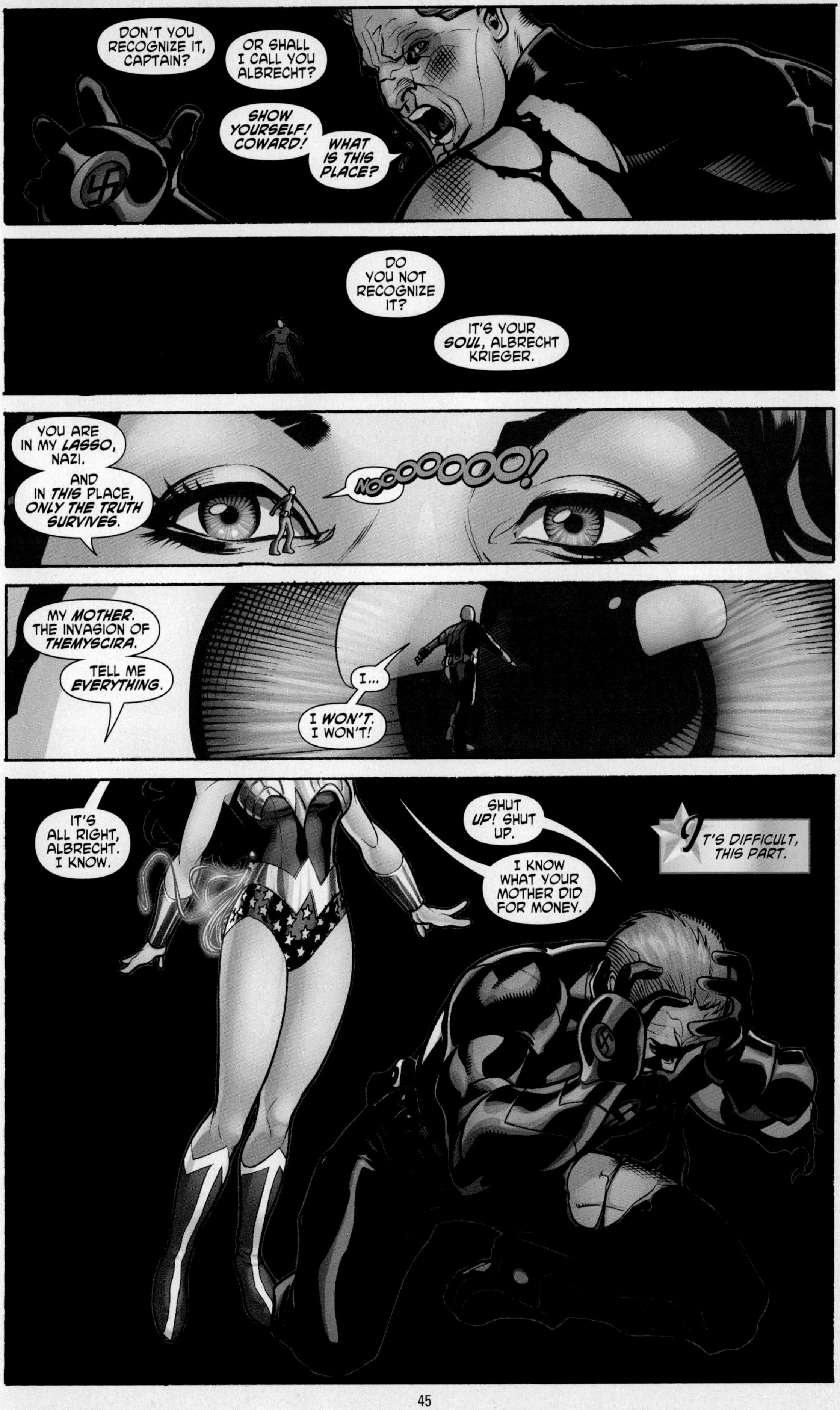
DON'T YOU RECOGNIZE IT, CAPTAIN?
OR SHALL I CALL YOU ALBRECHT?
SHOW YOURSELF! COWARD!
WHAT IS THIS PLACE?
DO YOU NOT RECOGNIZE IT?
IT'S YOUR SOUL, ALBRECHT KRIEGER.
YOU ARE IN MY LASSO, NAZI.
AND IN THIS PLACE, ONLY THE TRUTH SURVIVES.
NOOOOOOOO!
MY MOTHER. THE INVASION OF THEMYSCIRA.
TELL ME EVERYTHING.
I...
I WON'T. I WON'T!
IT'S ALL RIGHT, ALBRECHT. I KNOW.
SHUT UP! SHUT UP.
I KNOW WHAT YOUR MOTHER DID FOR MONEY.
IT'S DIFFICULT, THIS PART.

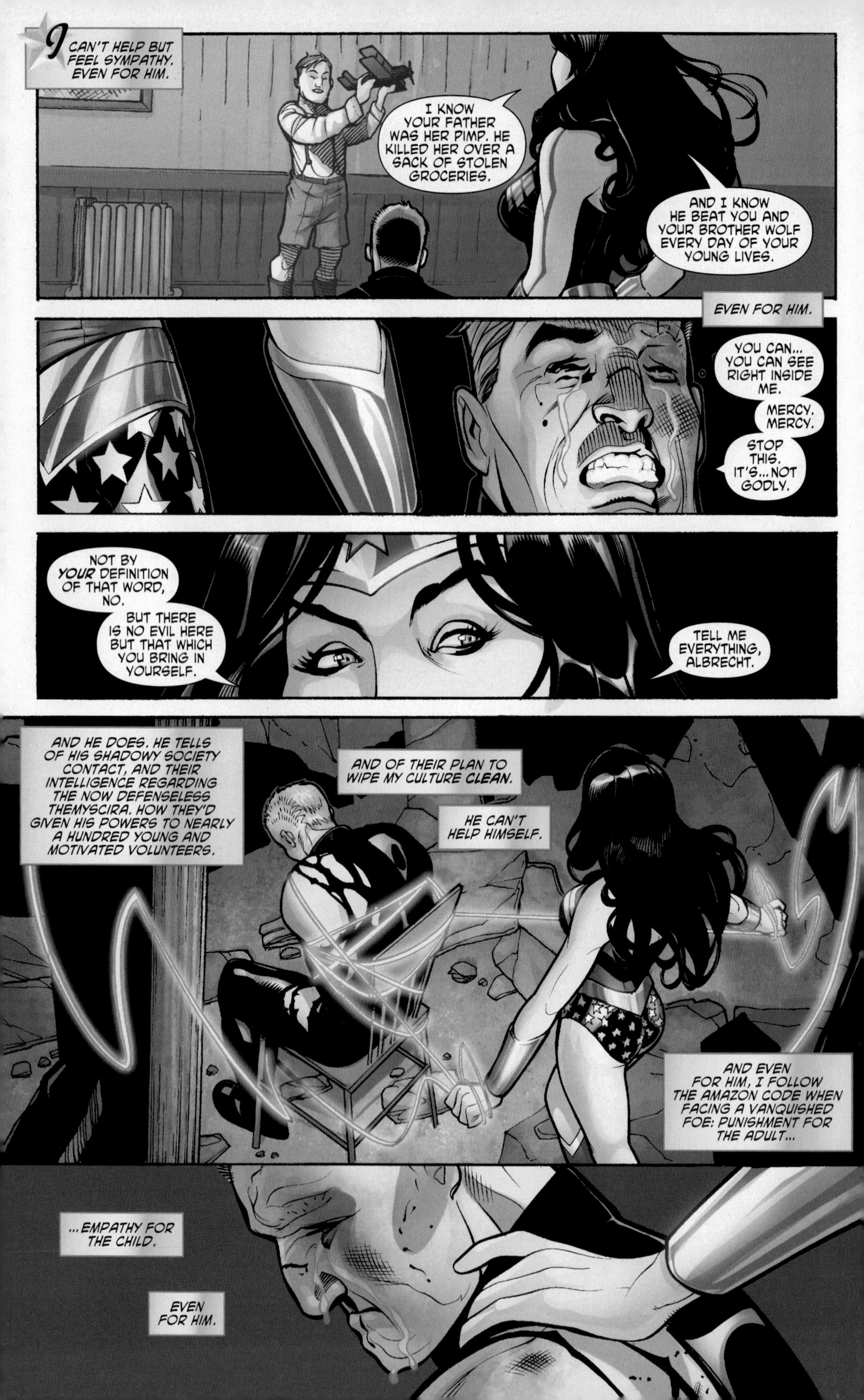
I CAN'T HELP BUT FEEL SYMPATHY. EVEN FOR HIM.
I KNOW YOUR FATHER WAS HER PIMP. HE KILLED HER OVER A SACK OF STOLEN GROCERIES.
AND I KNOW HE BEAT YOU AND YOUR BROTHER WOLF EVERY DAY OF YOUR YOUNG LIVES.
EVEN FOR HIM.
YOU CAN... YOU CAN SEE RIGHT INSIDE ME.
MERCY. MERCY.
STOP THIS. IT'S...NOT GODLY.
NOT BY YOUR DEFINITION OF THAT WORD, NO.
BUT THERE IS NO EVIL HERE BUT THAT WHICH YOU BRING IN YOURSELF.
TELL ME EVERYTHING, ALBRECHT.
AND HE DOES. HE TELLS OF HIS SHADOWY SOCIETY CONTACT, AND THEIR INTELLIGENCE REGARDING THE NOW DEFENSELESS THEMYSCIRA. HOW THEY'D GIVEN HIS POWERS TO NEARLY A HUNDRED YOUNG AND MOTIVATED VOLUNTEERS.
AND OF THEIR PLAN TO WIPE MY CULTURE CLEAN.
HE CAN'T HELP HIMSELF.
AND EVEN FOR HIM, I FOLLOW THE AMAZON CODE WHEN FACING A VANQUISHED FOE: PUNISHMENT FOR THE ADULT...
...EMPATHY FOR THE CHILD.
EVEN FOR HIM.

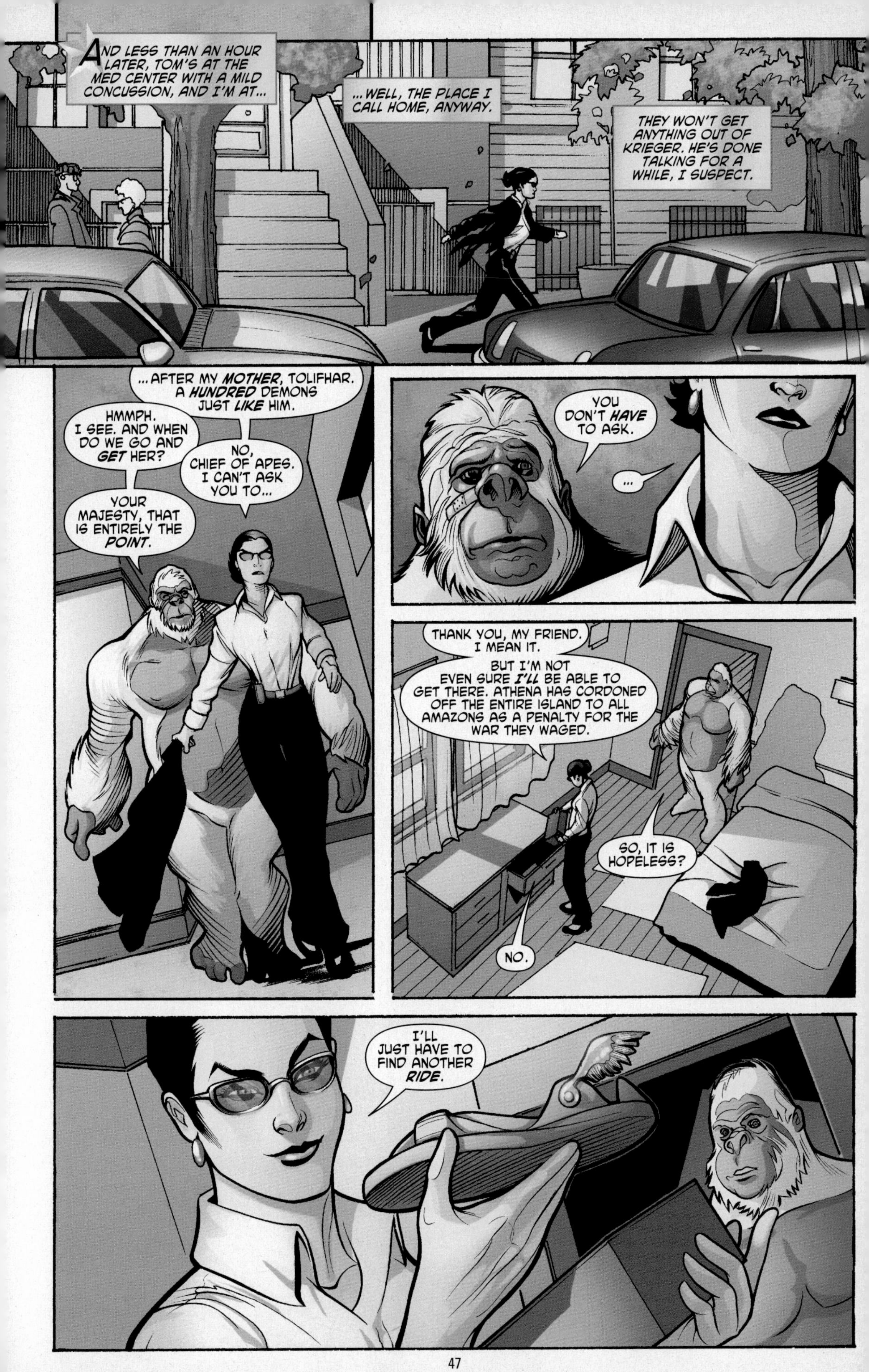
AND LESS THAN AN HOUR LATER, TOM'S AT THE MED CENTER WITH A MILD CONCUSSION, AND I'M AT...
...WELL, THE PLACE I CALL HOME, ANYWAY.
THEY WON'T GET ANYTHING OUT OF KRIEGER. HE'S DONE TALKING FOR A WHILE, I SUSPECT.
...AFTER MY MOTHER, TOLIFHAR. A HUNDRED DEMONS JUST LIKE HIM.
HMMPH. I SEE. AND WHEN DO WE GO AND GET HER?
NO, CHIEF OF APES. I CAN'T ASK YOU TO...
YOUR MAJESTY, THAT IS ENTIRELY THE POINT.
YOU DON'T HAVE TO ASK.
...
THANK YOU, MY FRIEND. I MEAN IT.
BUT I'M NOT EVEN SURE I'LL BE ABLE TO GET THERE. ATHENA HAS CORDONED OFF THE ENTIRE ISLAND TO ALL AMAZONS AS A PENALTY FOR THE WAR THEY WAGED.
SO, IT IS HOPELESS?
NO.
I'LL JUST HAVE TO FIND ANOTHER RIDE.

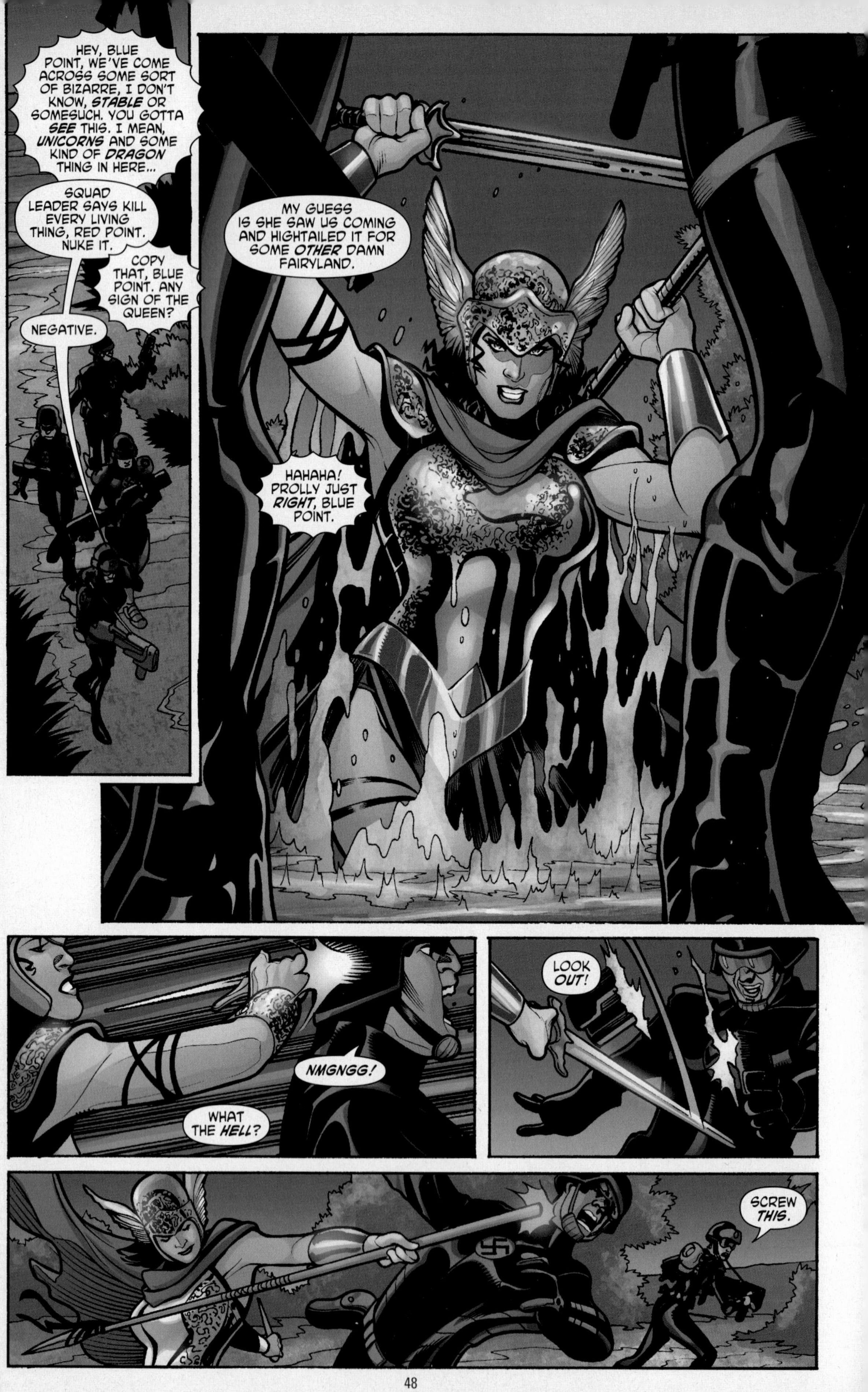
HEY, BLUE POINT, WE'VE COME ACROSS SOME SORT OF BIZARRE, I DON'T KNOW, STABLE OR SOMESUCH. YOU GOTTA SEE THIS. I MEAN, UNICORNS AND SOME KIND OF DRAGON THING IN HERE...
SQUAD LEADER SAYS KILL EVERY LIVING THING, RED POINT. NUKE IT.
COPY THAT, BLUE POINT. ANY SIGN OF THE QUEEN?
NEGATIVE.
MY GUESS IS SHE SAW US COMING AND HIGHTAILED IT FOR SOME OTHER DAMN FAIRYLAND.
HAHAHA! PROLLY JUST RIGHT, BLUE POINT.
NMGNGG!
WHAT THE HELL?
LOOK OUT!
SCREW THIS.

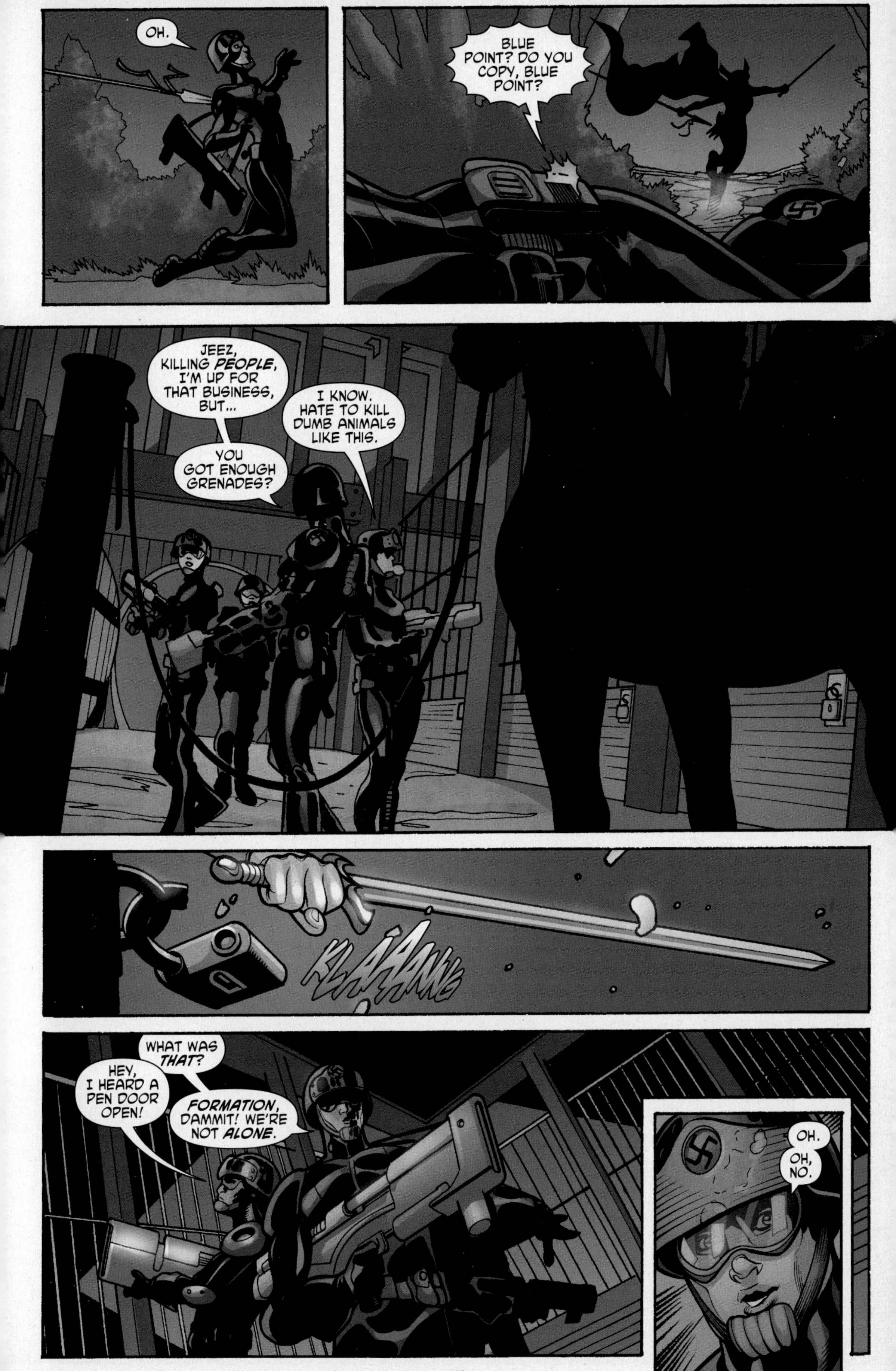
OH.
BLUE POINT? DO YOU COPY, BLUE POINT?
JEEZ, KILLING PEOPLE, I'M UP FOR THAT BUSINESS, BUT...
YOU GOT ENOUGH GRENADES?
I KNOW. HATE TO KILL DUMB ANIMALS LIKE THIS.
KLAAANG
WHAT WAS THAT?
HEY, I HEARD A PEN DOOR OPEN!
FORMATION, DAMMIT! WE'RE NOT ALONE.
OH. OH, NO.

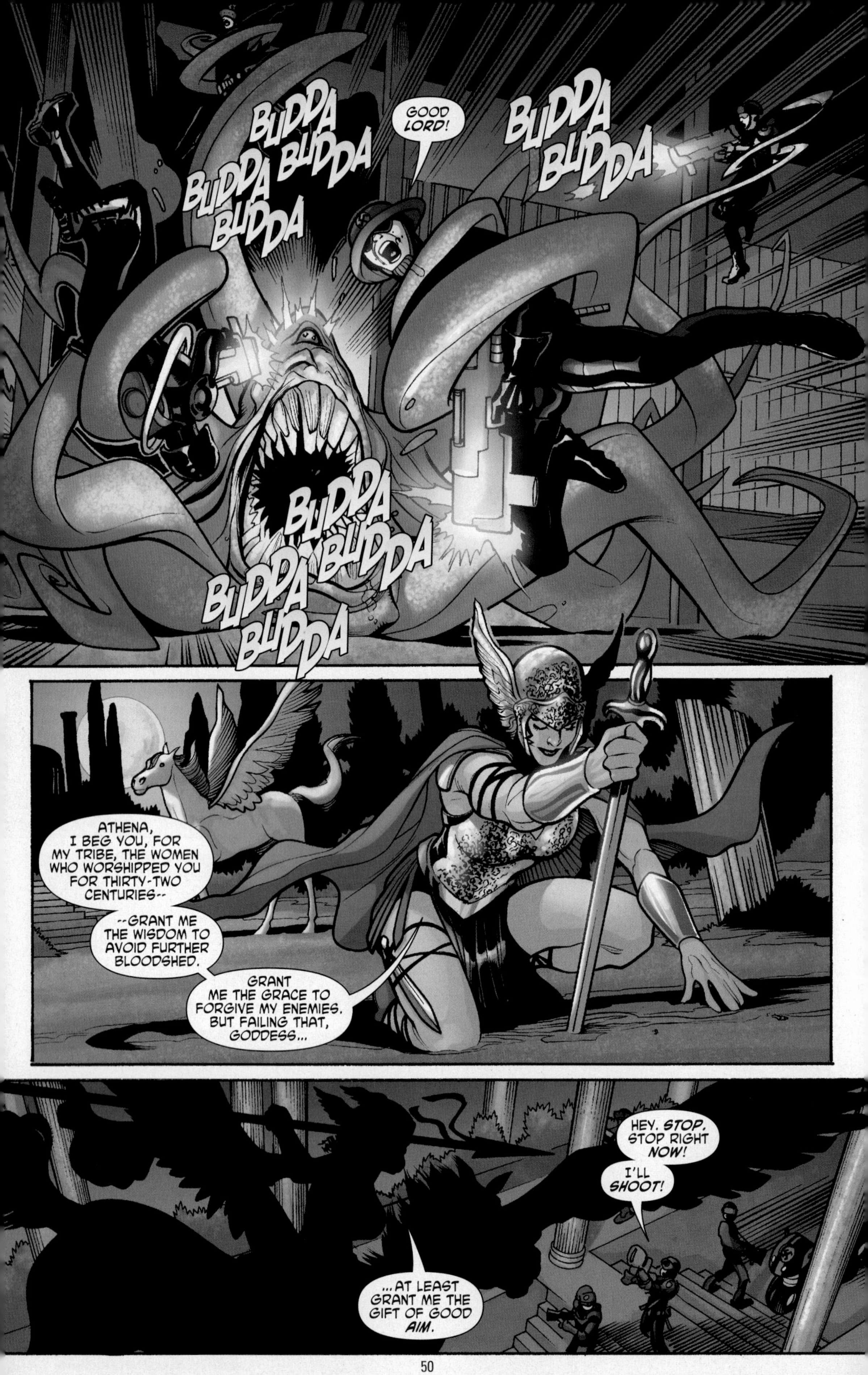
BUDDA BUDDA BUDDA BUDDA
GOOD LORD!
BUDDA BUDDA
BUDDA BUDDA BUDDA BUDDA
ATHENA, I BEG YOU, FOR MY TRIBE, THE WOMEN WHO WORSHIPPED YOU FOR THIRTY-TWO CENTURIES--
--GRANT ME THE WISDOM TO AVOID FURTHER BLOODSHED.
GRANT ME THE GRACE TO FORGIVE MY ENEMIES. BUT FAILING THAT, GODDESS...
HEY. STOP. STOP RIGHT NOW!
I'LL SHOOT!
...AT LEAST GRANT ME THE GIFT OF GOOD AIM.

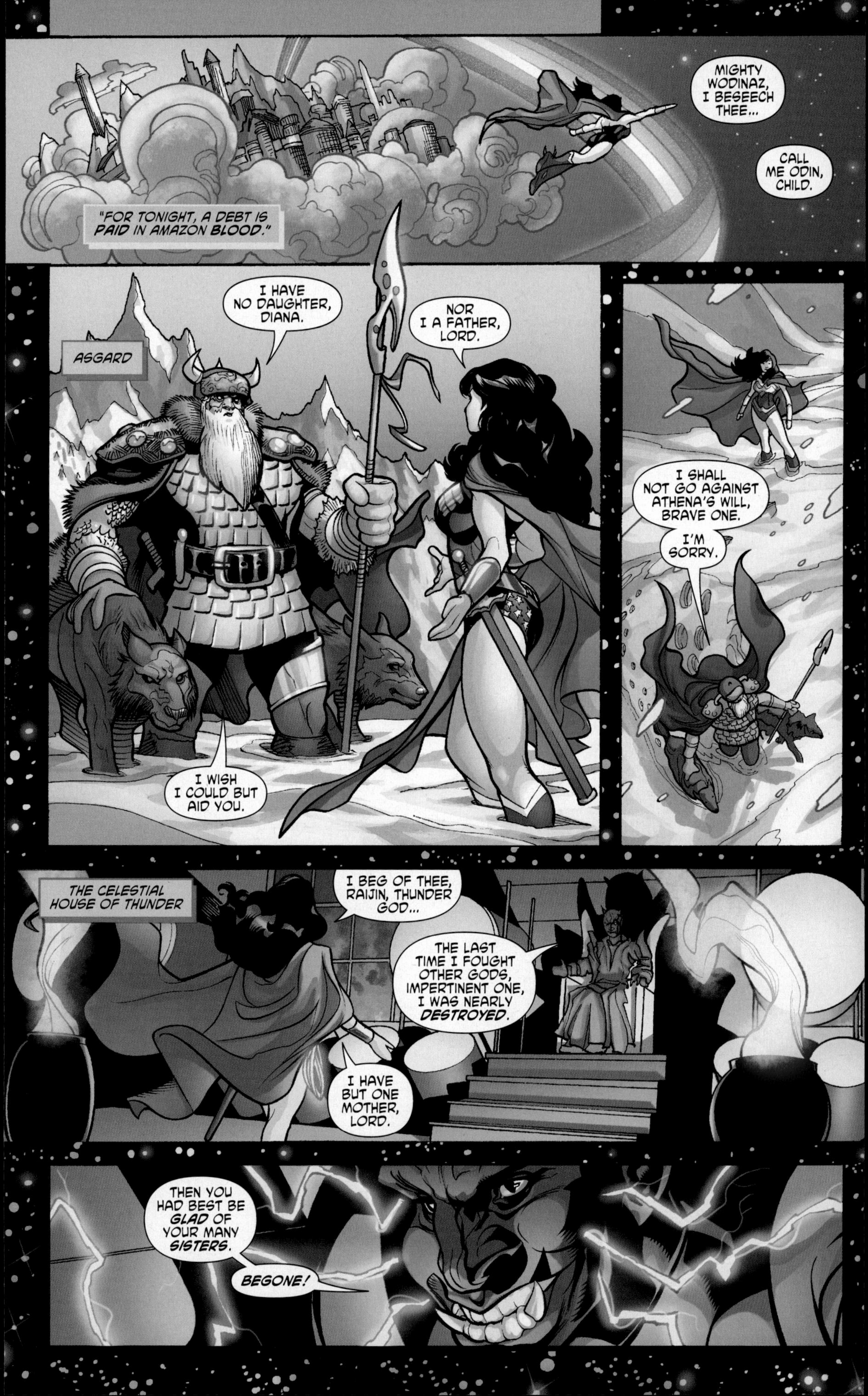
MIGHTY WODINAZ, I BESEECH THEE...
CALL ME ODIN, CHILD.
"FOR TONIGHT, A DEBT IS PAID IN AMAZON BLOOD."
ASGARD
I HAVE NO DAUGHTER, DIANA.
NOR I A FATHER, LORD.
I WISH I COULD BUT AID YOU.
I SHALL NOT GO AGAINST ATHENA'S WILL, BRAVE ONE.
I'M SORRY.
THE CELESTIAL HOUSE OF THUNDER
I BEG OF THEE, RAIJIN, THUNDER GOD...
THE LAST TIME I FOUGHT OTHER GODS, IMPERTINENT ONE, I WAS NEARLY DESTROYED.
I HAVE BUT ONE MOTHER, LORD.
THEN YOU HAD BEST BE GLAD OF YOUR MANY SISTERS.
BEGONE!

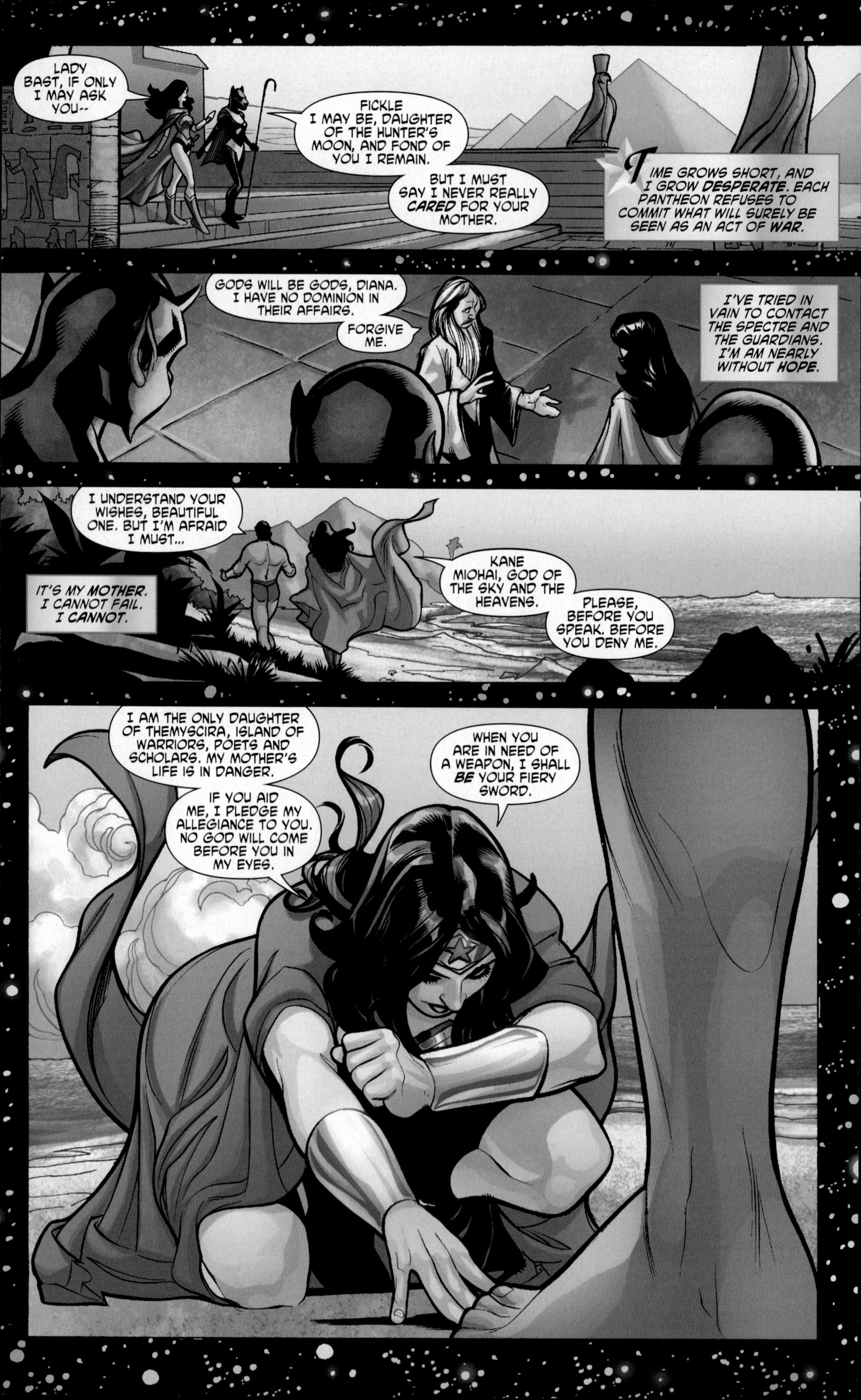
LADY BAST, IF ONLY I MAY ASK YOU--
FICKLE I MAY BE, DAUGHTER OF THE HUNTER'S MOON, AND FOND OF YOU I REMAIN.
BUT I MUST SAY I NEVER REALLY CARED FOR YOUR MOTHER.
TIME GROWS SHORT, AND I GROW DESPERATE. EACH PANTHEON REFUSES TO COMMIT WHAT WILL SURELY BE SEEN AS AN ACT OF WAR.
GODS WILL BE GODS, DIANA. I HAVE NO DOMINION IN THEIR AFFAIRS.
FORGIVE ME.
I'VE TRIED IN VAIN TO CONTACT THE SPECTRE AND THE GUARDIANS. I'M AM NEARLY WITHOUT HOPE.
I UNDERSTAND YOUR WISHES, BEAUTIFUL ONE. BUT I'M AFRAID I MUST...
IT'S MY MOTHER. I CANNOT FAIL. I CANNOT.
KANE MIOHAI, GOD OF THE SKY AND THE HEAVENS.
PLEASE, BEFORE YOU SPEAK. BEFORE YOU DENY ME.
I AM THE ONLY DAUGHTER OF THEMYSCIRA, ISLAND OF WARRIORS, POETS AND SCHOLARS. MY MOTHER'S LIFE IS IN DANGER.
IF YOU AID ME, I PLEDGE MY ALLEGIANCE TO YOU. NO GOD WILL COME BEFORE YOU IN MY EYES.
WHEN YOU ARE IN NEED OF A WEAPON, I SHALL BE YOUR FIERY SWORD.

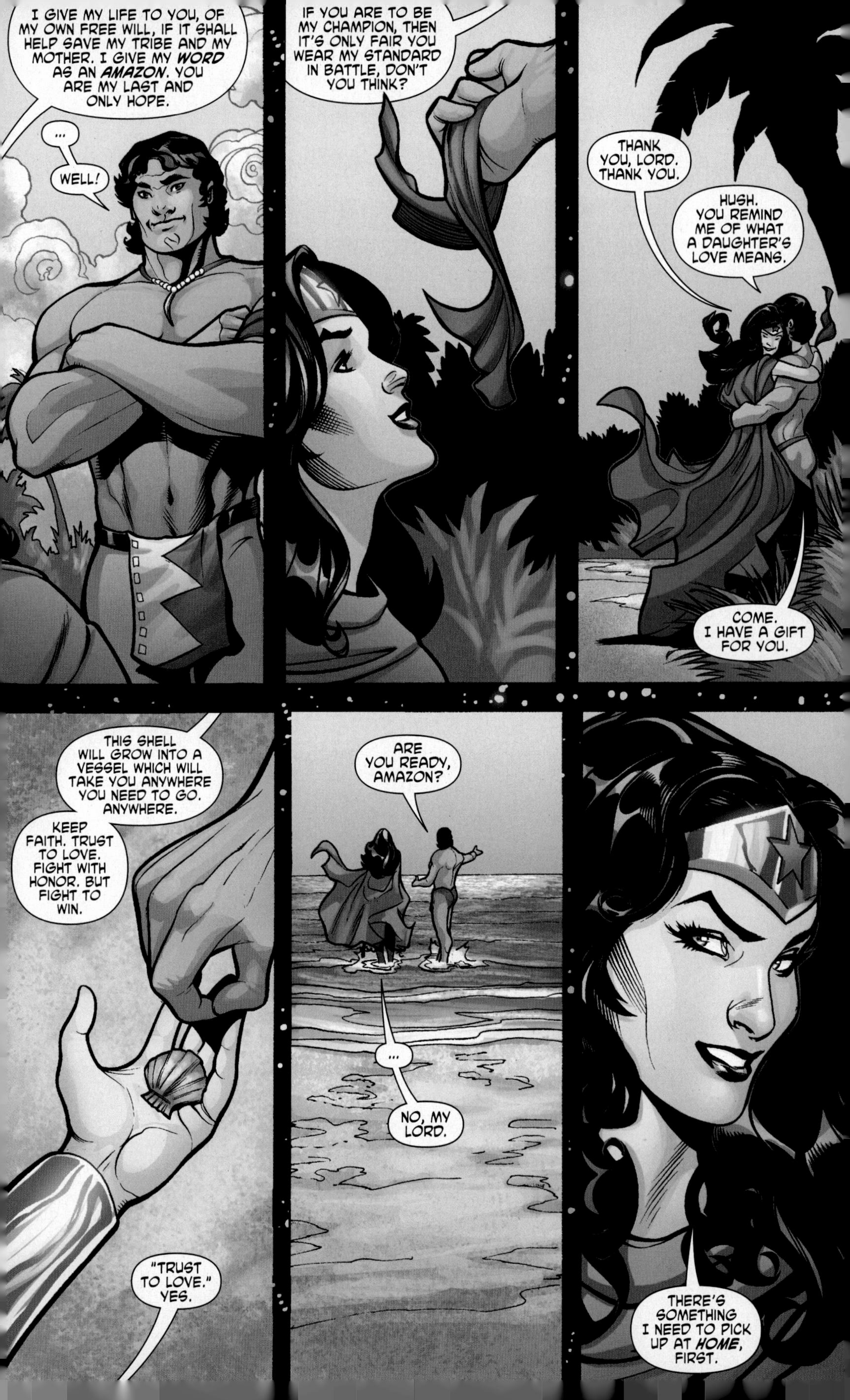
I GIVE MY LIFE TO YOU, OF MY OWN FREE WILL, IF IT SHALL HELP SAVE MY TRIBE AND MY MOTHER. I GIVE MY WORD AS AN AMAZON. YOU ARE MY LAST AND ONLY HOPE.
...
WELL!
IF YOU ARE TO BE MY CHAMPION, THEN IT'S ONLY FAIR YOU WEAR MY STANDARD IN BATTLE, DON'T YOU THINK?
THANK YOU, LORD. THANK YOU.
HUSH. YOU REMIND ME OF WHAT A DAUGHTER'S LOVE MEANS.
COME. I HAVE A GIFT FOR YOU.
THIS SHELL WILL GROW INTO A VESSEL WHICH WILL TAKE YOU ANYWHERE YOU NEED TO GO. ANYWHERE.
KEEP FAITH. TRUST TO LOVE. FIGHT WITH HONOR. BUT FIGHT TO WIN.
"TRUST TO LOVE." YES.
ARE YOU READY, AMAZON?
...
NO, MY LORD.
THERE'S SOMETHING I NEED TO PICK UP AT HOME, FIRST.

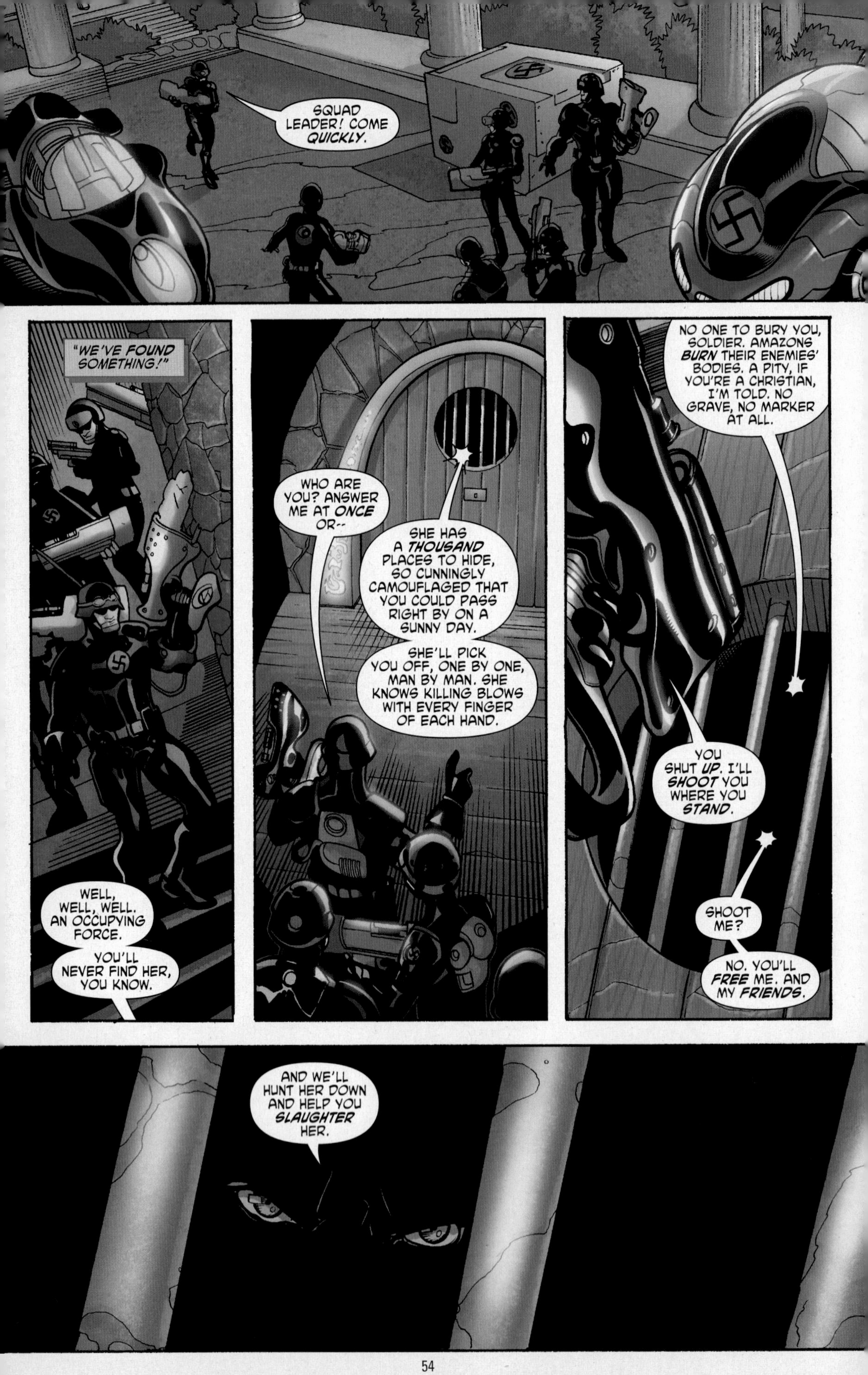

SQUAD LEADER! COME QUICKLY.
"WE'VE FOUND SOMETHING!"
WELL, WELL, WELL. AN OCCUPYING FORCE.
YOU'LL NEVER FIND HER, YOU KNOW.
WHO ARE YOU? ANSWER ME AT ONCE OR--
SHE HAS A THOUSAND PLACES TO HIDE, SO CUNNINGLY CAMOUFLAGED THAT YOU COULD PASS RIGHT BY ON A SUNNY DAY.
SHE'LL PICK YOU OFF, ONE BY ONE, MAN BY MAN. SHE KNOWS KILLING BLOWS WITH EVERY FINGER OF EACH HAND.
NO ONE TO BURY YOU, SOLDIER. AMAZONS BURN THEIR ENEMIES' BODIES. A PITY, IF YOU'RE A CHRISTIAN, I'M TOLD. NO GRAVE, NO MARKER AT ALL.
YOU SHUT UP. I'LL SHOOT YOU WHERE YOU STAND.
SHOOT ME?
NO. YOU'LL FREE ME. AND MY FRIENDS.
AND WE'LL HUNT HER DOWN AND HELP YOU SLAUGHTER HER.

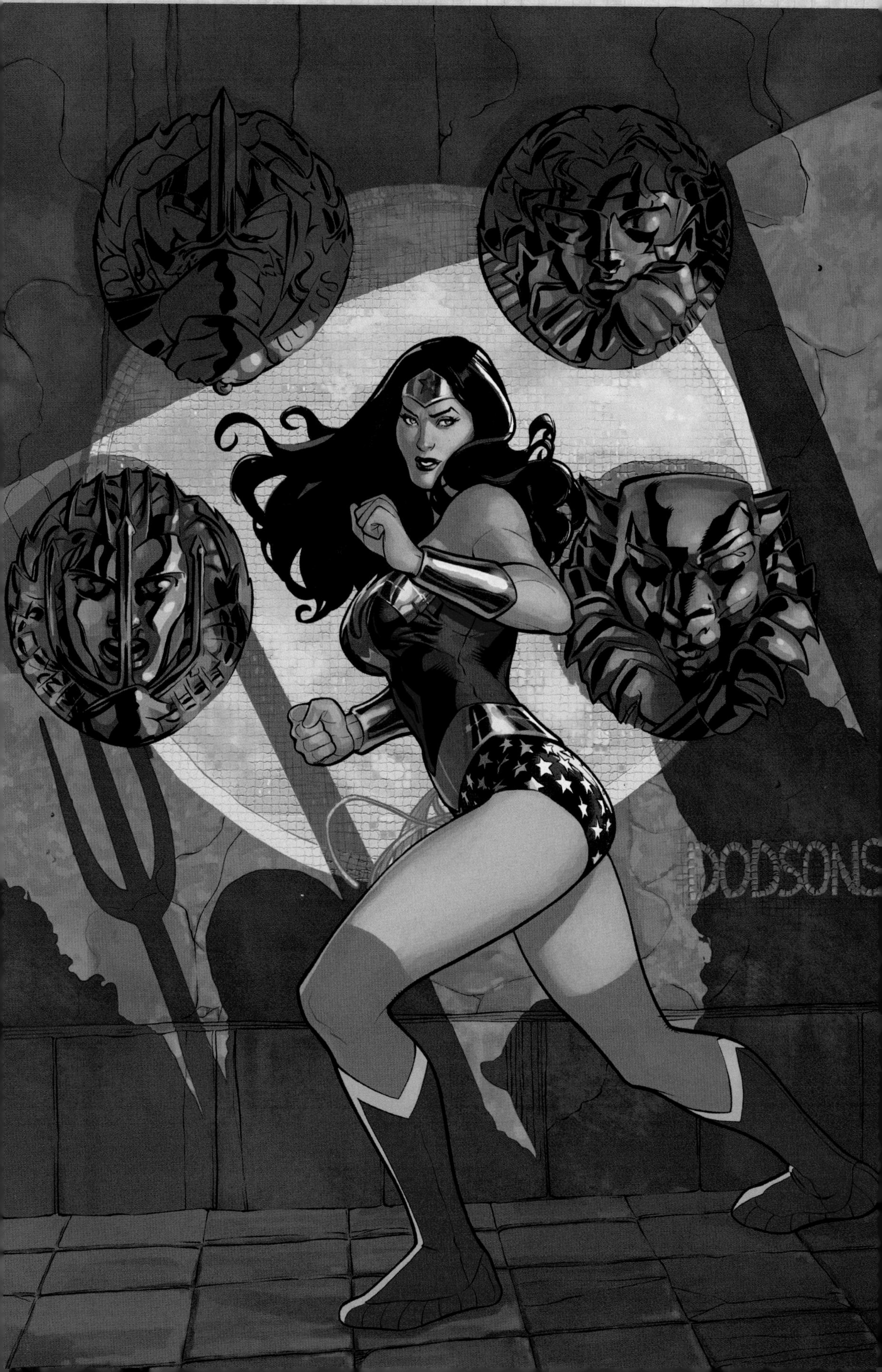
DODSONS

Art this issue by Terry Dodson & Rachel Dodson (pages 57-67, 75-78), and Ron Randall (pages 68-74)

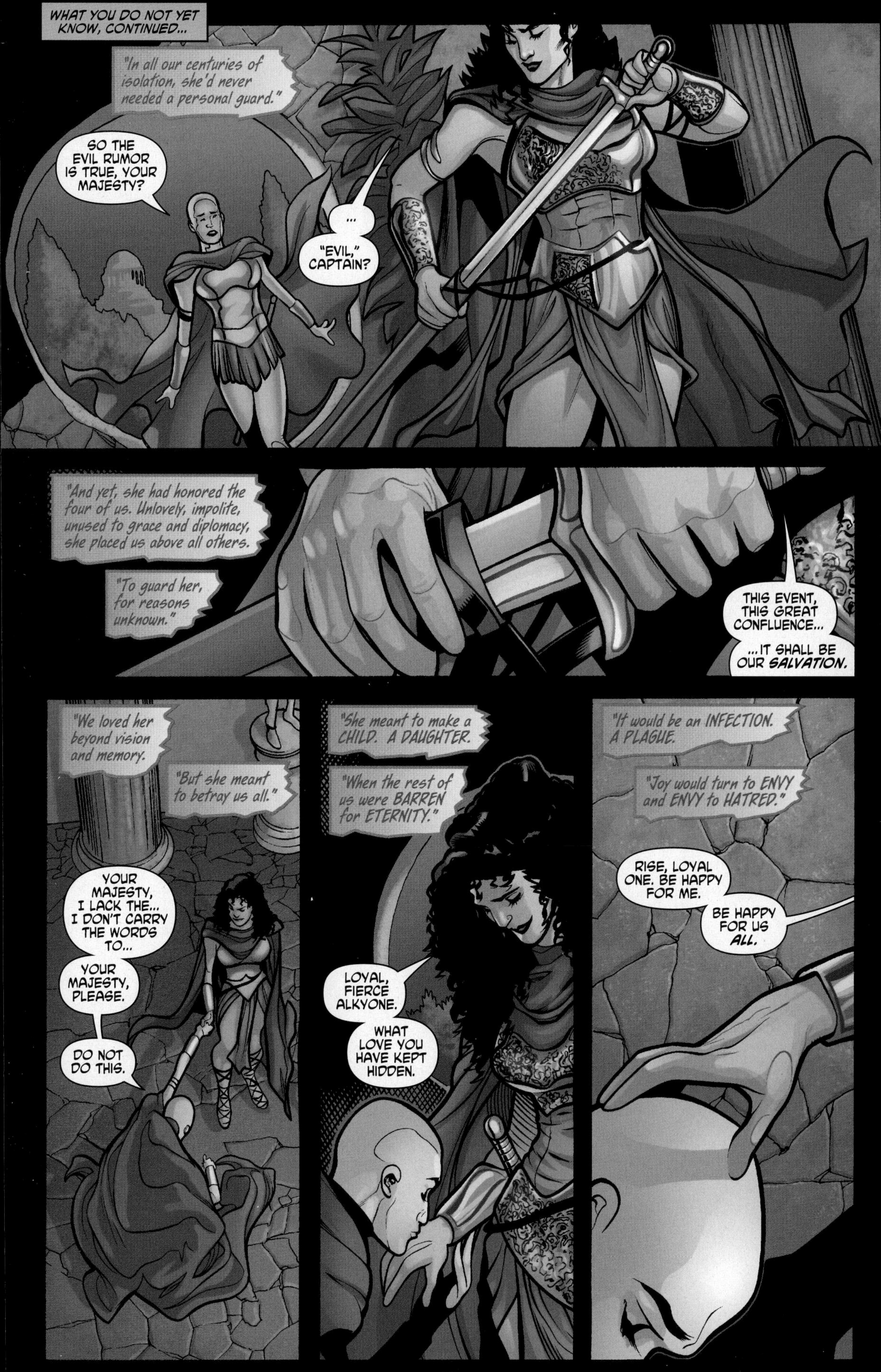
WHAT YOU DO NOT YET KNOW, CONTINUED...
"In all our centuries of isolation, she'd never needed a personal guard."
SO THE EVIL RUMOR IS TRUE, YOUR MAJESTY?
...
"EVIL," CAPTAIN?
"And yet, she had honored the four of us. Unlovely, impolite, unused to grace and diplomacy, she placed us above all others.
"To guard her, for reasons unknown."
THIS EVENT, THIS GREAT CONFLUENCE...
...IT SHALL BE OUR SALVATION.
"We loved her beyond vision and memory.
"But she meant to betray us all."
YOUR MAJESTY, I LACK THE... I DON'T CARRY THE WORDS TO...
YOUR MAJESTY, PLEASE.
DO NOT DO THIS.
"She meant to make a CHILD. A DAUGHTER.
"When the rest of us were BARREN for ETERNITY."
LOYAL, FIERCE ALKYONE.
WHAT LOVE YOU HAVE KEPT HIDDEN.
"It would be an INFECTION. A PLAGUE.
"Joy would turn to ENVY and ENVY to HATRED."
RISE, LOYAL ONE. BE HAPPY FOR ME.
BE HAPPY FOR US ALL.

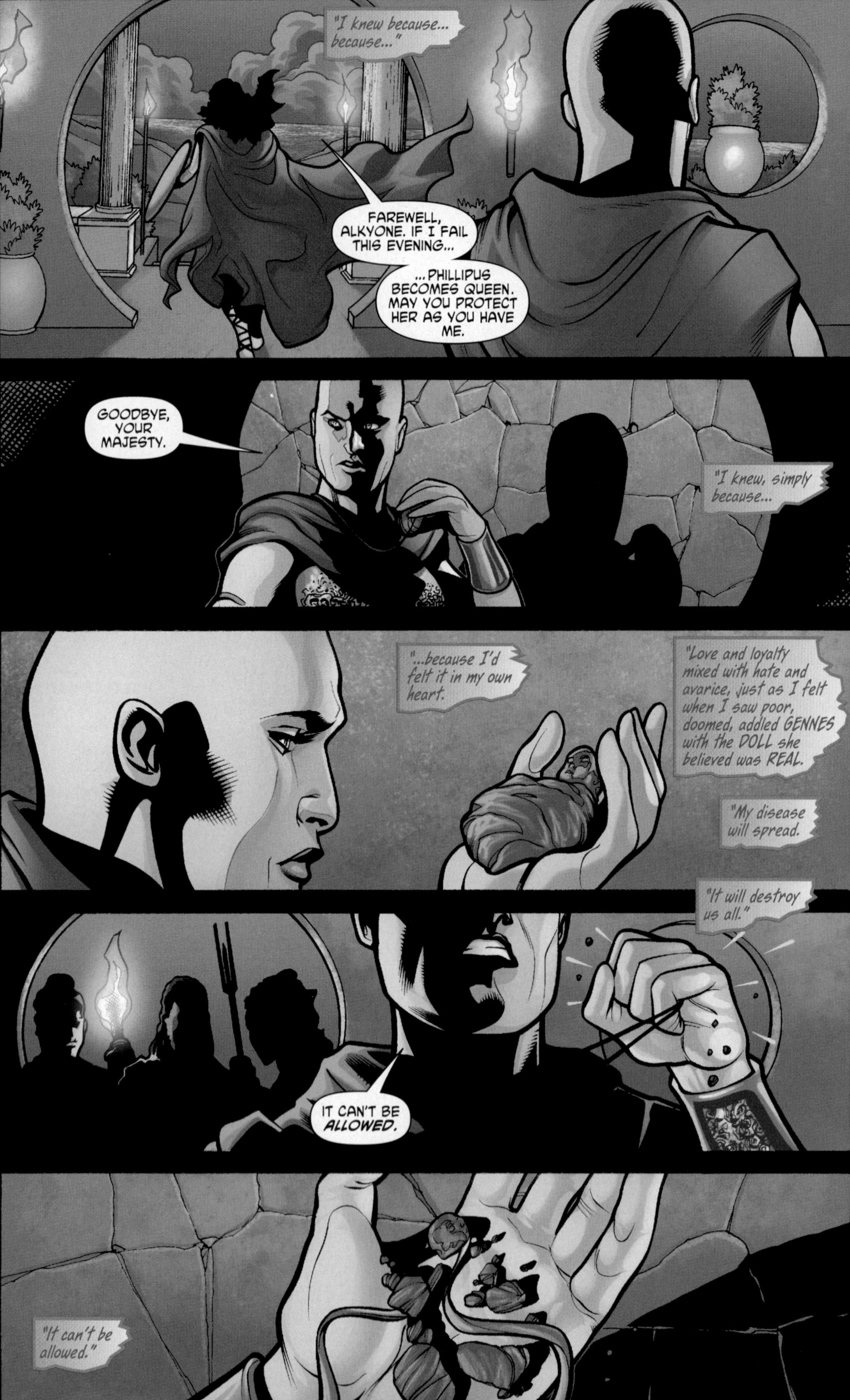
"I knew because... because..."
FAREWELL, ALKYONE. IF I FAIL THIS EVENING...
...PHILLIPUS BECOMES QUEEN. MAY YOU PROTECT HER AS YOU HAVE ME.
GOODBYE, YOUR MAJESTY.
"I knew, simply because...
"...because I'd felt it in my own heart.
"Love and loyalty mixed with hate and avarice, just as I felt when I saw poor, doomed, addled GENNES with the DOLL she believed was REAL.
"My disease will spread.
"It will destroy us all."
IT CAN'T BE ALLOWED.
"It can't be allowed."

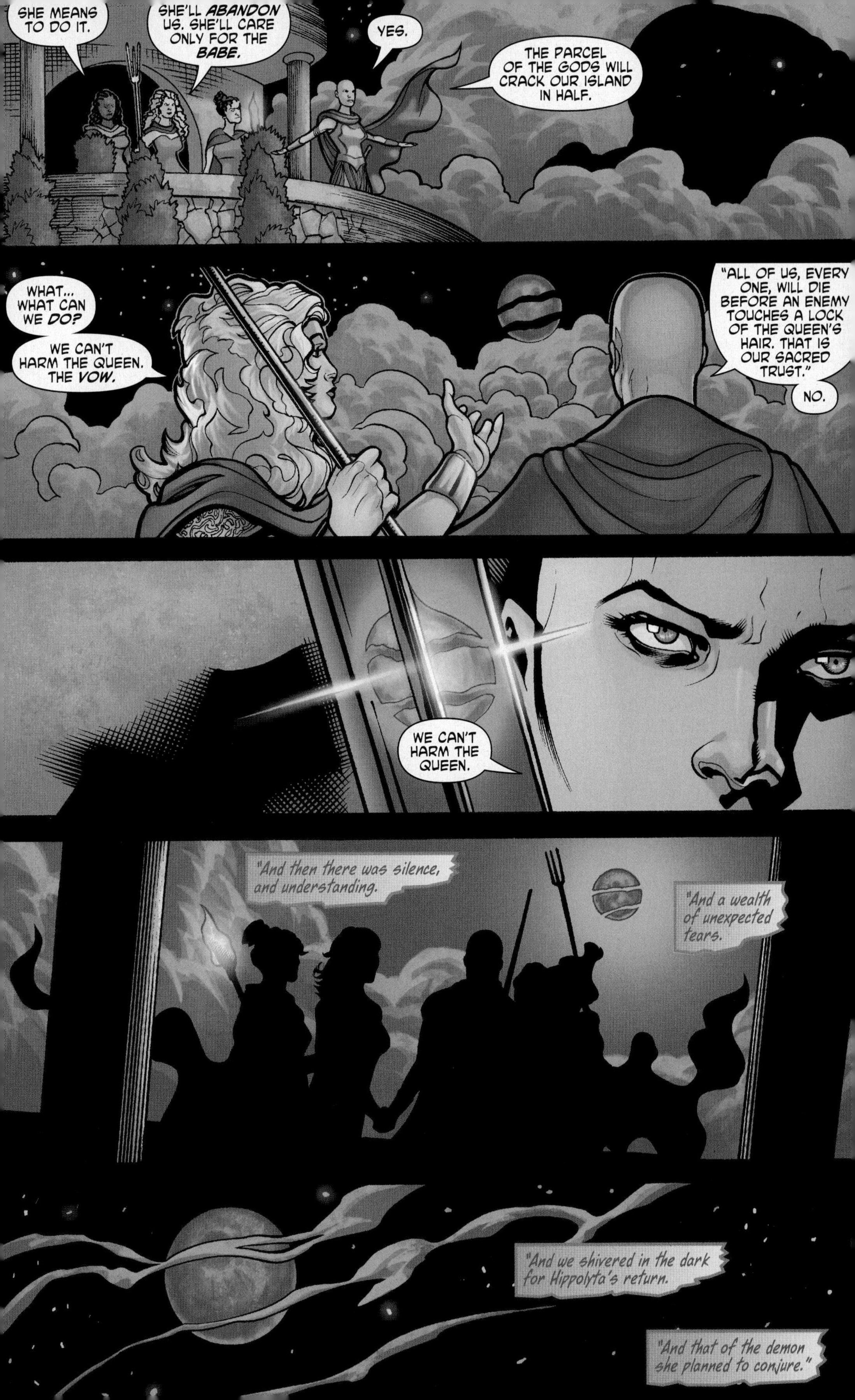
SHE MEANS TO DO IT.
SHE'LL ABANDON US. SHE'LL CARE ONLY FOR THE BABE.
YES.
THE PARCEL OF THE GODS WILL CRACK OUR ISLAND IN HALF.
WHAT... WHAT CAN WE DO?
WE CAN'T HARM THE QUEEN. THE VOW.
"ALL OF US, EVERY ONE, WILL DIE BEFORE AN ENEMY TOUCHES A LOCK OF THE QUEEN'S HAIR. THAT IS OUR SACRED TRUST."
NO.
WE CAN'T HARM THE QUEEN.
"And then there was silence, and understanding.
"And a wealth of unexpected tears.
"And we shivered in the dark for Hippolyta's return.
"And that of the demon she planned to conjure."

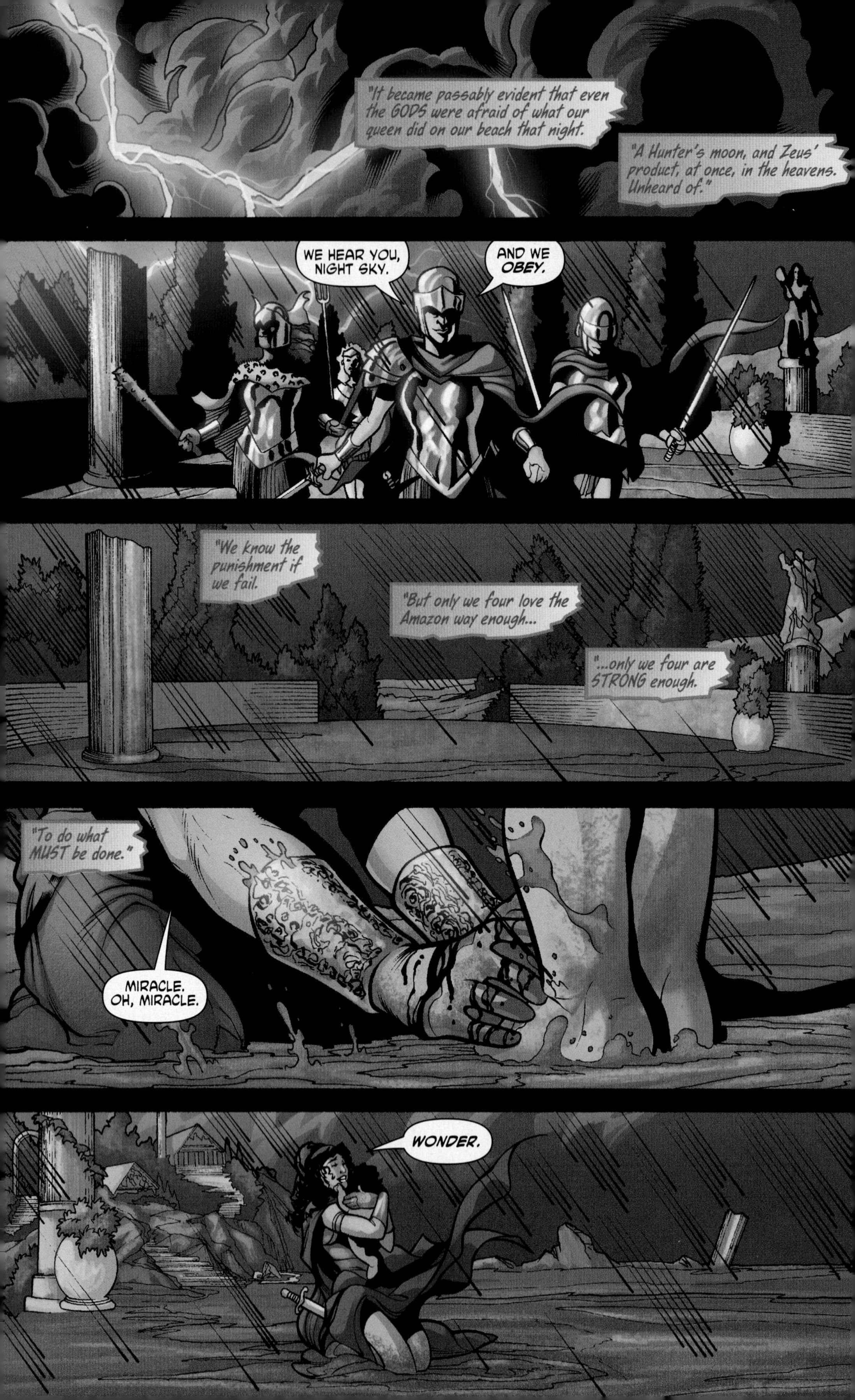
"It became passably evident that even the GODS were afraid of what our queen did on our beach that night.
"A Hunter's moon, and Zeus' product, at once, in the heavens. Unheard of."
WE HEAR YOU, NIGHT SKY.
AND WE OBEY.
"We know the punishment if we fail.
"But only we four love the Amazon way enough...
"...only we four are STRONG enough.
"To do what MUST be done."
MIRACLE. OH, MIRACLE.
WONDER.

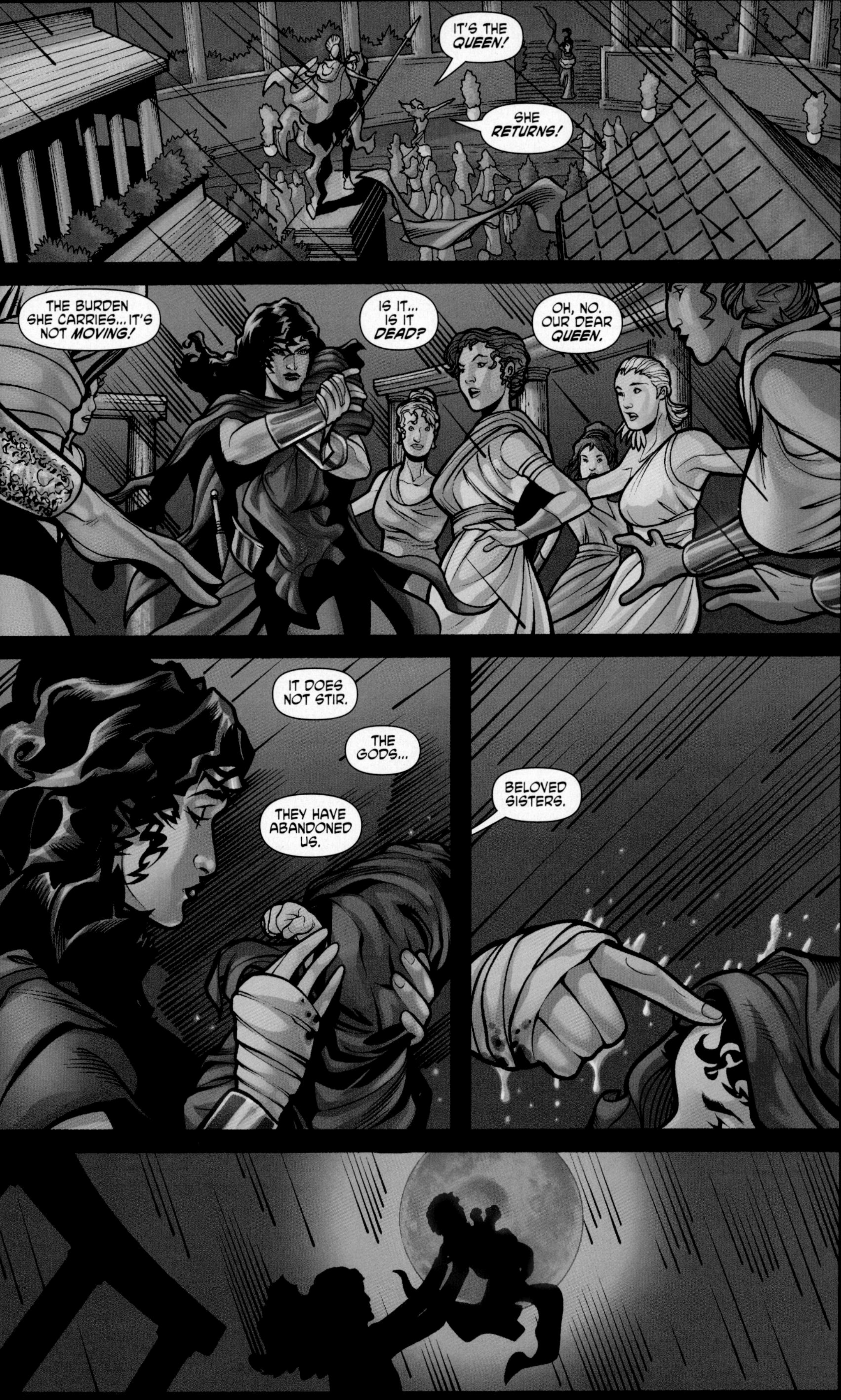
IT'S THE QUEEN!
SHE RETURNS!
THE BURDEN SHE CARRIES...IT'S NOT MOVING!
IS IT... IS IT DEAD?
OH, NO. OUR DEAR QUEEN.
IT DOES NOT STIR.
THE GODS...
THEY HAVE ABANDONED US.
BELOVED SISTERS.

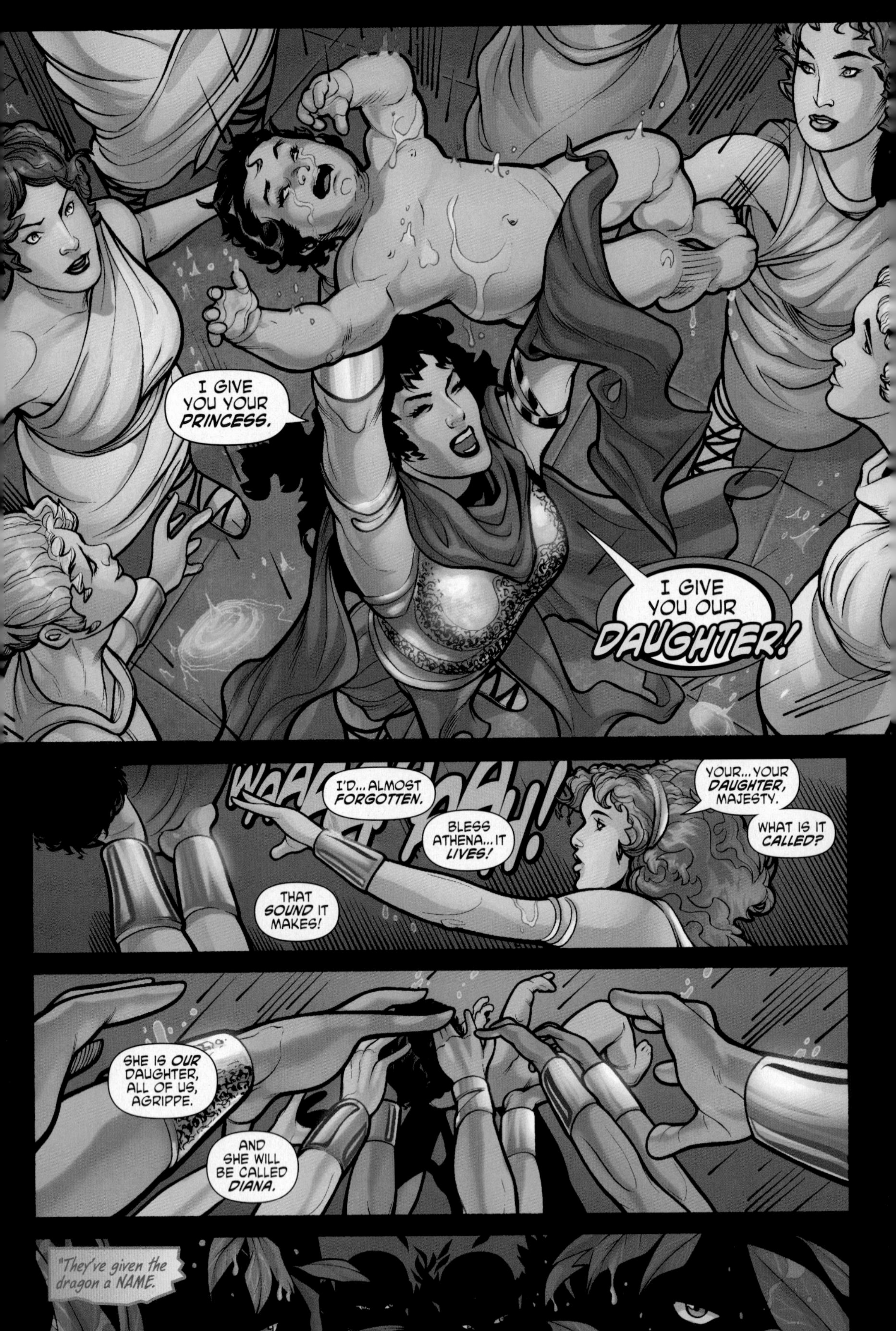
I GIVE YOU YOUR PRINCESS.
I GIVE YOU OUR DAUGHTER!
I'D... ALMOST FORGOTTEN.
BLESS ATHENA... IT LIVES!
THAT SOUND IT MAKES!
YOUR... YOUR DAUGHTER, MAJESTY.
WHAT IS IT CALLED?
SHE IS OUR DAUGHTER, ALL OF US, AGRIPPE.
AND SHE WILL BE CALLED DIANA.
"They've given the dragon a NAME.
"Forgive us, my queen, what we must do this night.
"Forgive us."

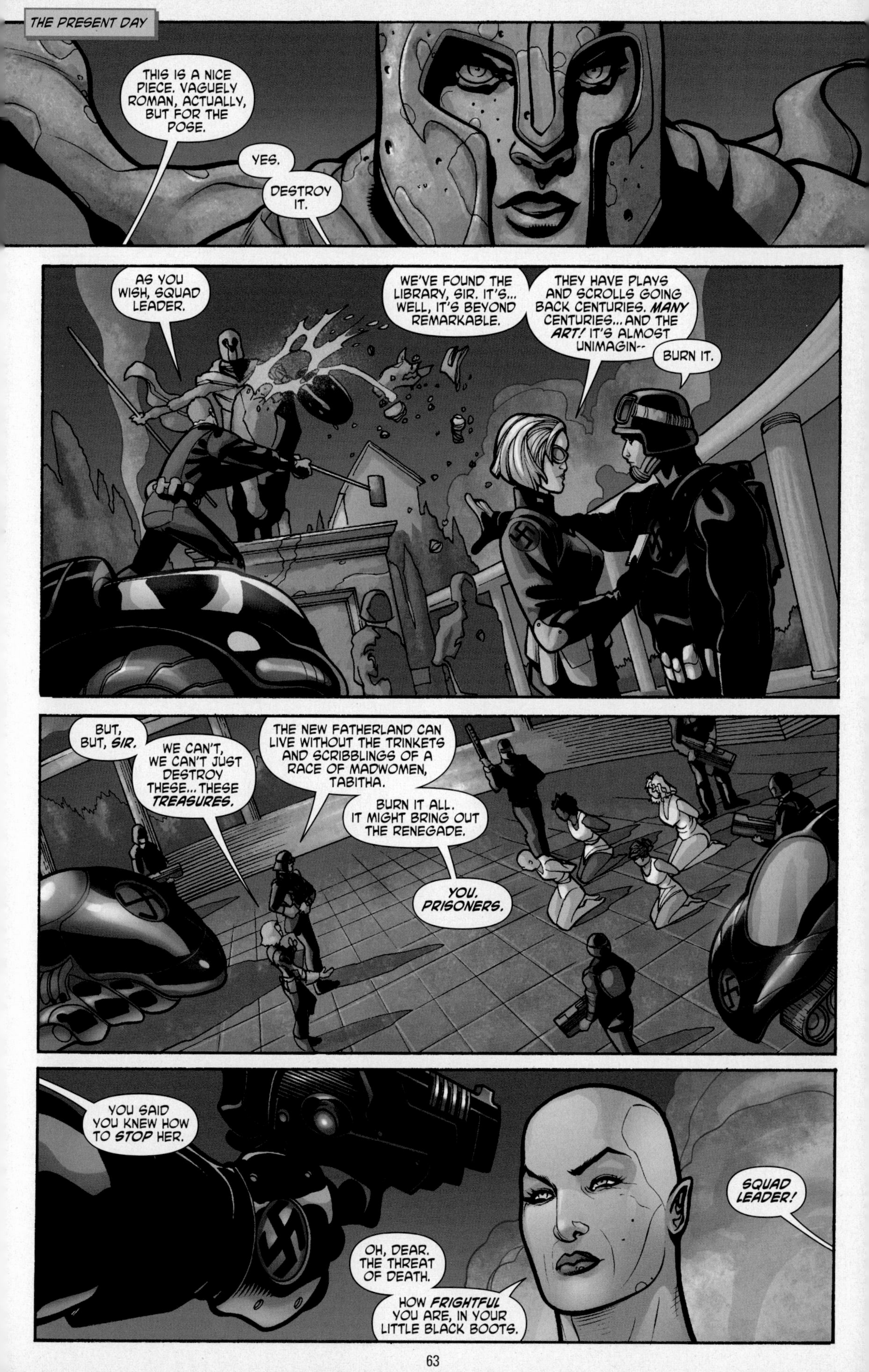
THE PRESENT DAY
THIS IS A NICE PIECE. VAGUELY ROMAN, ACTUALLY, BUT FOR THE POSE.
YES.
DESTROY IT.
AS YOU WISH, SQUAD LEADER.
WE'VE FOUND THE LIBRARY, SIR. IT'S... WELL, IT'S BEYOND REMARKABLE.
THEY HAVE PLAYS AND SCROLLS GOING BACK CENTURIES. MANY CENTURIES... AND THE ART! IT'S ALMOST UNIMAGIN--
BURN IT.
BUT, BUT, SIR.
WE CAN'T, WE CAN'T JUST DESTROY THESE... THESE TREASURES.
THE NEW FATHERLAND CAN LIVE WITHOUT THE TRINKETS AND SCRIBBLINGS OF A RACE OF MADWOMEN, TABITHA.
BURN IT ALL. IT MIGHT BRING OUT THE RENEGADE.
YOU. PRISONERS.
YOU SAID YOU KNEW HOW TO STOP HER.
SQUAD LEADER!
OH, DEAR. THE THREAT OF DEATH.
HOW FRIGHTFUL YOU ARE, IN YOUR LITTLE BLACK BOOTS.

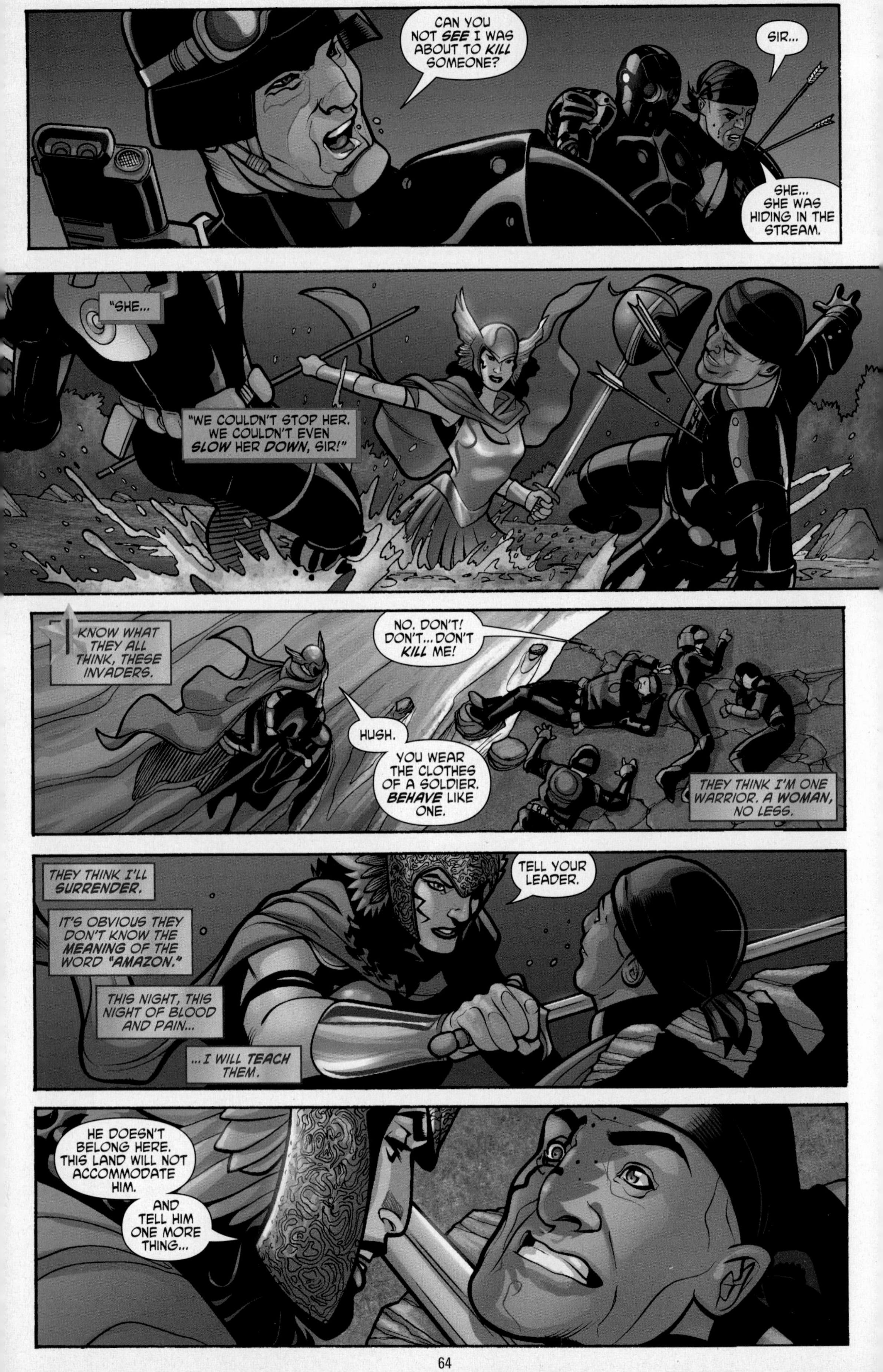
CAN YOU NOT SEE I WAS ABOUT TO KILL SOMEONE?
SIR...
SHE... SHE WAS HIDING IN THE STREAM.
"SHE...
"WE COULDN'T STOP HER. WE COULDN'T EVEN SLOW HER DOWN, SIR!"
I KNOW WHAT THEY ALL THINK, THESE INVADERS.
NO. DON'T! DON'T...DON'T KILL ME!
HUSH.
YOU WEAR THE CLOTHES OF A SOLDIER. BEHAVE LIKE ONE.
THEY THINK I'M ONE WARRIOR. A WOMAN, NO LESS.
THEY THINK I'LL SURRENDER.
IT'S OBVIOUS THEY DON'T KNOW THE MEANING OF THE WORD "AMAZON."
TELL YOUR LEADER.
THIS NIGHT, THIS NIGHT OF BLOOD AND PAIN...
...I WILL TEACH THEM.
HE DOESN'T BELONG HERE. THIS LAND WILL NOT ACCOMMODATE HIM.
AND TELL HIM ONE MORE THING...

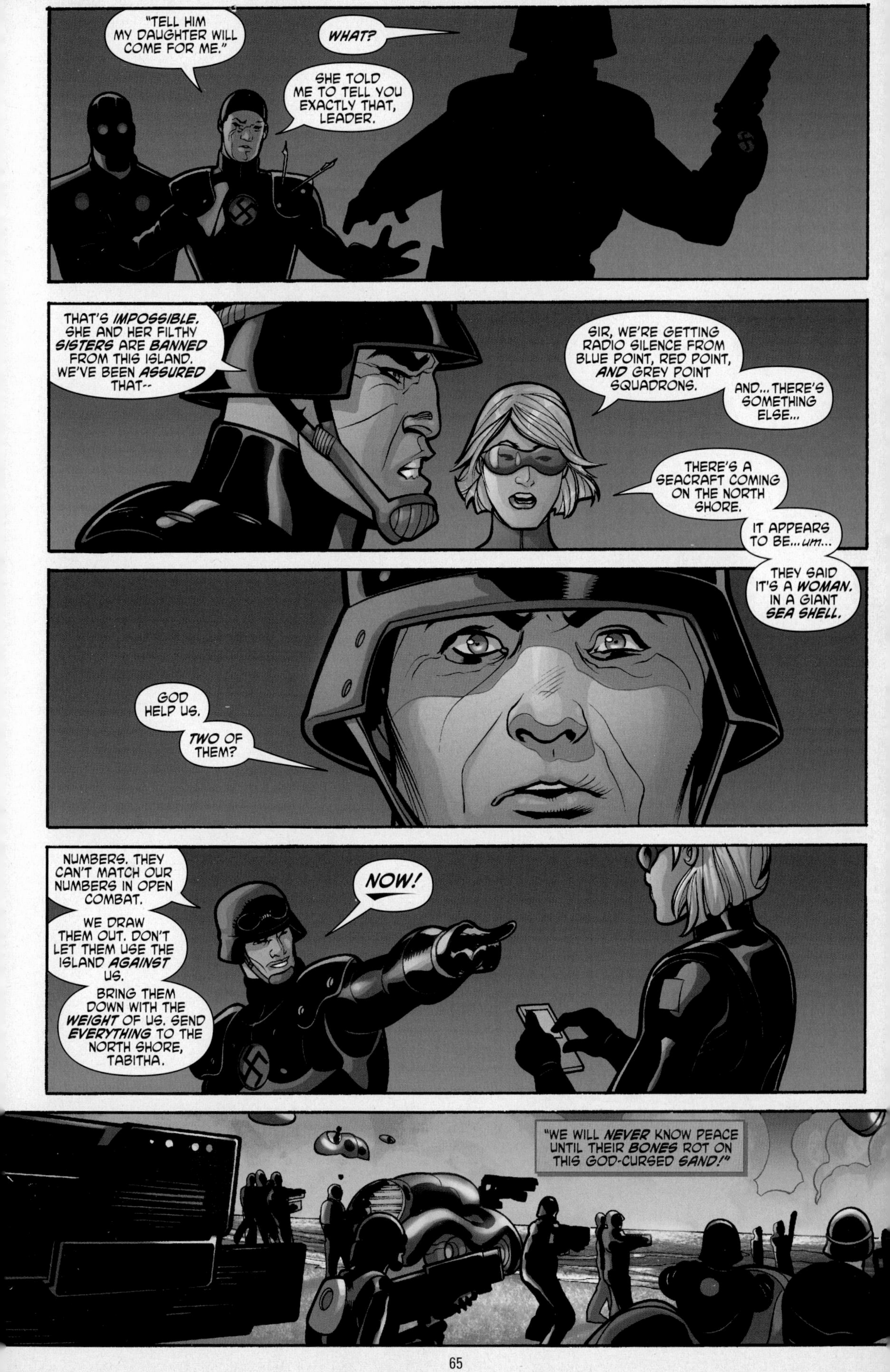
"TELL HIM MY DAUGHTER WILL COME FOR ME."
WHAT?
SHE TOLD ME TO TELL YOU EXACTLY THAT, LEADER.
THAT'S IMPOSSIBLE. SHE AND HER FILTHY SISTERS ARE BANNED FROM THIS ISLAND. WE'VE BEEN ASSURED THAT--
SIR, WE'RE GETTING RADIO SILENCE FROM BLUE POINT, RED POINT, AND GREY POINT SQUADRONS.
AND... THERE'S SOMETHING ELSE...
THERE'S A SEACRAFT COMING ON THE NORTH SHORE.
IT APPEARS TO BE... um...
THEY SAID IT'S A WOMAN. IN A GIANT SEA SHELL.
GOD HELP US.
TWO OF THEM?
NUMBERS. THEY CAN'T MATCH OUR NUMBERS IN OPEN COMBAT.
WE DRAW THEM OUT. DON'T LET THEM USE THE ISLAND AGAINST US.
BRING THEM DOWN WITH THE WEIGHT OF US. SEND EVERYTHING TO THE NORTH SHORE, TABITHA.
NOW!
"WE WILL NEVER KNOW PEACE UNTIL THEIR BONES ROT ON THIS GOD-CURSED SAND!"

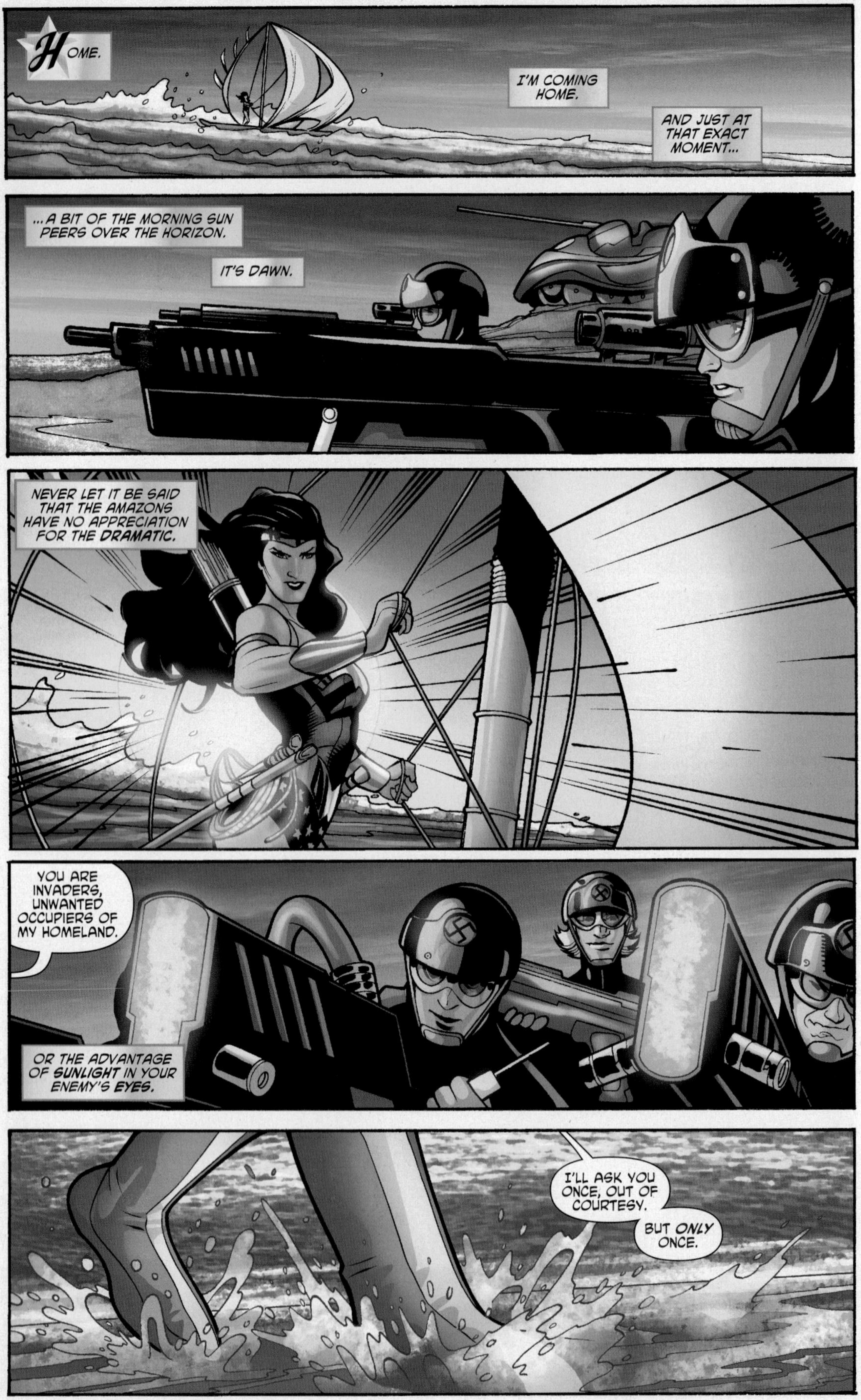
HOME.
I'M COMING HOME.
AND JUST AT THAT EXACT MOMENT...
...A BIT OF THE MORNING SUN PEERS OVER THE HORIZON.
IT'S DAWN.
NEVER LET IT BE SAID THAT THE AMAZONS HAVE NO APPRECIATION FOR THE DRAMATIC.
YOU ARE INVADERS, UNWANTED OCCUPIERS OF MY HOMELAND.
OR THE ADVANTAGE OF SUNLIGHT IN YOUR ENEMY'S EYES.
I'LL ASK YOU ONCE, OUT OF COURTESY.
BUT ONLY ONCE.

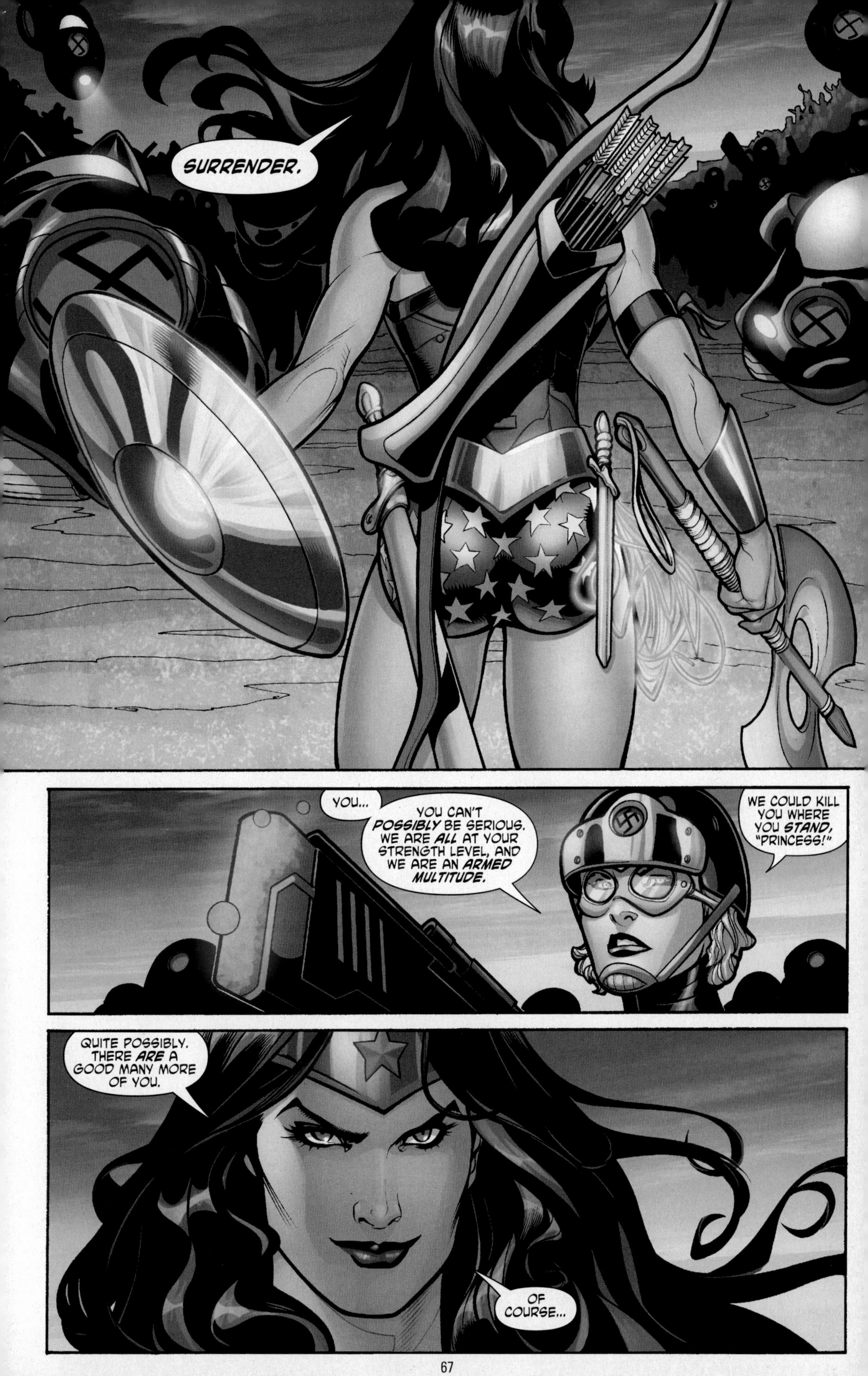
SURRENDER.
YOU...
YOU CAN'T *POSSIBLY* BE SERIOUS. WE ARE *ALL* AT YOUR STRENGTH LEVEL, AND WE ARE AN *ARMED MULTITUDE.*
WE COULD KILL YOU WHERE YOU *STAND,* "PRINCESS!"
QUITE POSSIBLY. THERE *ARE* A GOOD MANY MORE OF YOU.
OF COURSE...

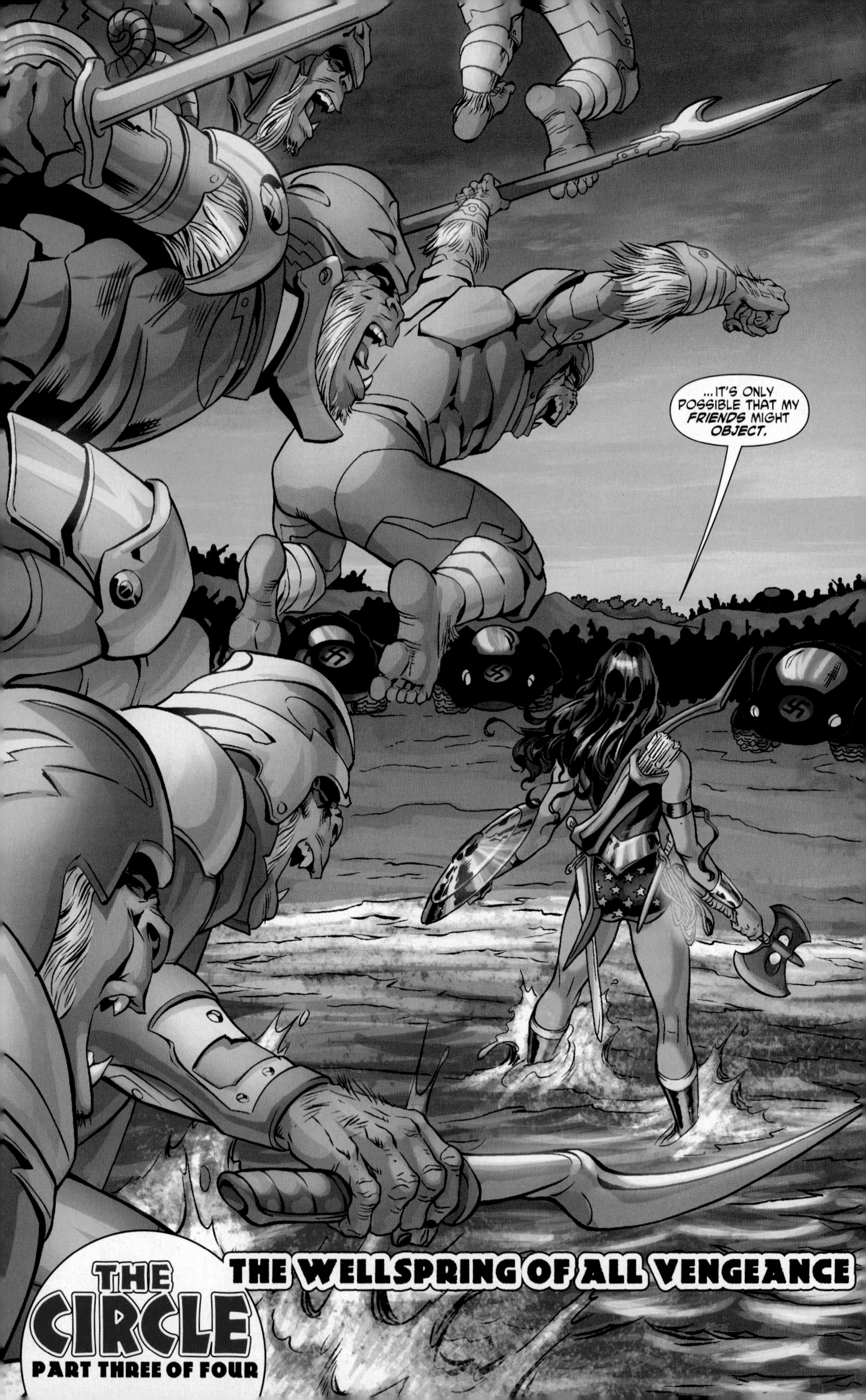
...IT'S ONLY POSSIBLE THAT MY FRIENDS MIGHT OBJECT.
THE CIRCLE
PART THREE OF FOUR
THE WELLSPRING OF ALL VENGEANCE

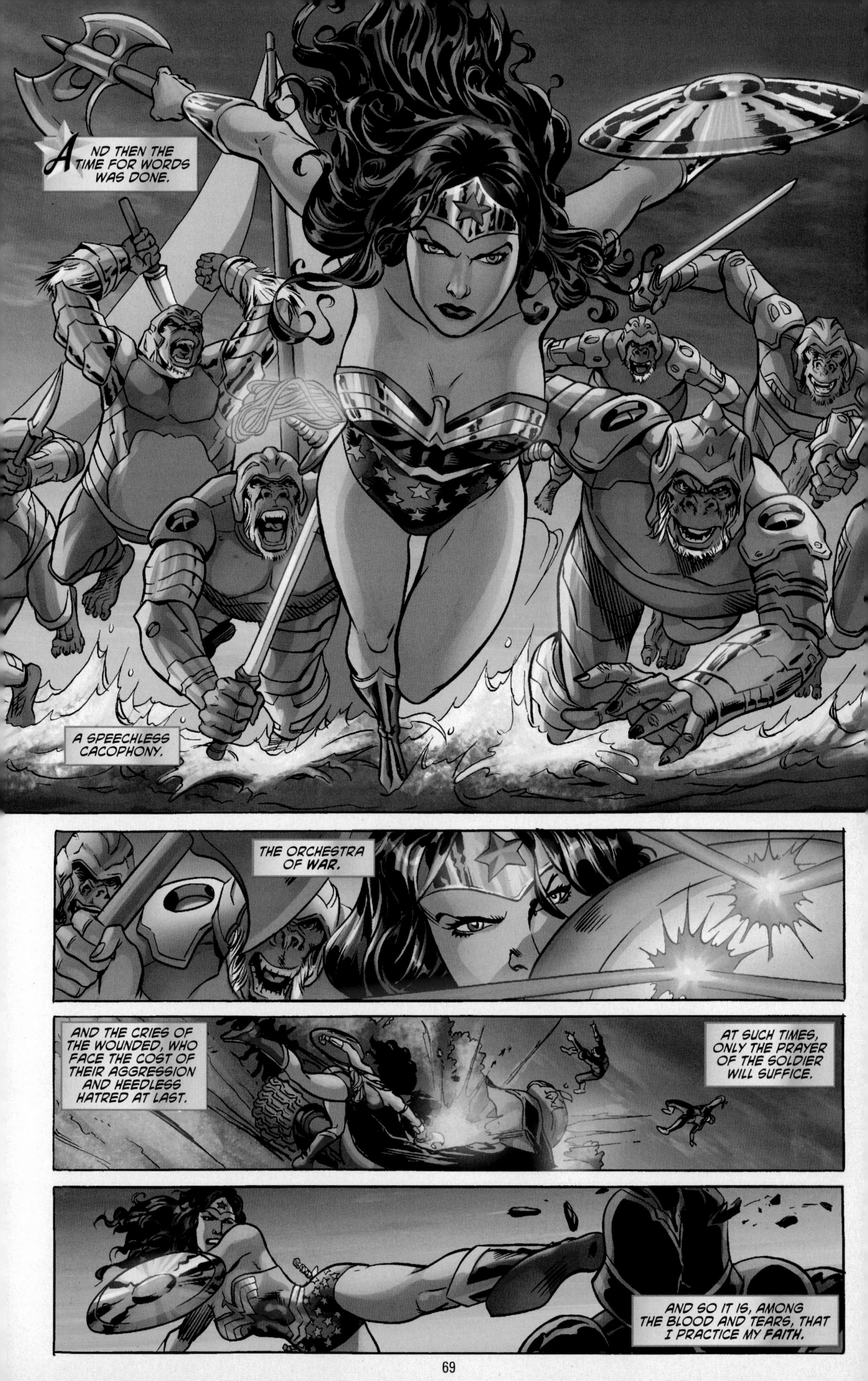
AND THEN THE TIME FOR WORDS WAS DONE.
A SPEECHLESS CACOPHONY.
THE ORCHESTRA OF WAR.
AND THE CRIES OF THE WOUNDED, WHO FACE THE COST OF THEIR AGGRESSION AND HEEDLESS HATRED AT LAST.
AT SUCH TIMES, ONLY THE PRAYER OF THE SOLDIER WILL SUFFICE.
AND SO IT IS, AMONG THE BLOOD AND TEARS, THAT I PRACTICE MY FAITH.

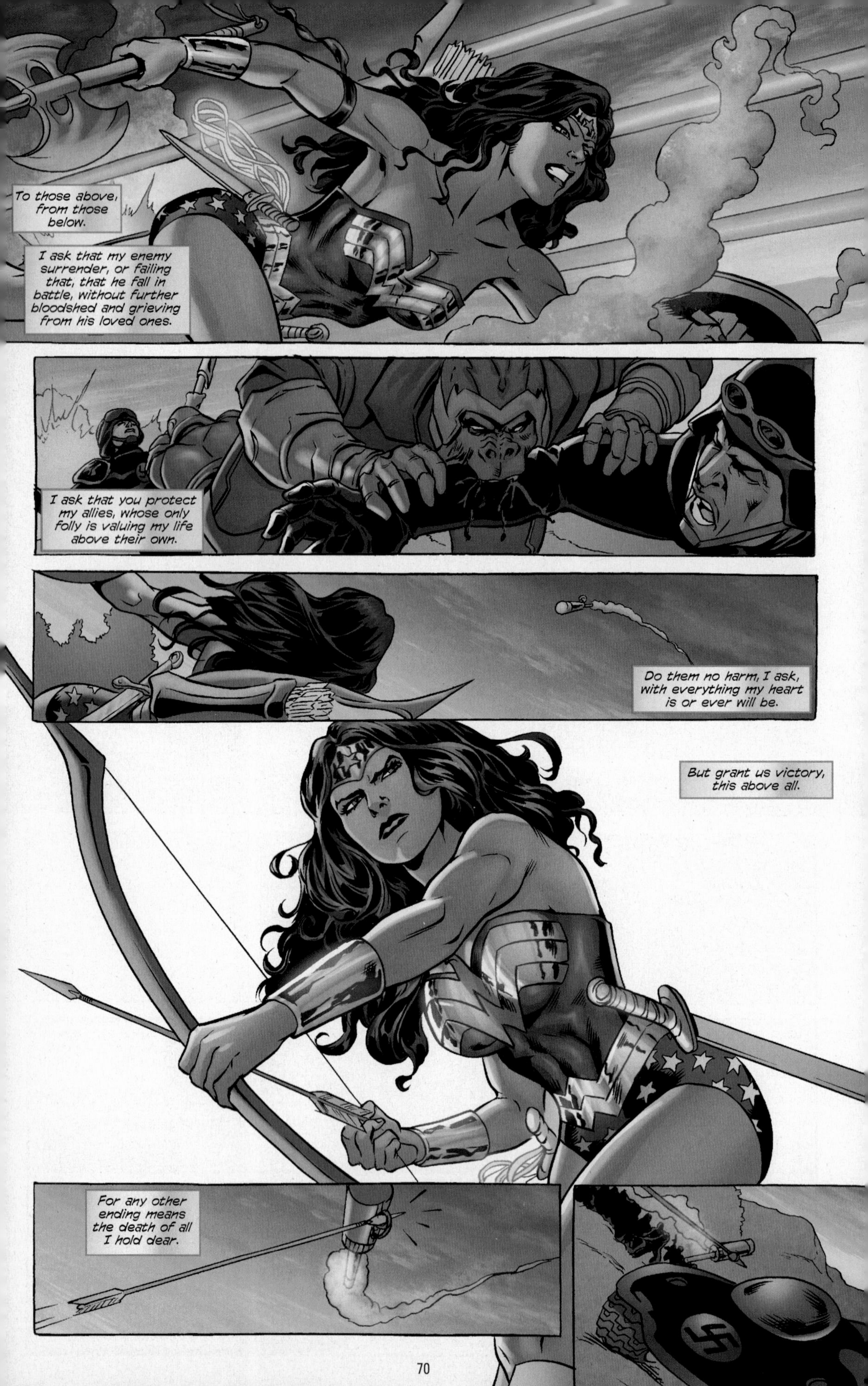
To those above, from those below.
I ask that my enemy surrender, or failing that, that he fall in battle, without further bloodshed and grieving from his loved ones.
I ask that you protect my allies, whose only folly is valuing my life above their own.
Do them no harm, I ask, with everything my heart is or ever will be.
But grant us victory, this above all.
For any other ending means the death of all I hold dear.

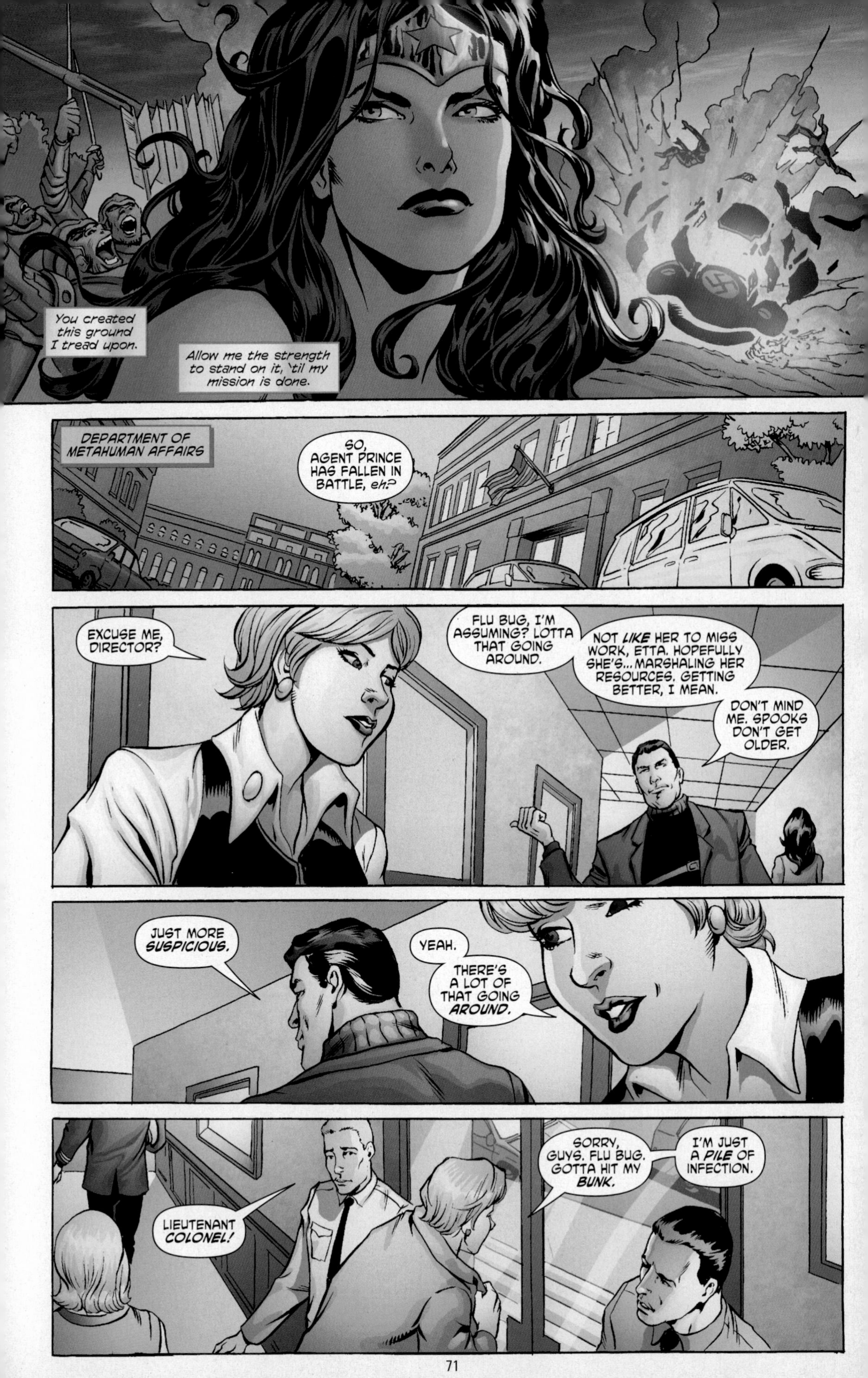
You created this ground I tread upon.
Allow me the strength to stand on it, 'til my mission is done.
DEPARTMENT OF METAHUMAN AFFAIRS
SO, AGENT PRINCE HAS FALLEN IN BATTLE, eh?
EXCUSE ME, DIRECTOR?
FLU BUG, I'M ASSUMING? LOTTA THAT GOING AROUND.
NOT LIKE HER TO MISS WORK, ETTA. HOPEFULLY SHE'S... MARSHALING HER RESOURCES. GETTING BETTER, I MEAN.
DON'T MIND ME. SPOOKS DON'T GET OLDER.
JUST MORE SUSPICIOUS.
YEAH.
THERE'S A LOT OF THAT GOING AROUND.
LIEUTENANT COLONEL!
SORRY, GUYS. FLU BUG. GOTTA HIT MY BUNK.
I'M JUST A PILE OF INFECTION.

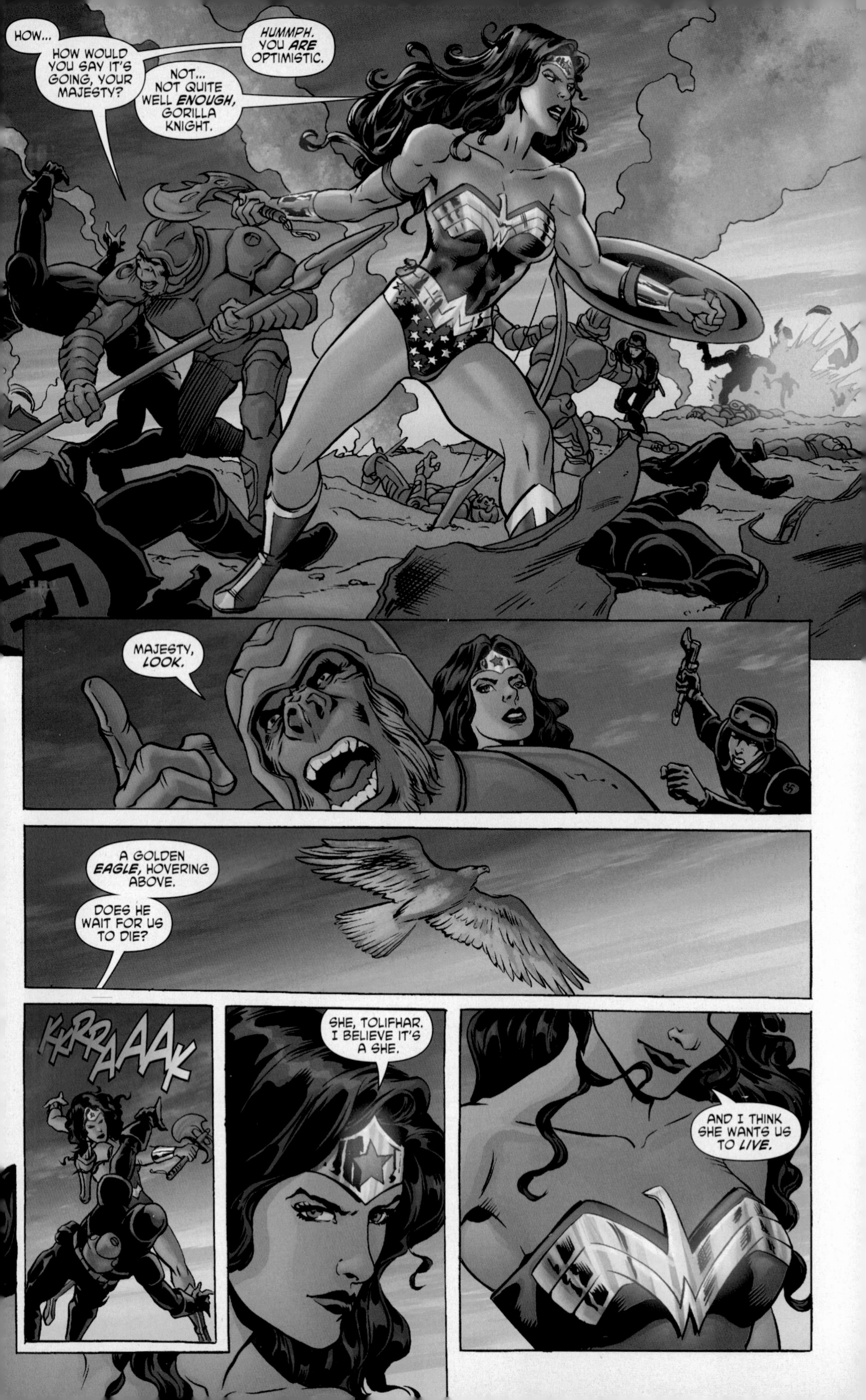
HOW...
HOW WOULD YOU SAY IT'S GOING, YOUR MAJESTY?
HUMMPH. YOU *ARE* OPTIMISTIC.
NOT... NOT QUITE WELL *ENOUGH,* GORILLA KNIGHT.
MAJESTY, *LOOK.*
A GOLDEN *EAGLE,* HOVERING ABOVE.
DOES HE WAIT FOR US TO DIE?
KARRAAAK
SHE, TOLIFHAR. I BELIEVE IT'S A SHE.
AND I THINK SHE WANTS US TO *LIVE.*

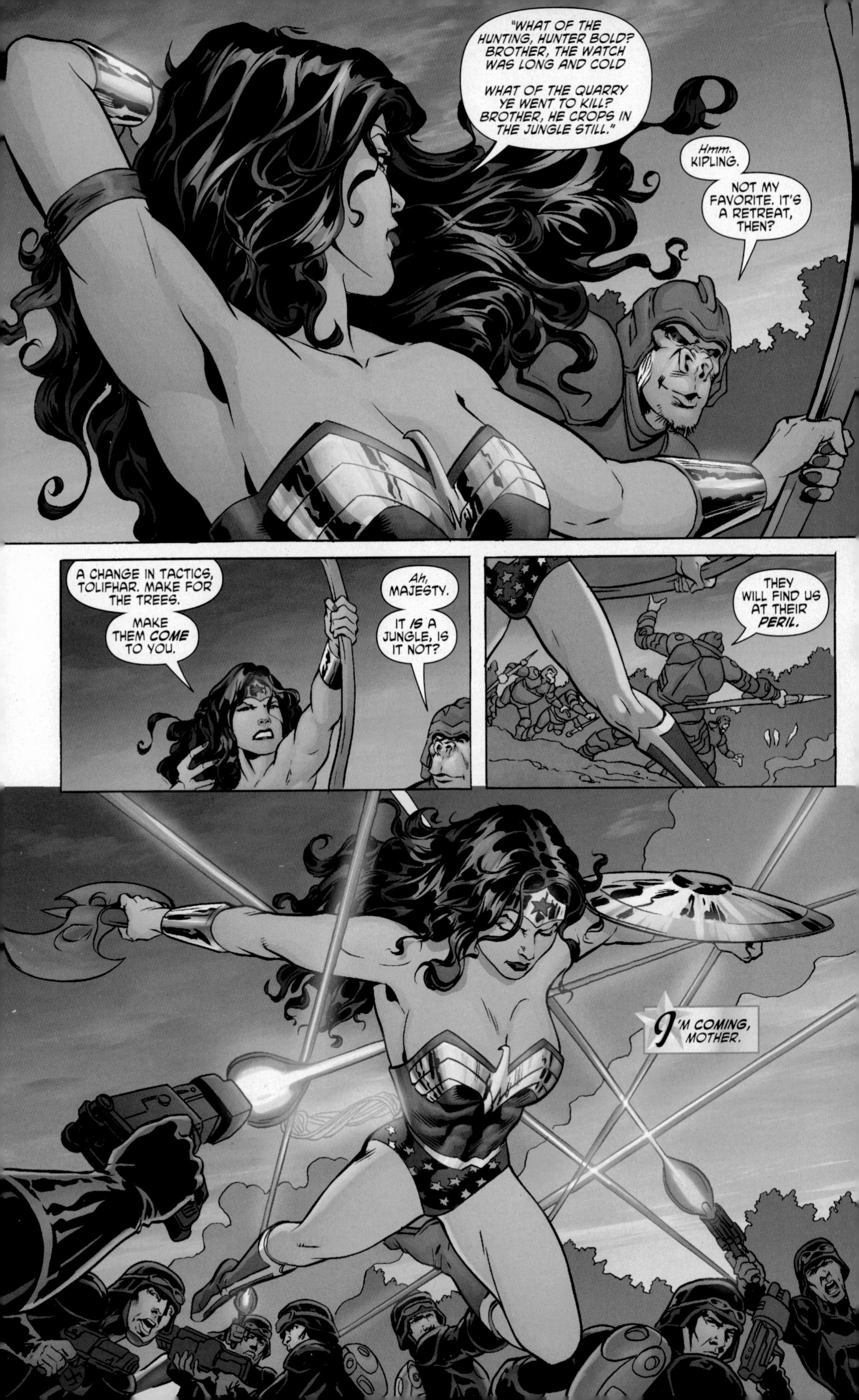
"WHAT OF THE HUNTING, HUNTER BOLD? BROTHER, THE WATCH WAS LONG AND COLD

WHAT OF THE QUARRY YE WENT TO KILL? BROTHER, HE CROPS IN THE JUNGLE STILL."
Hmm. KIPLING.
NOT MY FAVORITE. IT'S A RETREAT, THEN?
A CHANGE IN TACTICS, TOLIFHAR. MAKE FOR THE TREES.
MAKE THEM COME TO YOU.
Ah, MAJESTY.
IT IS A JUNGLE, IS IT NOT?
THEY WILL FIND US AT THEIR PERIL.
I'M COMING, MOTHER.

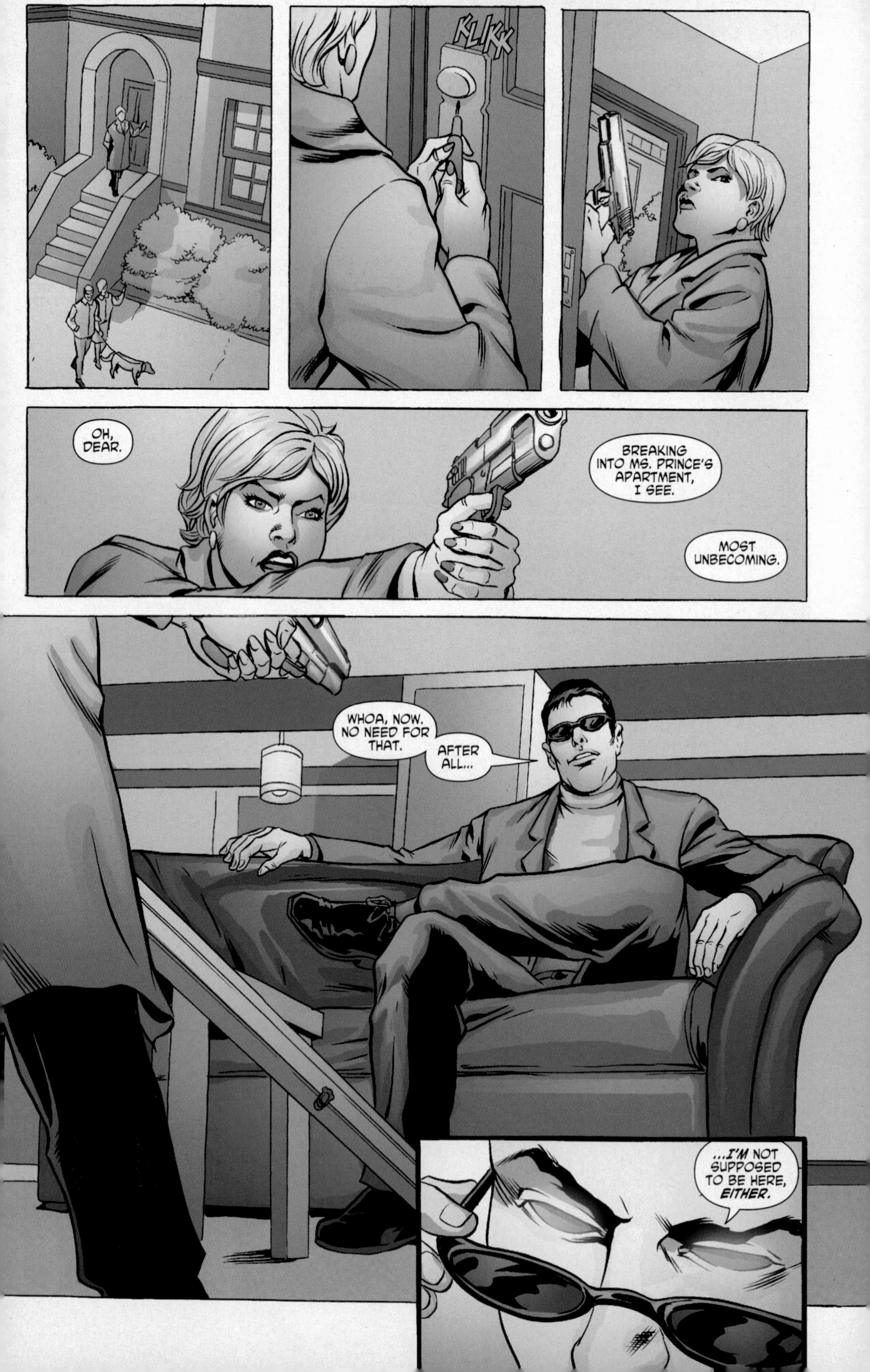
KLIKK
OH, DEAR.
BREAKING INTO MS. PRINCE'S APARTMENT, I SEE.
MOST UNBECOMING.
WHOA, NOW. NO NEED FOR THAT.
AFTER ALL...
...I'M NOT SUPPOSED TO BE HERE, EITHER.

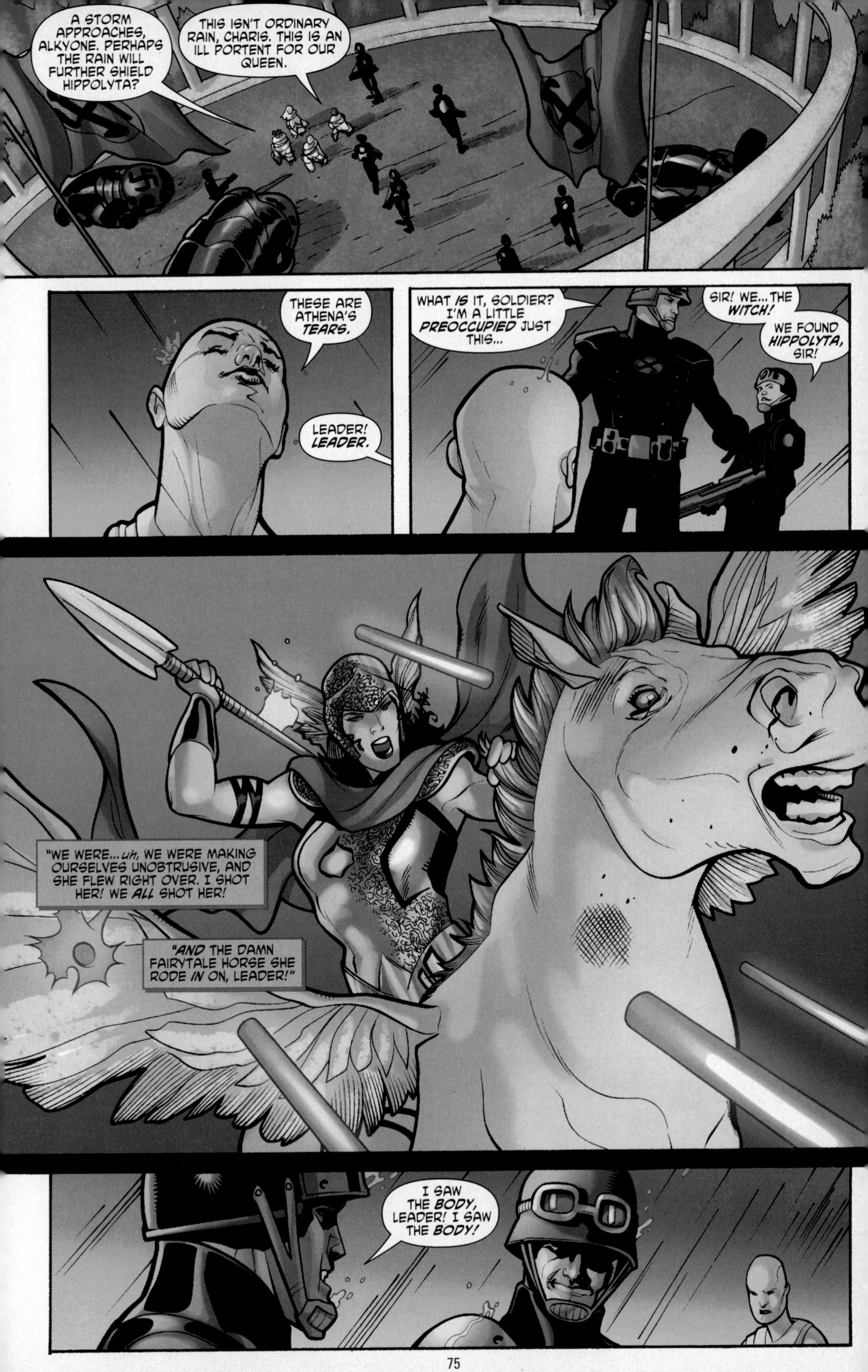
A STORM APPROACHES, ALKYONE. PERHAPS THE RAIN WILL FURTHER SHIELD HIPPOLYTA?
THIS ISN'T ORDINARY RAIN, CHARIS. THIS IS AN ILL PORTENT FOR OUR QUEEN.
THESE ARE ATHENA'S *TEARS.*
LEADER! *LEADER.*
WHAT *IS* IT, SOLDIER? I'M A LITTLE *PREOCCUPIED* JUST THIS...
SIR! WE... THE *WITCH!*
WE FOUND *HIPPOLYTA,* SIR!
"WE WERE... *uh,* WE WERE MAKING OURSELVES UNOBTRUSIVE, AND SHE FLEW RIGHT OVER. I SHOT HER! WE *ALL* SHOT HER!
"*AND* THE DAMN FAIRYTALE HORSE SHE RODE *IN* ON, LEADER!"
I SAW THE *BODY,* LEADER! I SAW THE *BODY!*

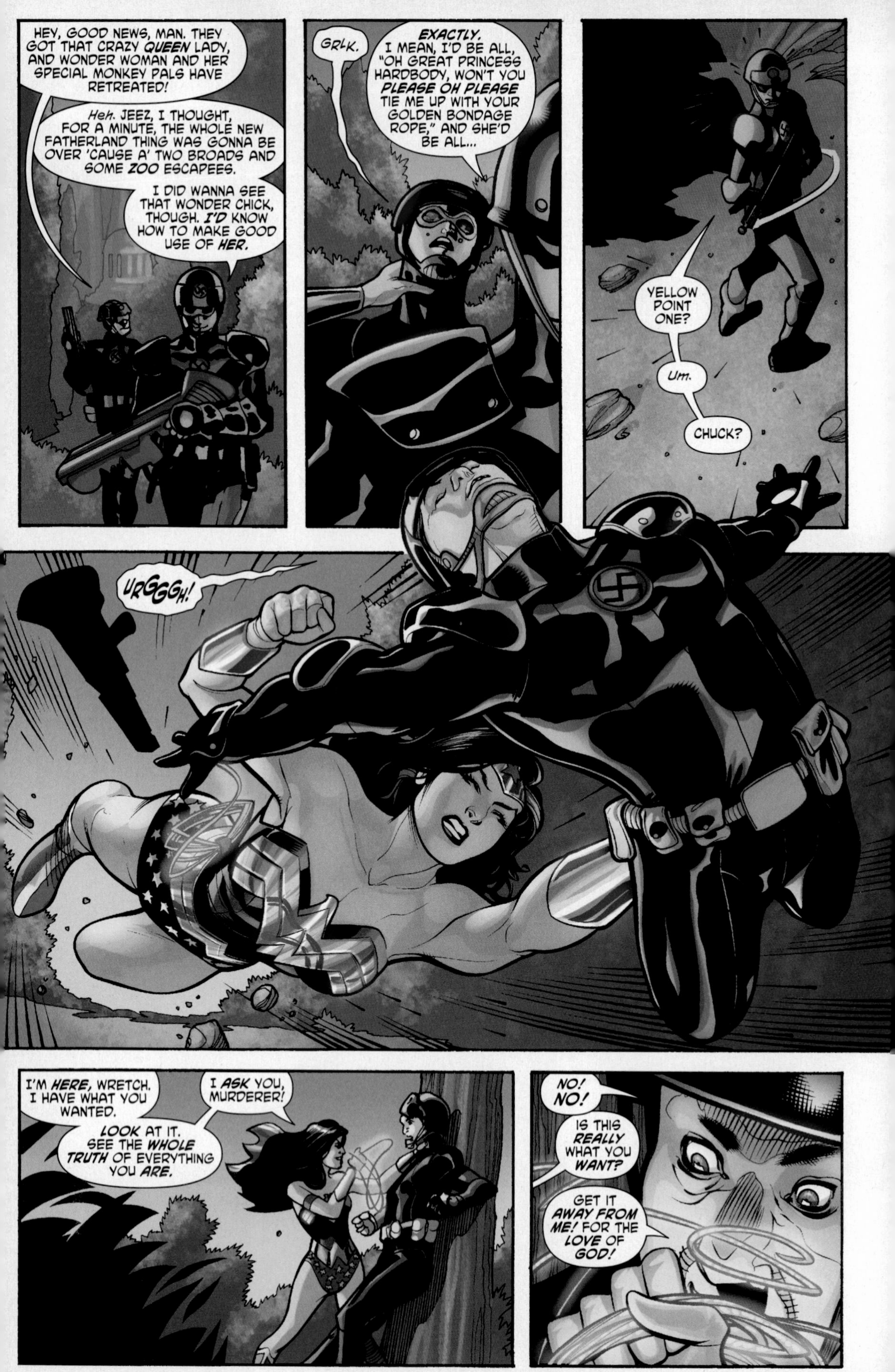
HEY, GOOD NEWS, MAN. THEY GOT THAT CRAZY QUEEN LADY, AND WONDER WOMAN AND HER SPECIAL MONKEY PALS HAVE RETREATED!
Heh. JEEZ, I THOUGHT, FOR A MINUTE, THE WHOLE NEW FATHERLAND THING WAS GONNA BE OVER 'CAUSE A' TWO BROADS AND SOME ZOO ESCAPEES.
I DID WANNA SEE THAT WONDER CHICK, THOUGH. I'D KNOW HOW TO MAKE GOOD USE OF HER.
GRLK.
EXACTLY. I MEAN, I'D BE ALL, "OH GREAT PRINCESS HARDBODY, WON'T YOU PLEASE OH PLEASE TIE ME UP WITH YOUR GOLDEN BONDAGE ROPE," AND SHE'D BE ALL...
YELLOW POINT ONE?
Um.
CHUCK?
URGGGH!
I'M HERE, WRETCH. I HAVE WHAT YOU WANTED.
LOOK AT IT. SEE THE WHOLE TRUTH OF EVERYTHING YOU ARE.
I ASK YOU, MURDERER!
NO! NO!
IS THIS REALLY WHAT YOU WANT?
GET IT AWAY FROM ME! FOR THE LOVE OF GOD!

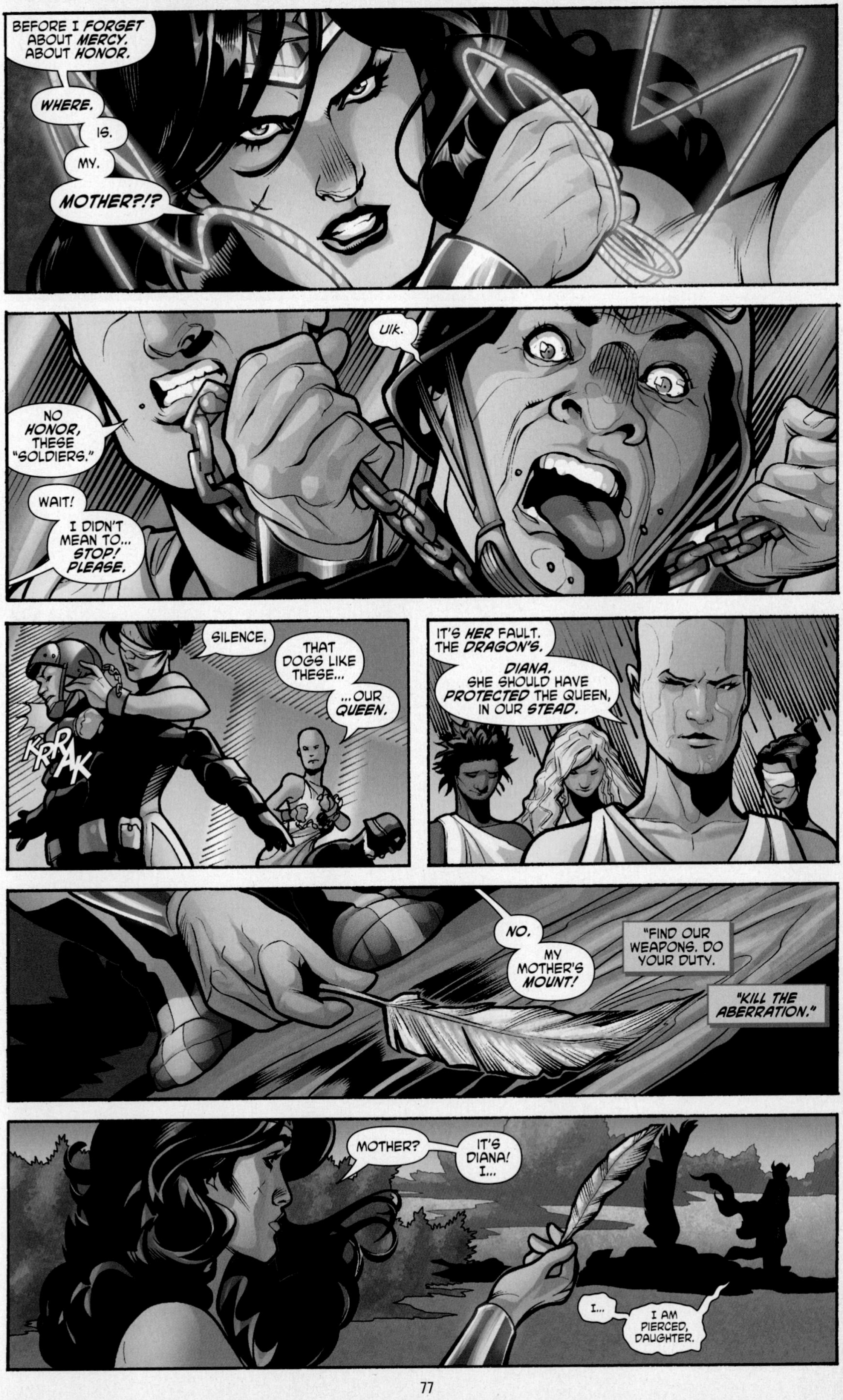
BEFORE I FORGET ABOUT MERCY. ABOUT HONOR.
WHERE.
IS.
MY.
MOTHER?!?
ULK.
NO HONOR, THESE "SOLDIERS."
WAIT!
I DIDN'T MEAN TO... STOP! PLEASE.
SILENCE.
THAT DOGS LIKE THESE...
...OUR QUEEN.
KRRAK
IT'S HER FAULT. THE DRAGON'S.
DIANA. SHE SHOULD HAVE PROTECTED THE QUEEN, IN OUR STEAD.
NO.
MY MOTHER'S MOUNT!
"FIND OUR WEAPONS. DO YOUR DUTY.
"KILL THE ABERRATION."
MOTHER?
IT'S DIANA! I...
I...
I AM PIERCED, DAUGHTER.

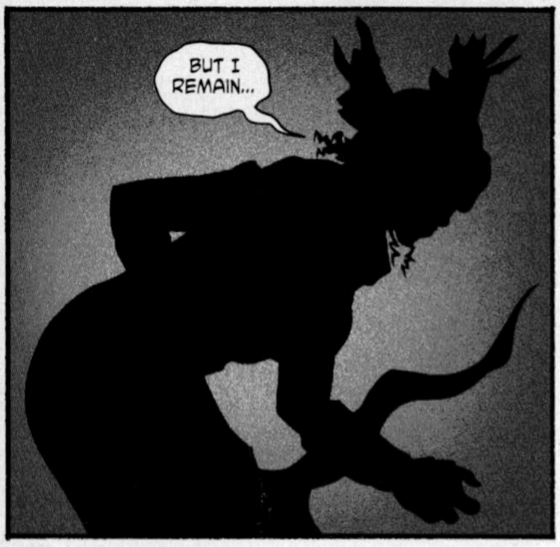
BUT I REMAIN...

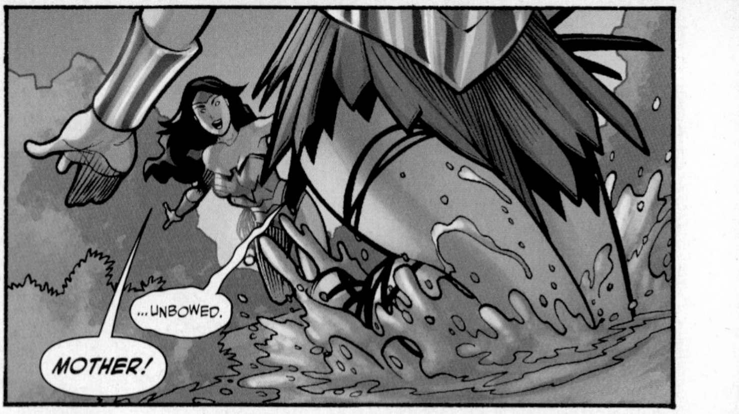
...UNBOWED.
MOTHER!

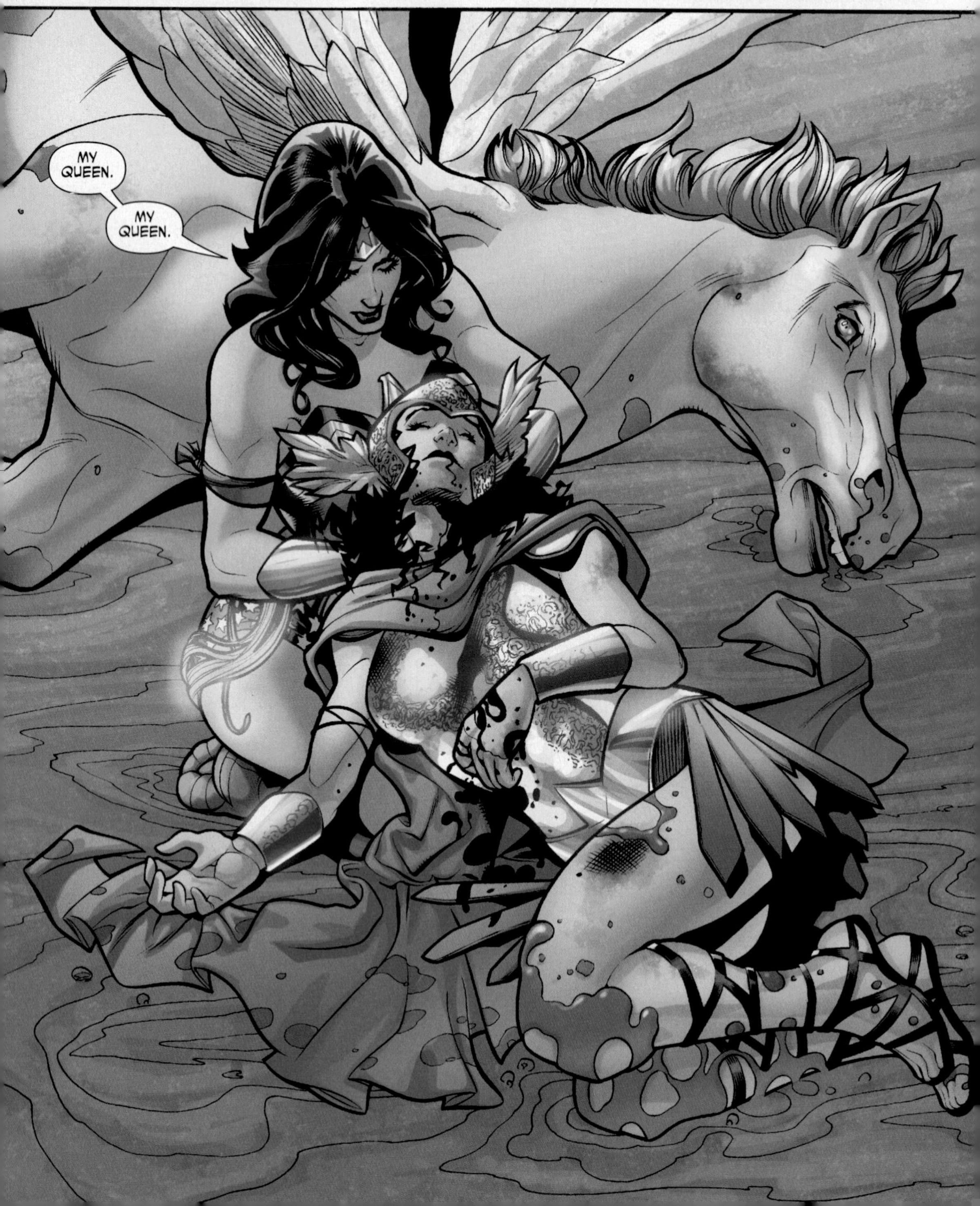
MY QUEEN.
MY QUEEN.

WONDER WOMAN #17 Cover by Terry & Rachel Dodson with Alex Sinclair

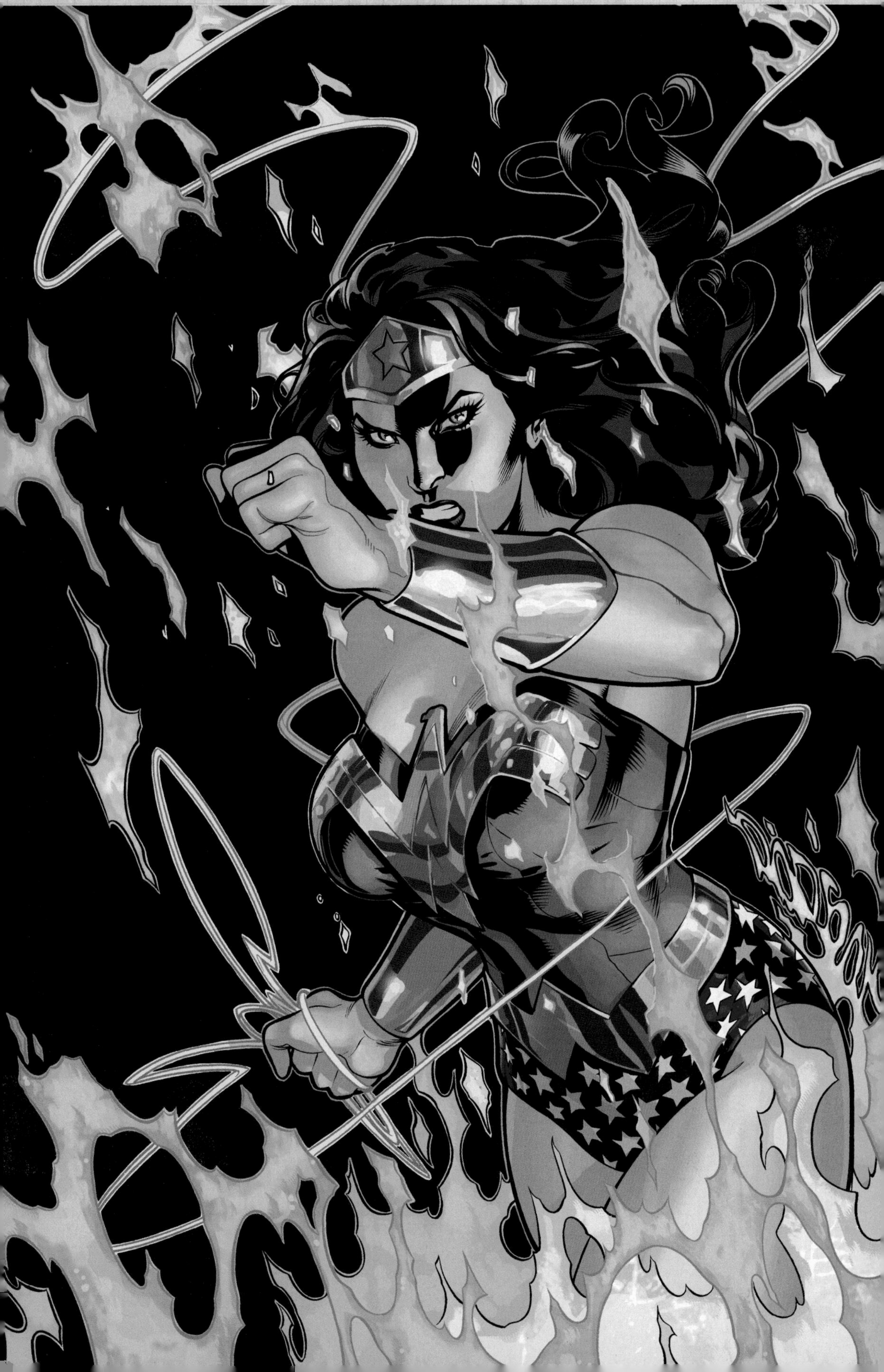

Art this issue by Ron Randall (pages 81-86, 92-98),
and Terry Dodson & Rachel Dodson
(pages 87-91, 99-102)

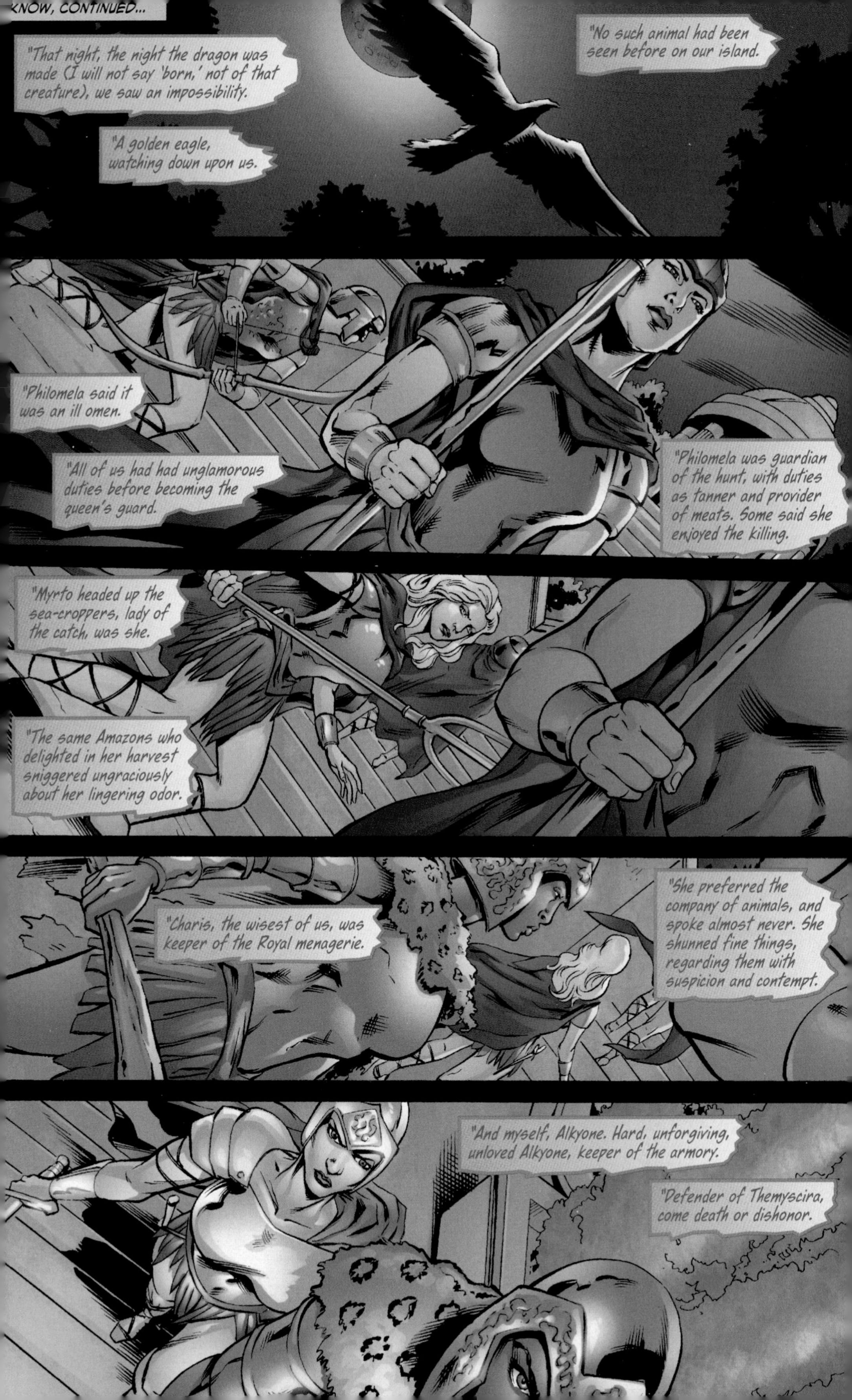
KNOW, CONTINUED...
"That night, the night the dragon was made (I will not say 'born,' not of that creature), we saw an impossibility.
"A golden eagle, watching down upon us.
"No such animal had been seen before on our island.
"Philomela said it was an ill omen.
"All of us had had unglamorous duties before becoming the queen's guard.
"Philomela was guardian of the hunt, with duties as tanner and provider of meats. Some said she enjoyed the killing.
"Myrto headed up the sea-croppers, lady of the catch, was she.
"The same Amazons who delighted in her harvest sniggered ungraciously about her lingering odor.
"Charis, the wisest of us, was keeper of the Royal menagerie.
"She preferred the company of animals, and spoke almost never. She shunned fine things, regarding them with suspicion and contempt.
"And myself, Alkyone. Hard, unforgiving, unloved Alkyone, keeper of the armory.
"Defender of Themyscira, come death or dishonor.

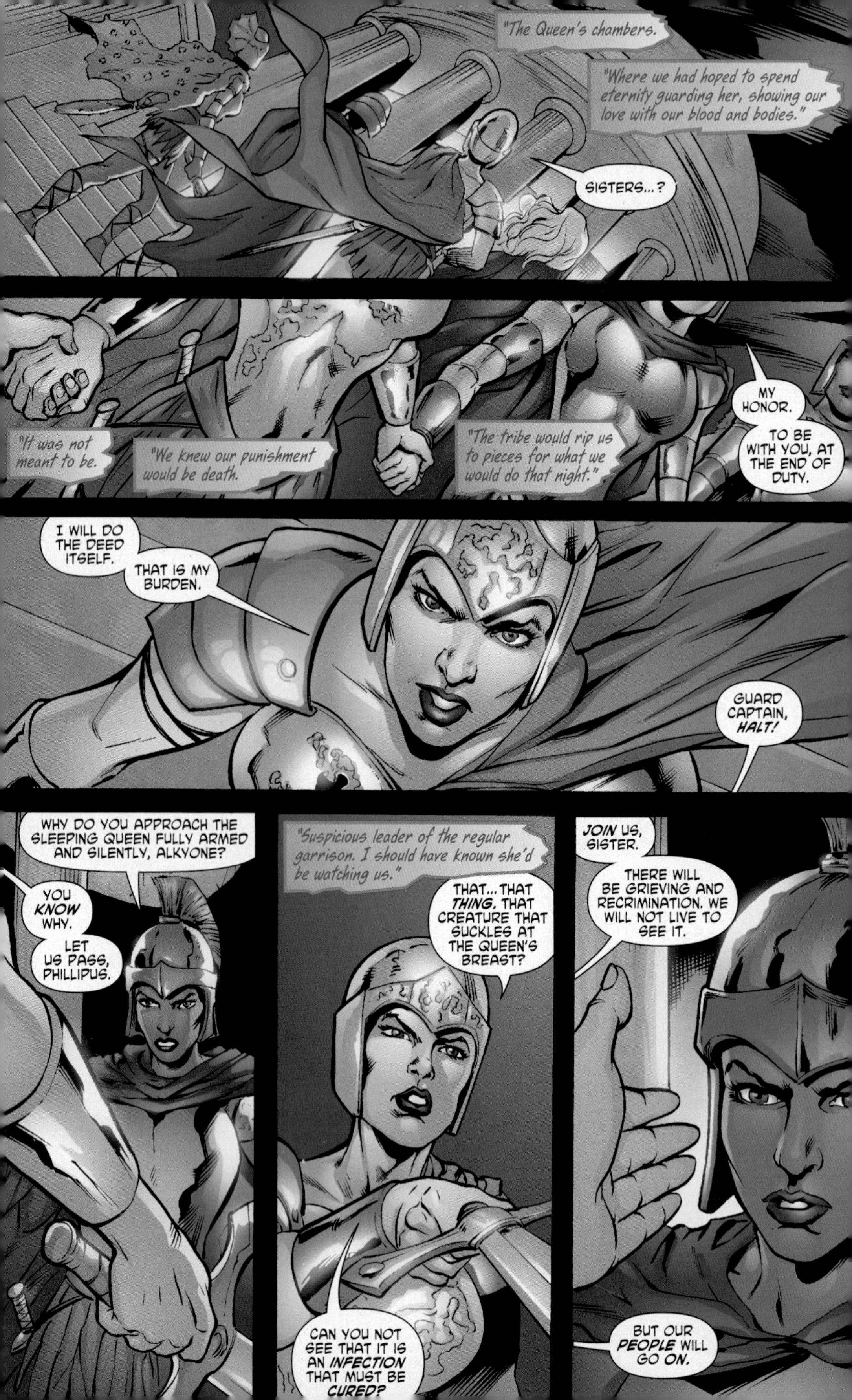
"The Queen's chambers.
"Where we had hoped to spend eternity guarding her, showing our love with our blood and bodies."
SISTERS...?
"It was not meant to be.
"We knew our punishment would be death.
"The tribe would rip us to pieces for what we would do that night."
MY HONOR.
TO BE WITH YOU, AT THE END OF DUTY.
I WILL DO THE DEED ITSELF.
THAT IS MY BURDEN.
GUARD CAPTAIN, HALT!
WHY DO YOU APPROACH THE SLEEPING QUEEN FULLY ARMED AND SILENTLY, ALKYONE?
YOU KNOW WHY.
LET US PASS, PHILLIPUS.
"Suspicious leader of the regular garrison. I should have known she'd be watching us."
THAT... THAT THING. THAT CREATURE THAT SUCKLES AT THE QUEEN'S BREAST?
CAN YOU NOT SEE THAT IT IS AN INFECTION THAT MUST BE CURED?
JOIN US, SISTER.
THERE WILL BE GRIEVING AND RECRIMINATION. WE WILL NOT LIVE TO SEE IT.
BUT OUR PEOPLE WILL GO ON.

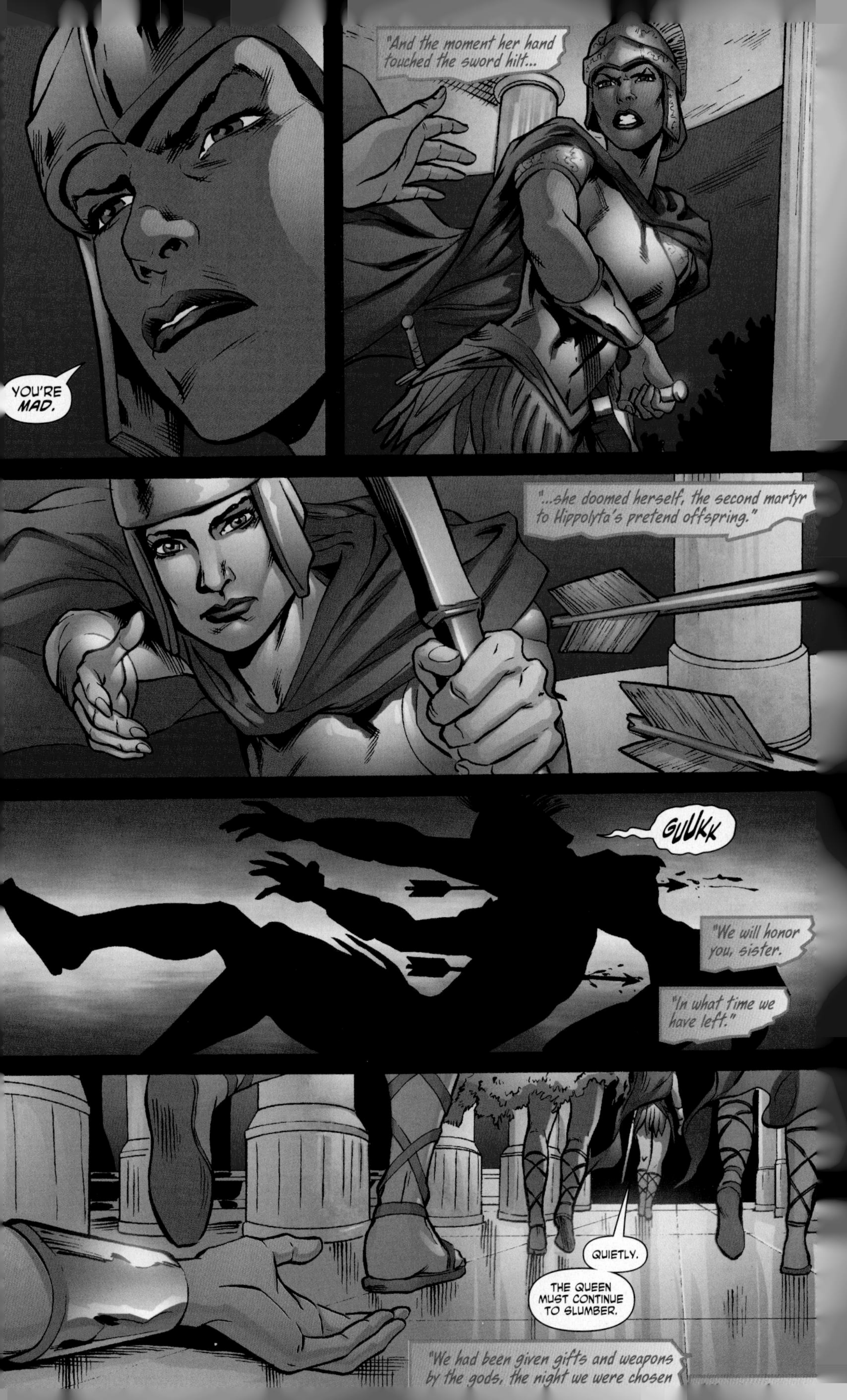
YOU'RE MAD.
"And the moment her hand touched the sword hilt...
"...she doomed herself, the second martyr to Hippolyta's pretend offspring."
GUUKK
"We will honor you, sister.
"In what time we have left."
QUIETLY.
THE QUEEN MUST CONTINUE TO SLUMBER.
"We had been given gifts and weapons by the gods, the night we were chosen

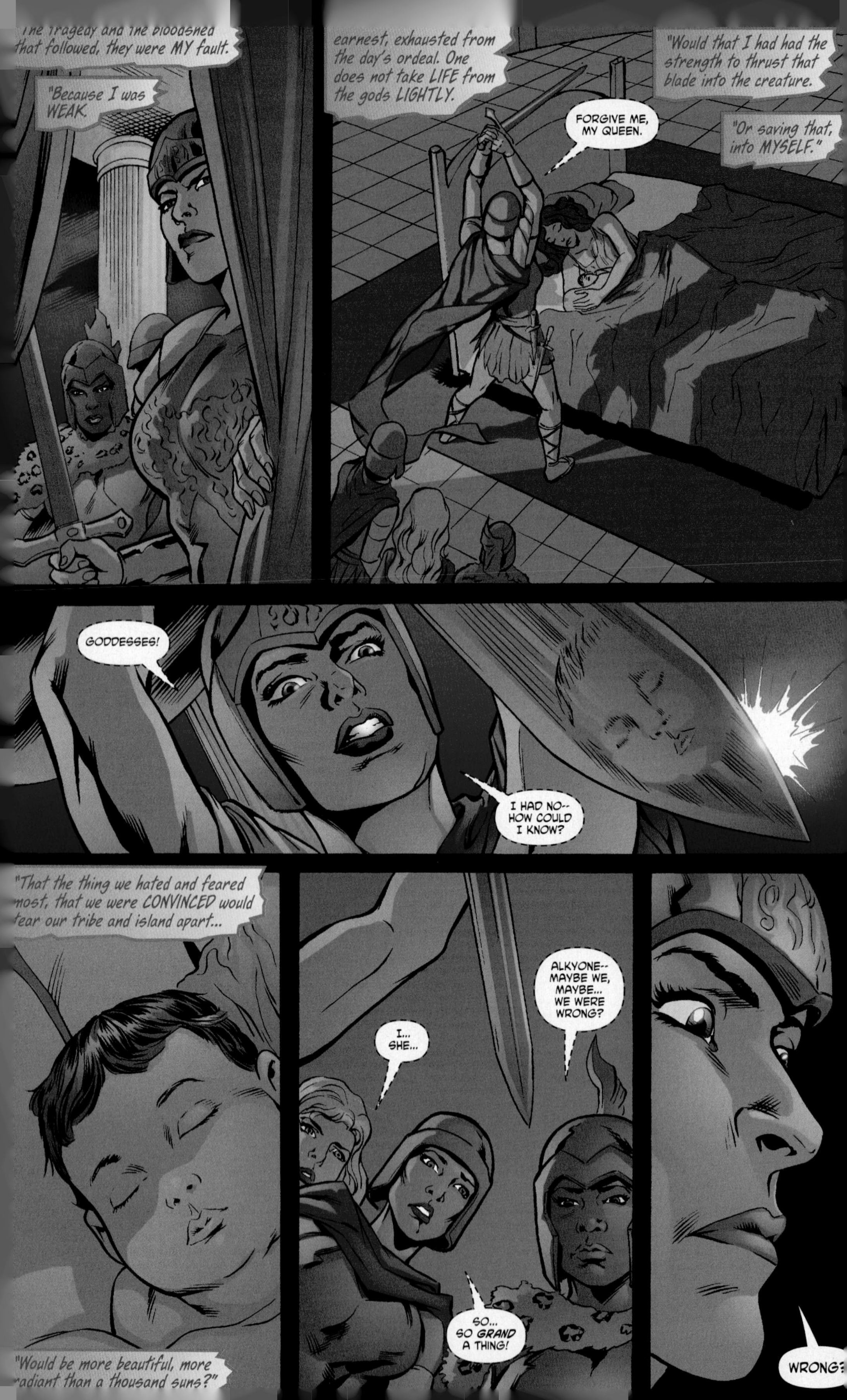
The tragedy and the bloodshed that followed, they were MY fault.
"Because I was WEAK.
earnest, exhausted from the day's ordeal. One does not take LIFE from the gods LIGHTLY.
"Would that I had had the strength to thrust that blade into the creature.
FORGIVE ME, MY QUEEN.
"Or saving that, into MYSELF."
GODDESSES!
I HAD NO-- HOW COULD I KNOW?
"That the thing we hated and feared most, that we were CONVINCED would tear our tribe and island apart...
"Would be more beautiful, more radiant than a thousand suns?"
I... SHE...
ALKYONE-- MAYBE WE, MAYBE... WE WERE WRONG?
SO... SO GRAND A THING!
WRONG?

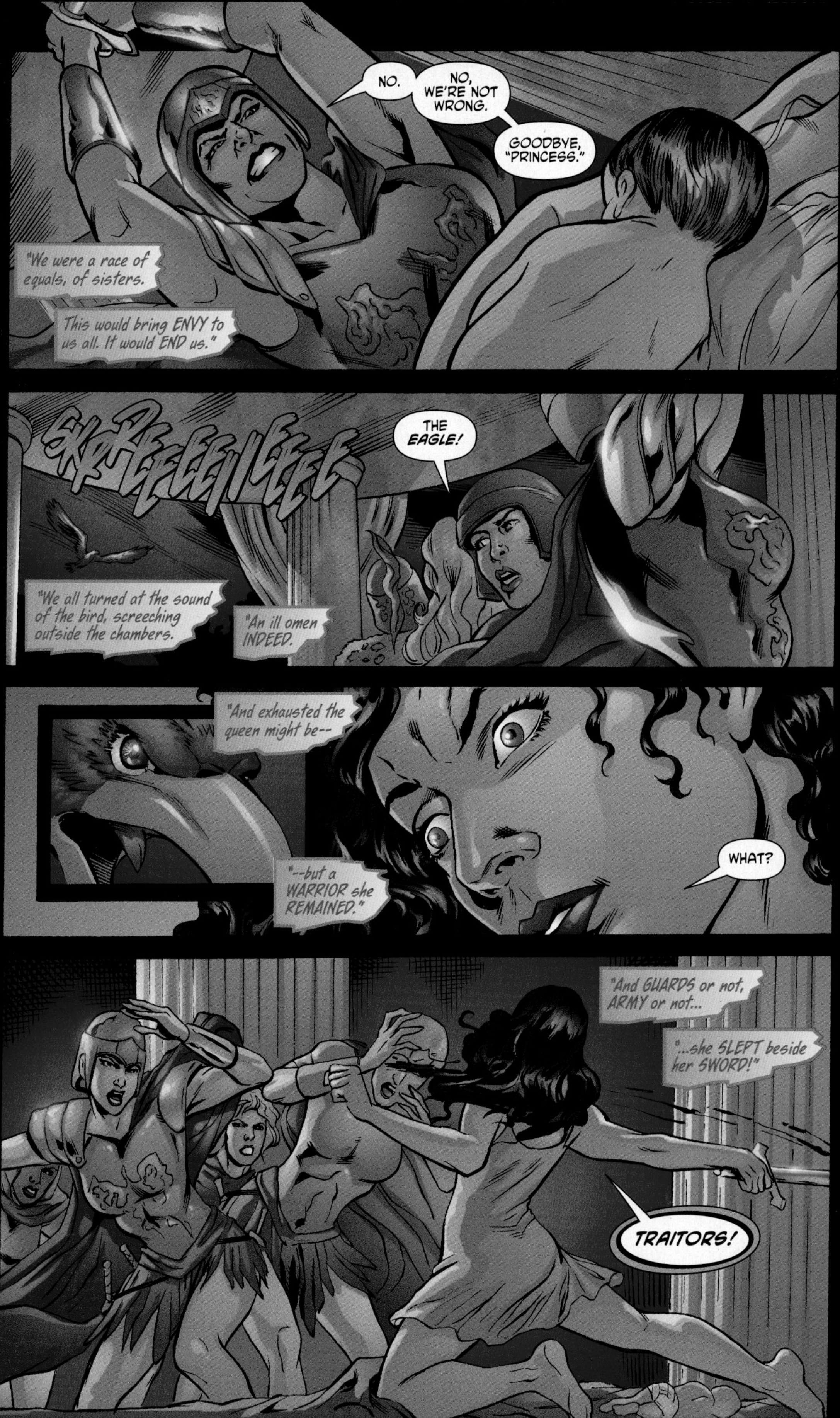
NO.
NO, WE'RE NOT WRONG.
GOODBYE, "PRINCESS."
"We were a race of equals, of sisters.
This would bring ENVY to us all. It would END us."
THE EAGLE!
"We all turned at the sound of the bird, screeching outside the chambers.
"An ill omen INDEED.
"And exhausted the queen might be--
"--but a WARRIOR she REMAINED."
WHAT?
"And GUARDS or not, ARMY or not...
"...she SLEPT beside her SWORD!"
TRAITORS!

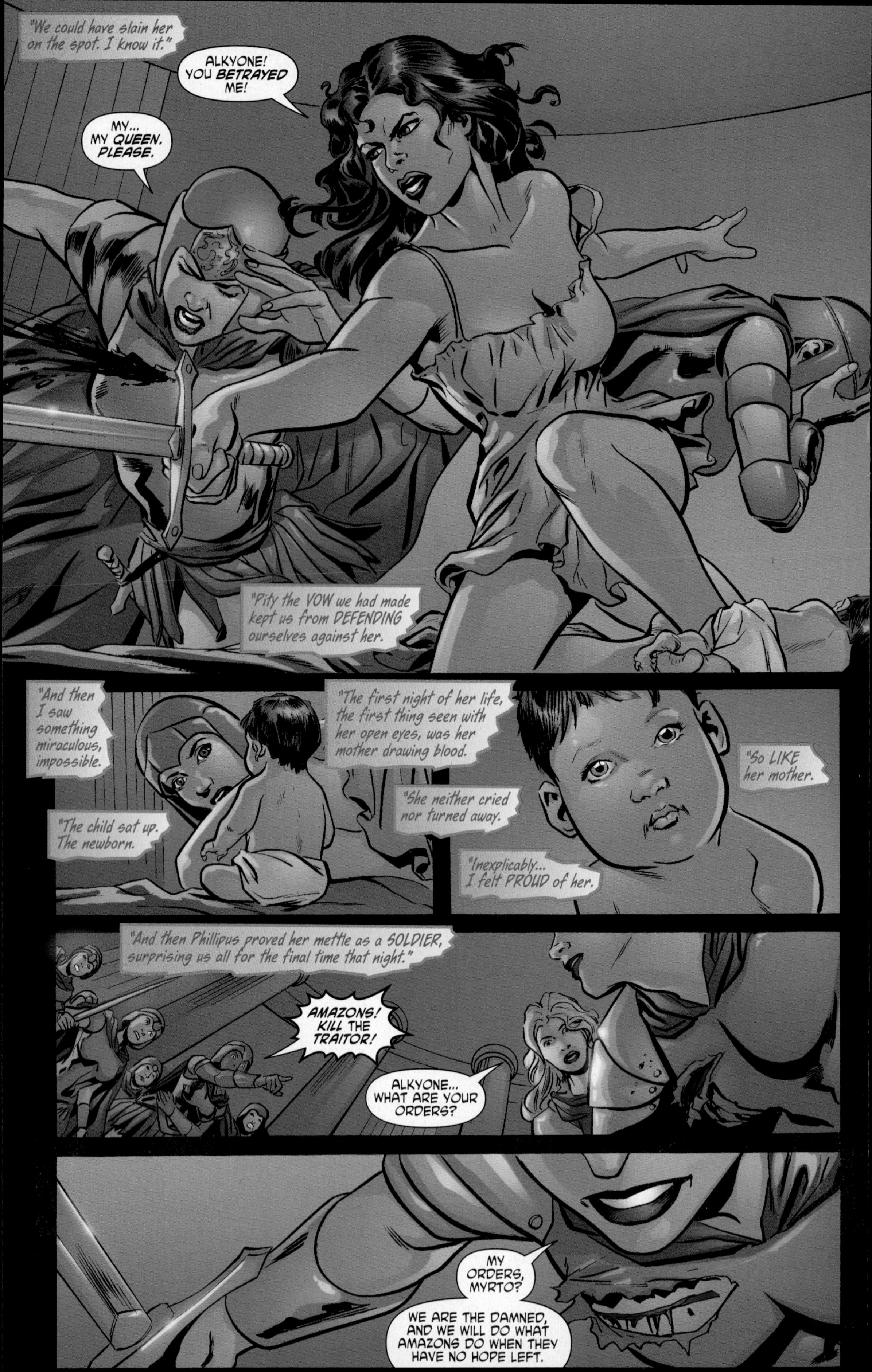
"We could have slain her on the spot. I know it."
ALKYONE! YOU BETRAYED ME!
MY... MY QUEEN. PLEASE.
"Pity the VOW we had made kept us from DEFENDING ourselves against her.
"And then I saw something miraculous, impossible.
"The child sat up. The newborn.
"The first night of her life, the first thing seen with her open eyes, was her mother drawing blood.
"She neither cried nor turned away.
"So LIKE her mother.
"Inexplicably... I felt PROUD of her.
"And then Phillipus proved her mettle as a SOLDIER, surprising us all for the final time that night."
AMAZONS! KILL THE TRAITOR!
ALKYONE... WHAT ARE YOUR ORDERS?
MY ORDERS, MYRTO?
WE ARE THE DAMNED, AND WE WILL DO WHAT AMAZONS DO WHEN THEY HAVE NO HOPE LEFT.

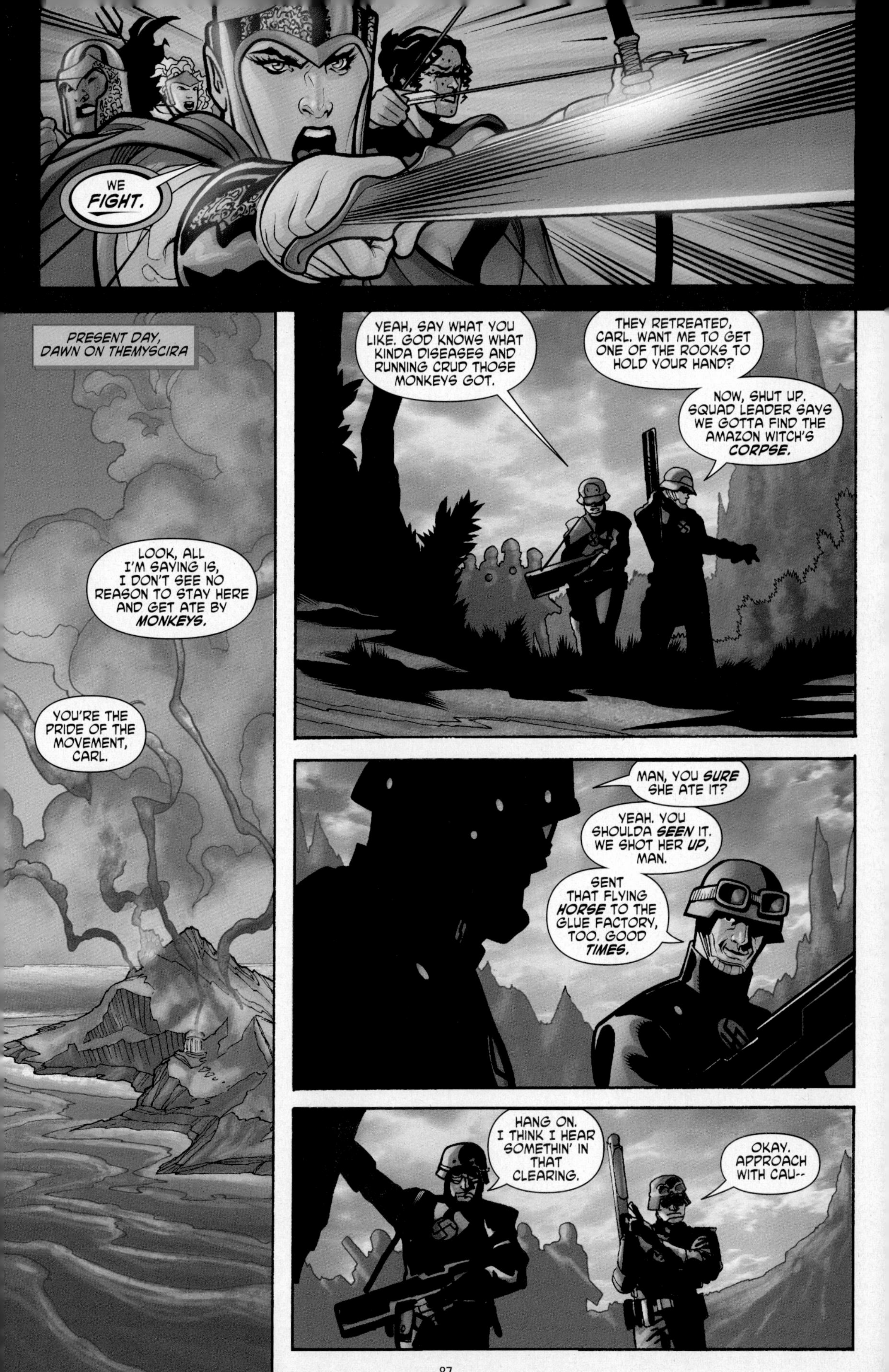
WE FIGHT.
PRESENT DAY, DAWN ON THEMYSCIRA
LOOK, ALL I'M SAYING IS, I DON'T SEE NO REASON TO STAY HERE AND GET ATE BY MONKEYS.
YOU'RE THE PRIDE OF THE MOVEMENT, CARL.
YEAH, SAY WHAT YOU LIKE. GOD KNOWS WHAT KINDA DISEASES AND RUNNING CRUD THOSE MONKEYS GOT.
THEY RETREATED, CARL. WANT ME TO GET ONE OF THE ROOKS TO HOLD YOUR HAND?
NOW, SHUT UP. SQUAD LEADER SAYS WE GOTTA FIND THE AMAZON WITCH'S CORPSE.
MAN, YOU SURE SHE ATE IT?
YEAH. YOU SHOULDA SEEN IT. WE SHOT HER UP, MAN.
SENT THAT FLYING HORSE TO THE GLUE FACTORY, TOO. GOOD TIMES.
HANG ON. I THINK I HEAR SOMETHIN' IN THAT CLEARING.
OKAY. APPROACH WITH CAU--

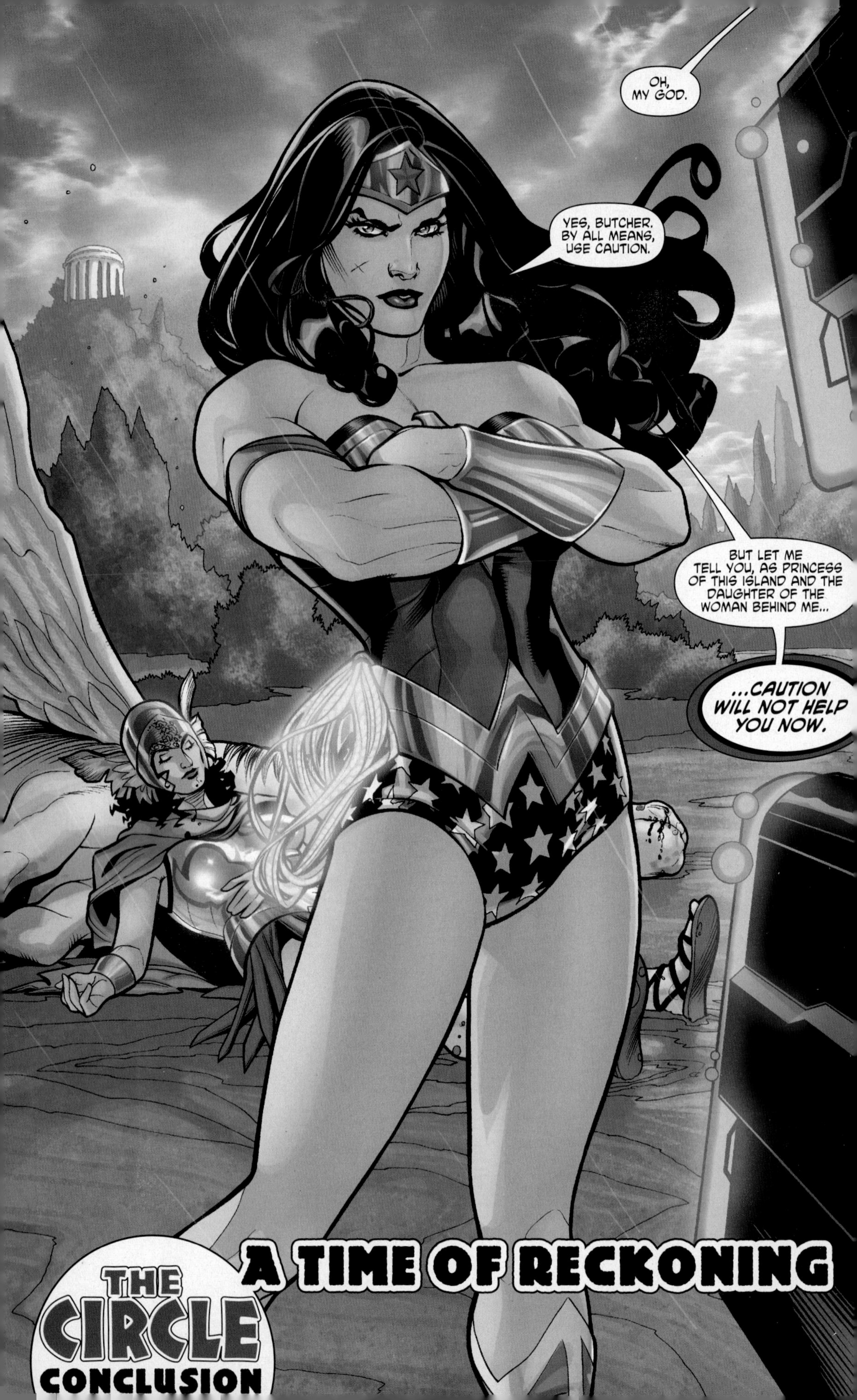
OH, MY GOD.
YES, BUTCHER. BY ALL MEANS, USE CAUTION.
BUT LET ME TELL YOU, AS PRINCESS OF THIS ISLAND AND THE DAUGHTER OF THE WOMAN BEHIND ME...
...CAUTION WILL NOT HELP YOU NOW.
A TIME OF RECKONING
THE CIRCLE CONCLUSION

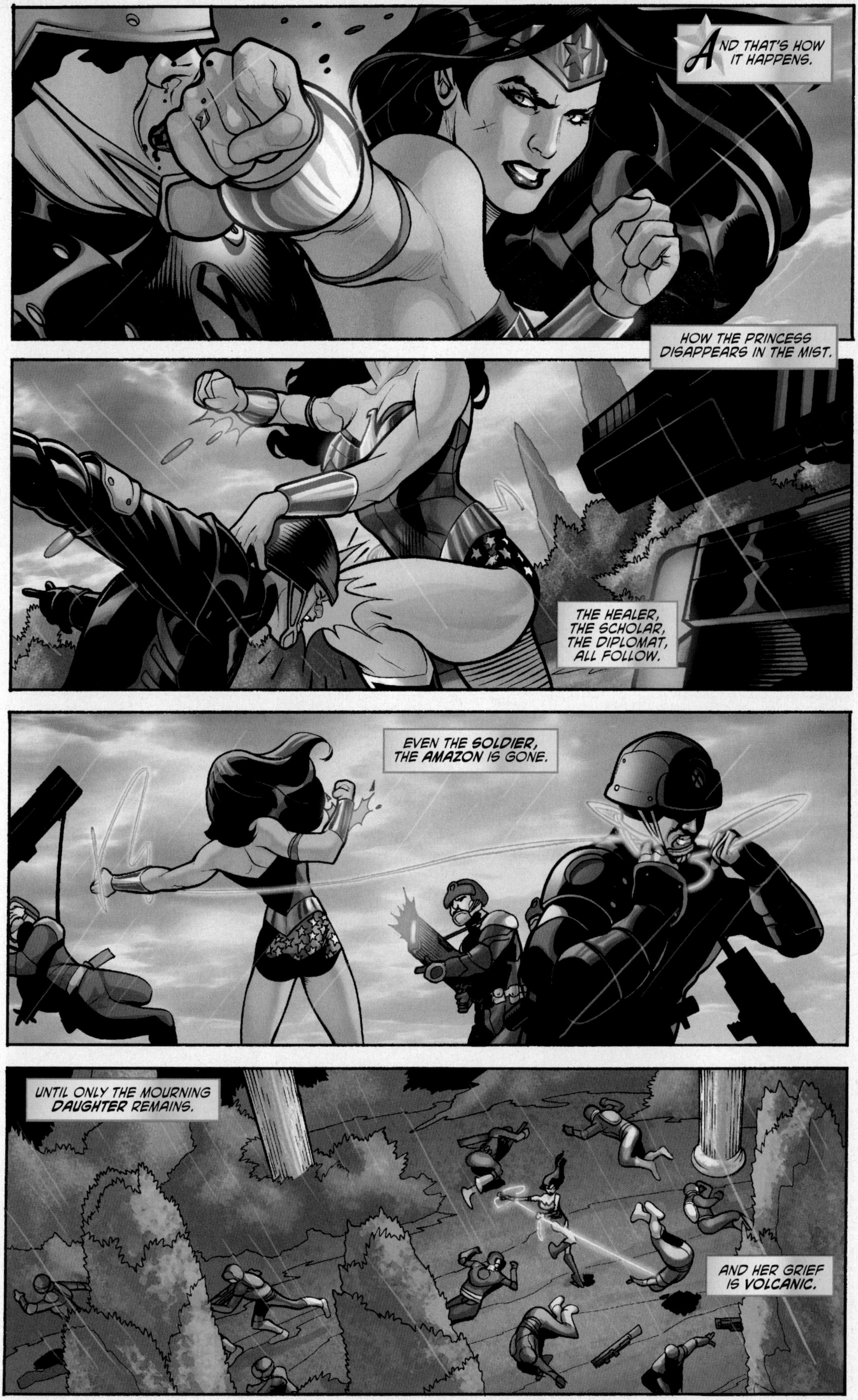
AND THAT'S HOW IT HAPPENS.
HOW THE PRINCESS DISAPPEARS IN THE MIST.
THE HEALER, THE SCHOLAR, THE DIPLOMAT, ALL FOLLOW.
EVEN THE SOLDIER, THE AMAZON IS GONE.
UNTIL ONLY THE MOURNING DAUGHTER REMAINS.
AND HER GRIEF IS VOLCANIC.

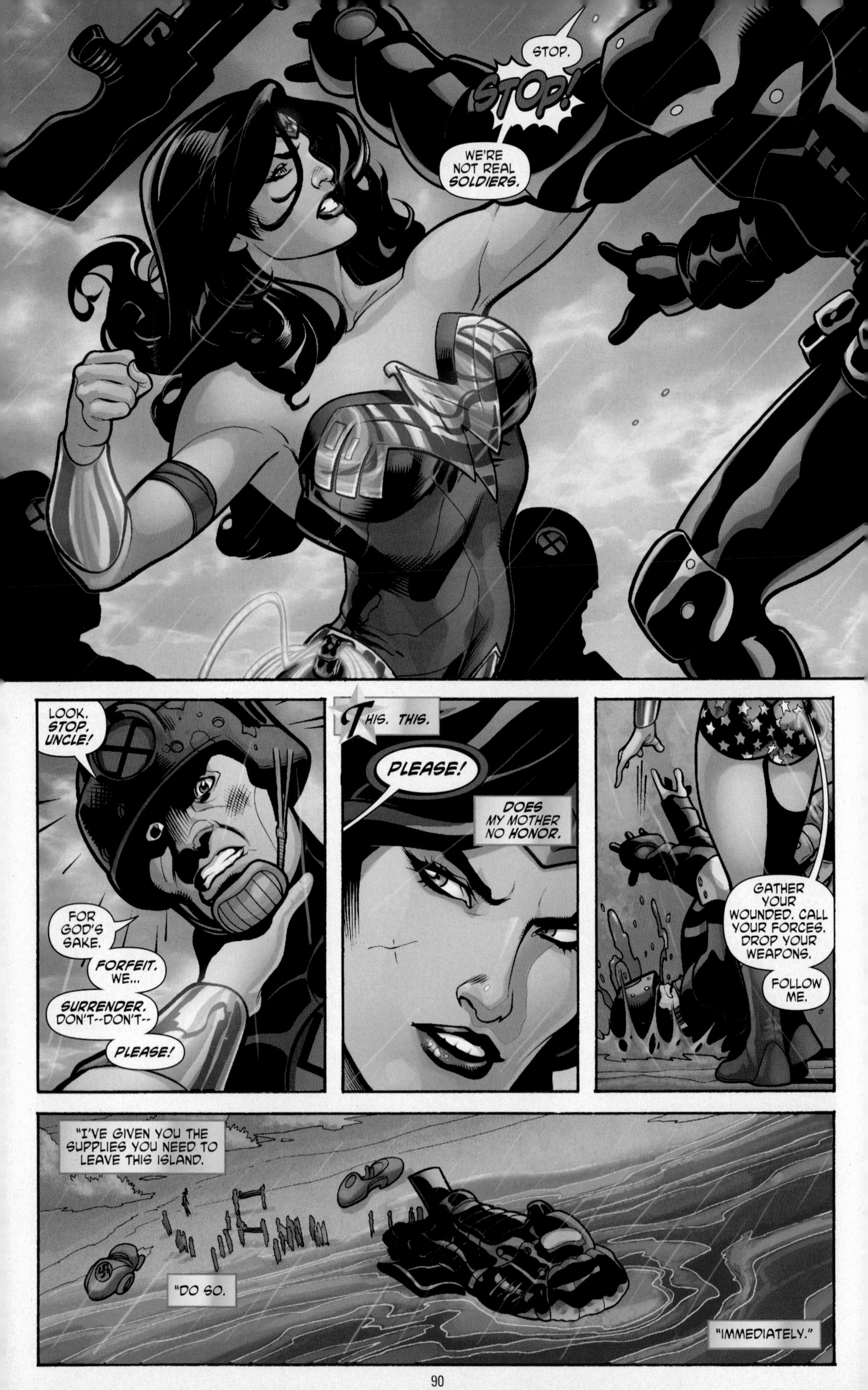
STOP.
STOP!
WE'RE NOT REAL SOLDIERS.
LOOK. STOP. UNCLE!
FOR GOD'S SAKE.
FORFEIT. WE...
SURRENDER. DON'T--DON'T--
PLEASE!
THIS. THIS.
PLEASE!
DOES MY MOTHER NO HONOR.
GATHER YOUR WOUNDED. CALL YOUR FORCES. DROP YOUR WEAPONS.
FOLLOW ME.
"I'VE GIVEN YOU THE SUPPLIES YOU NEED TO LEAVE THIS ISLAND.
"DO SO.
"IMMEDIATELY."

GO. I'LL LET SOMEONE KNOW YOUR COORDINATES FOR YOUR PICKUP AND ARREST.

WE... WITH THE SOCIETY'S HELP, WE GOT HERE *ONCE*. WE COULD FIND YOU *AGAIN*, AMAZON.

YOU COULD.

I WOULDN'T.

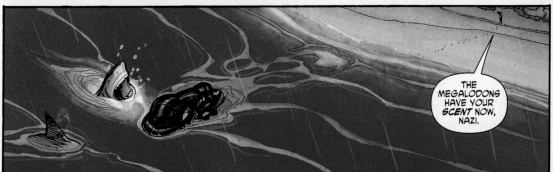

THE MEGALODONS HAVE YOUR *SCENT* NOW, NAZI.

SHE FIGHTS LIKE HER MOTHER.

YES.

LET HER KNOW WE'RE HERE, PHILOMELA.

"Philomela may have lost her eyes in battle the night this dragon was created.

"It would not *OCCUR* to her to complain."

UNNNGH.

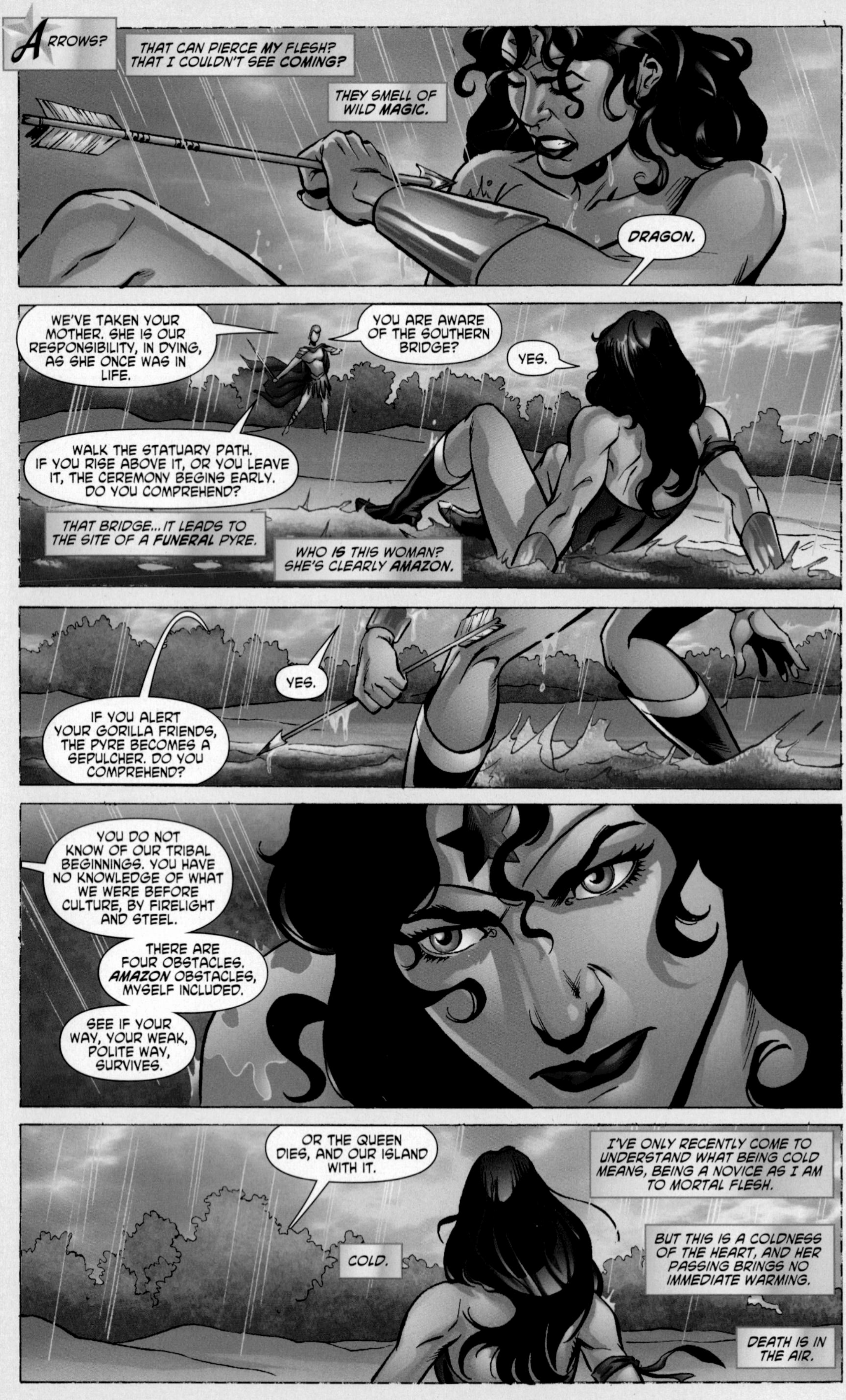
ARROWS?
THAT CAN PIERCE MY FLESH? THAT I COULDN'T SEE COMING?
THEY SMELL OF WILD MAGIC.
DRAGON.
WE'VE TAKEN YOUR MOTHER. SHE IS OUR RESPONSIBILITY, IN DYING, AS SHE ONCE WAS IN LIFE.
YOU ARE AWARE OF THE SOUTHERN BRIDGE?
YES.
WALK THE STATUARY PATH. IF YOU RISE ABOVE IT, OR YOU LEAVE IT, THE CEREMONY BEGINS EARLY. DO YOU COMPREHEND?
THAT BRIDGE... IT LEADS TO THE SITE OF A FUNERAL PYRE.
WHO IS THIS WOMAN? SHE'S CLEARLY AMAZON.
YES.
IF YOU ALERT YOUR GORILLA FRIENDS, THE PYRE BECOMES A SEPULCHER. DO YOU COMPREHEND?
YOU DO NOT KNOW OF OUR TRIBAL BEGINNINGS. YOU HAVE NO KNOWLEDGE OF WHAT WE WERE BEFORE CULTURE, BY FIRELIGHT AND STEEL.
THERE ARE FOUR OBSTACLES. AMAZON OBSTACLES, MYSELF INCLUDED.
SEE IF YOUR WAY, YOUR WEAK, POLITE WAY, SURVIVES.
OR THE QUEEN DIES, AND OUR ISLAND WITH IT.
COLD.
I'VE ONLY RECENTLY COME TO UNDERSTAND WHAT BEING COLD MEANS, BEING A NOVICE AS I AM TO MORTAL FLESH.
BUT THIS IS A COLDNESS OF THE HEART, AND HER PASSING BRINGS NO IMMEDIATE WARMING.
DEATH IS IN THE AIR.

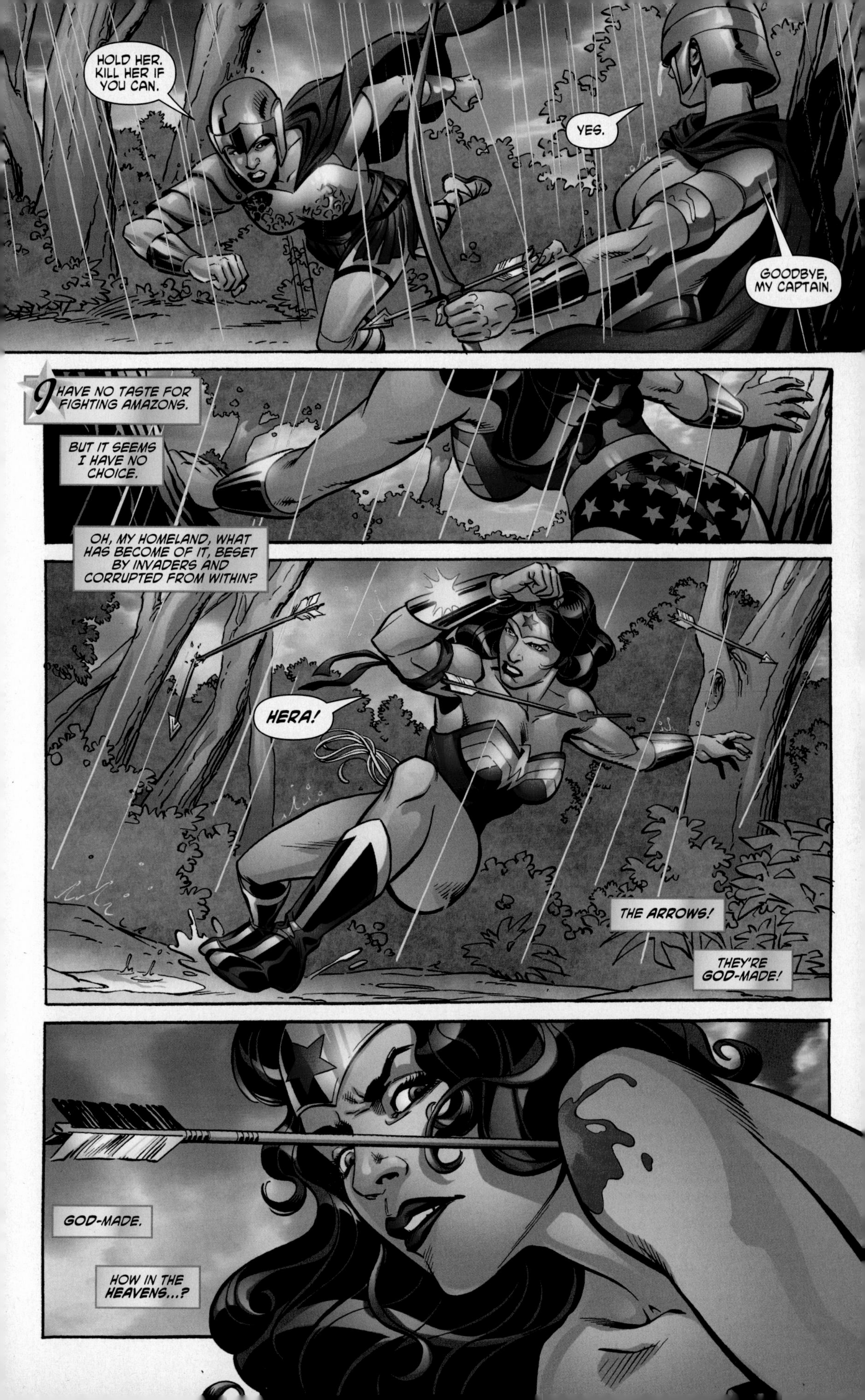
HOLD HER. KILL HER IF YOU CAN.
YES.
GOODBYE, MY CAPTAIN.
I HAVE NO TASTE FOR FIGHTING AMAZONS.
BUT IT SEEMS I HAVE NO CHOICE.
OH, MY HOMELAND, WHAT HAS BECOME OF IT, BESET BY INVADERS AND CORRUPTED FROM WITHIN?
HERA!
THE ARROWS!
THEY'RE GOD-MADE!
GOD-MADE.
HOW IN THE HEAVENS...?

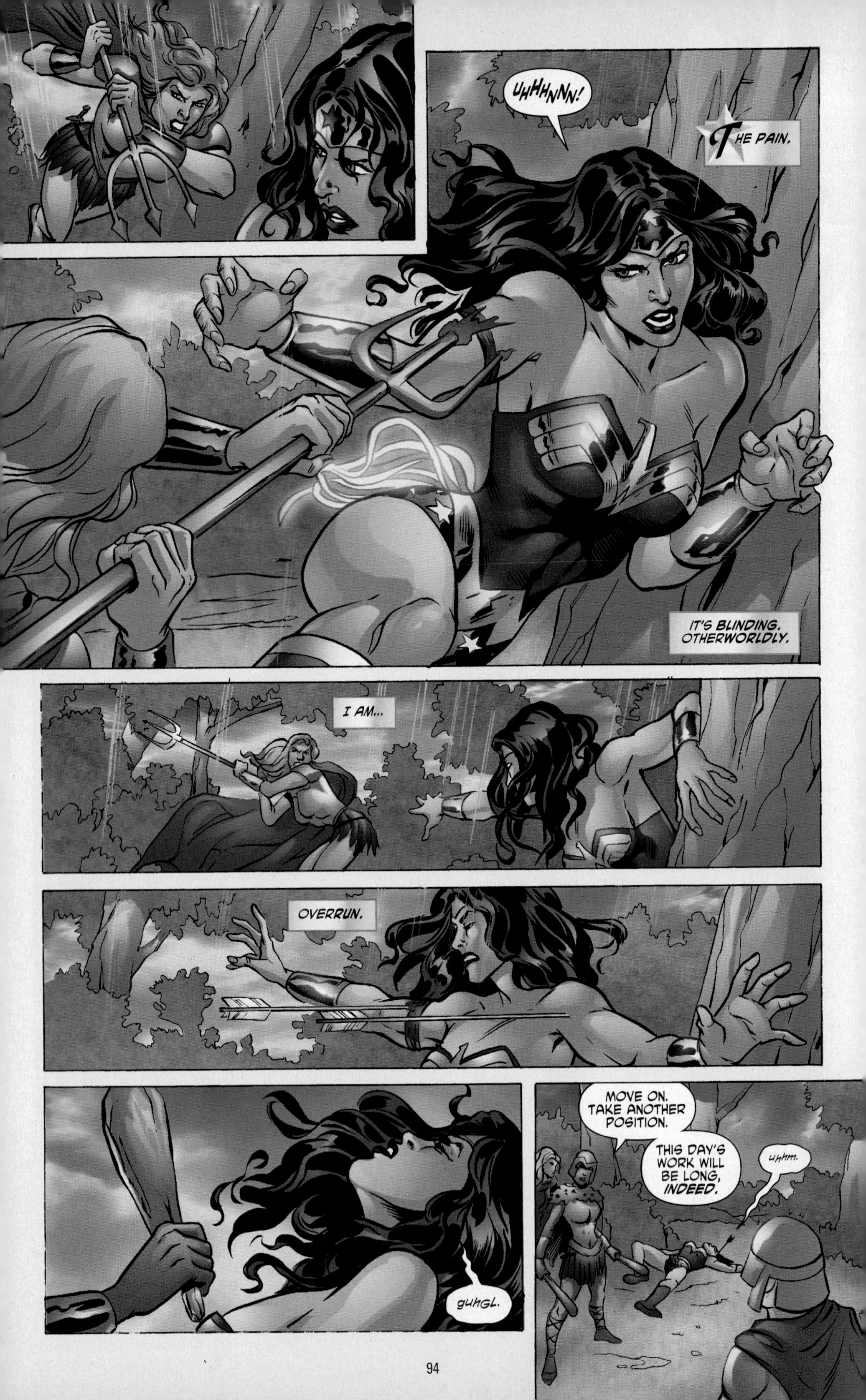
UHHHNNN!
THE PAIN.
IT'S BLINDING. OTHERWORLDLY.
I AM...
OVERRUN.
guhGL.
MOVE ON. TAKE ANOTHER POSITION.
THIS DAY'S WORK WILL BE LONG, INDEED.
uhhm.

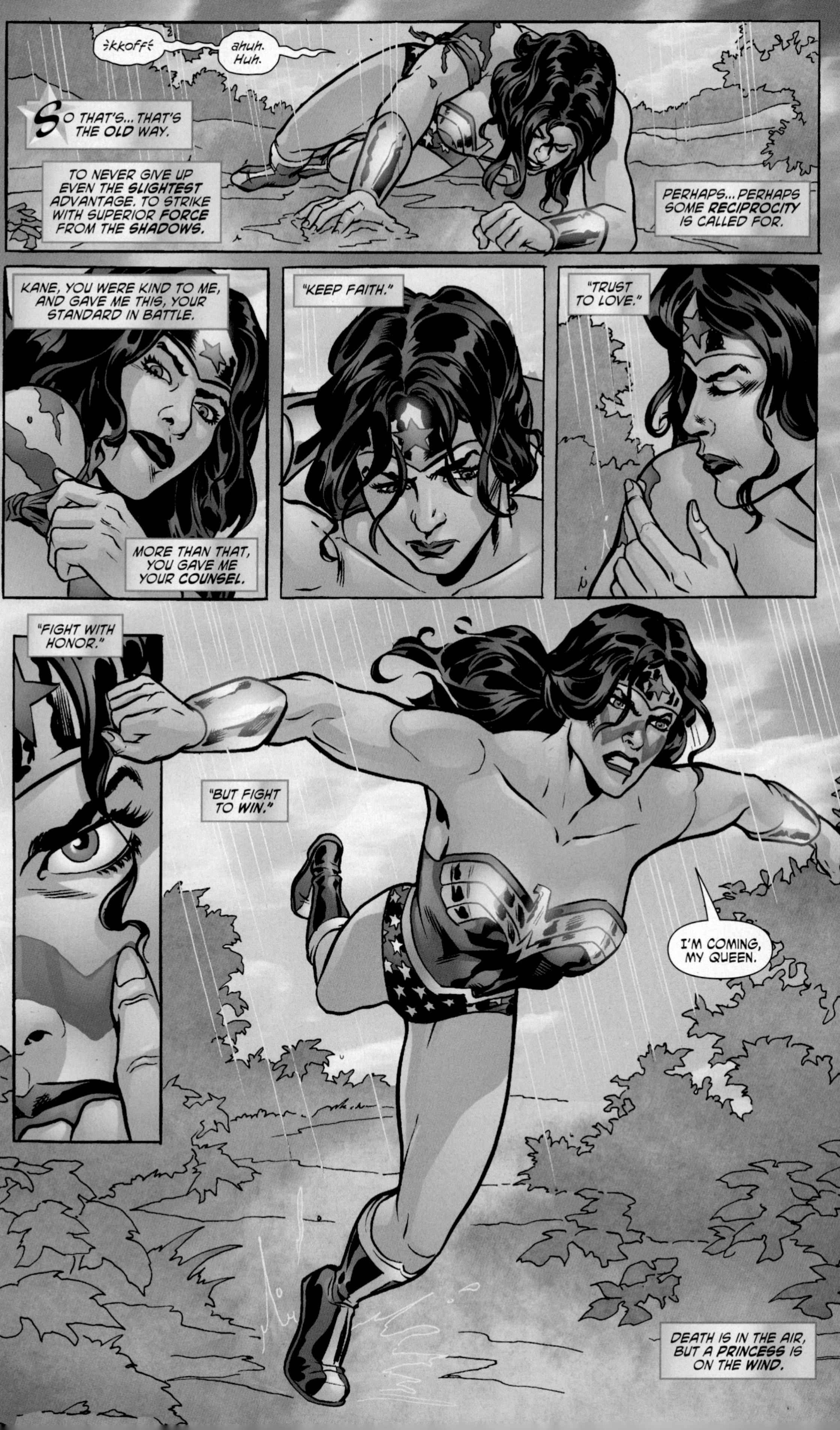

kkoff
ahuh. Huh.
SO THAT'S... THAT'S THE OLD WAY.
TO NEVER GIVE UP EVEN THE SLIGHTEST ADVANTAGE. TO STRIKE WITH SUPERIOR FORCE FROM THE SHADOWS.
PERHAPS... PERHAPS SOME RECIPROCITY IS CALLED FOR.
KANE, YOU WERE KIND TO ME, AND GAVE ME THIS, YOUR STANDARD IN BATTLE.
MORE THAN THAT, YOU GAVE ME YOUR COUNSEL.
"KEEP FAITH."
"TRUST TO LOVE."
"FIGHT WITH HONOR."
"BUT FIGHT TO WIN."
I'M COMING, MY QUEEN.
DEATH IS IN THE AIR, BUT A PRINCESS IS ON THE WIND.

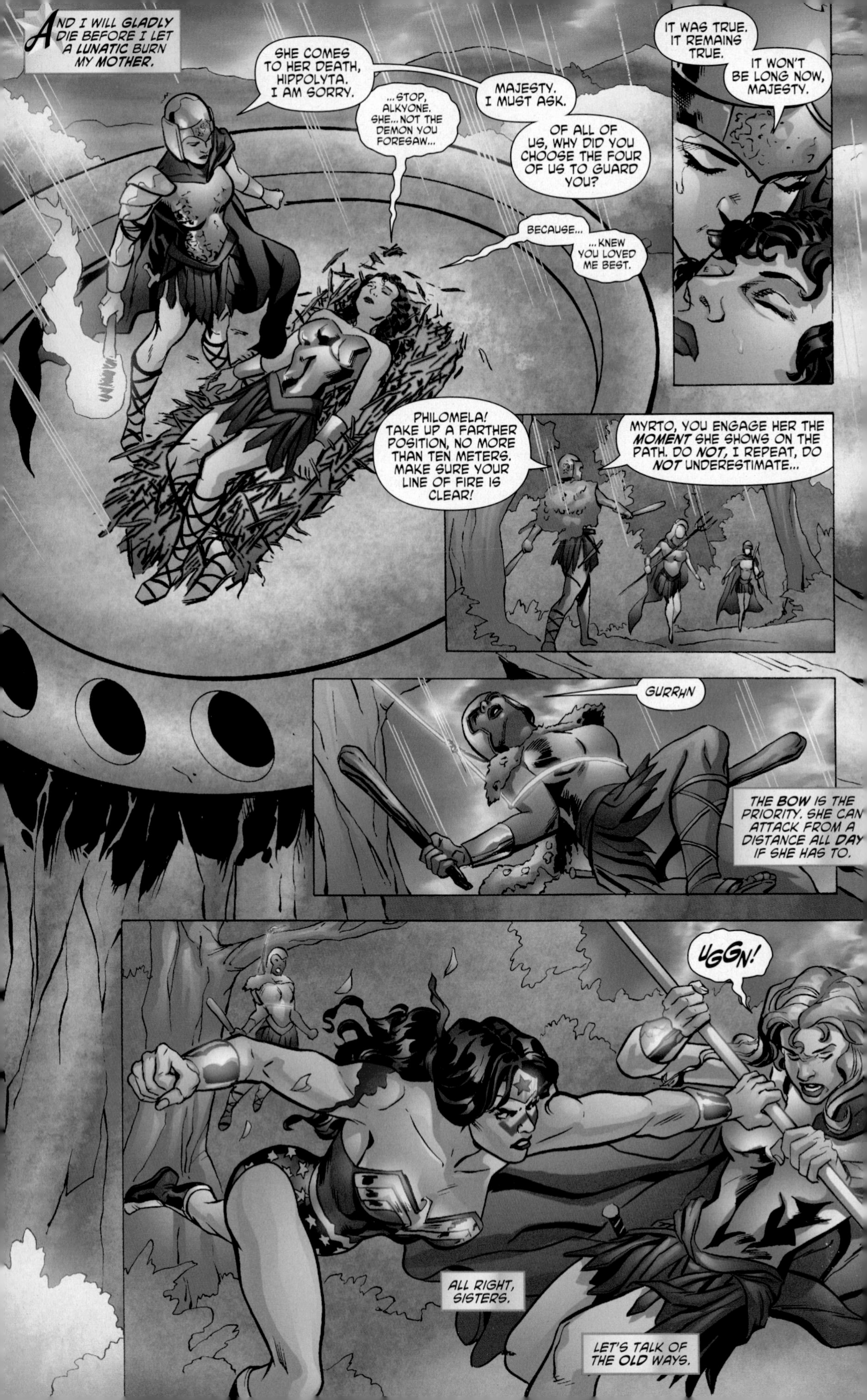
AND I WILL GLADLY DIE BEFORE I LET A LUNATIC BURN MY MOTHER.
SHE COMES TO HER DEATH, HIPPOLYTA. I AM SORRY.
...STOP, ALKYONE. SHE...NOT THE DEMON YOU FORESAW...
MAJESTY. I MUST ASK.
OF ALL OF US, WHY DID YOU CHOOSE THE FOUR OF US TO GUARD YOU?
BECAUSE...
...KNEW YOU LOVED ME BEST.
IT WAS TRUE. IT REMAINS TRUE.
IT WON'T BE LONG NOW, MAJESTY.
PHILOMELA! TAKE UP A FARTHER POSITION, NO MORE THAN TEN METERS. MAKE SURE YOUR LINE OF FIRE IS CLEAR!
MYRTO, YOU ENGAGE HER THE MOMENT SHE SHOWS ON THE PATH. DO NOT, I REPEAT, DO NOT UNDERESTIMATE...
GURRHN
THE BOW IS THE PRIORITY. SHE CAN ATTACK FROM A DISTANCE ALL DAY IF SHE HAS TO.
UGGN!
ALL RIGHT, SISTERS.
LET'S TALK OF THE OLD WAYS.

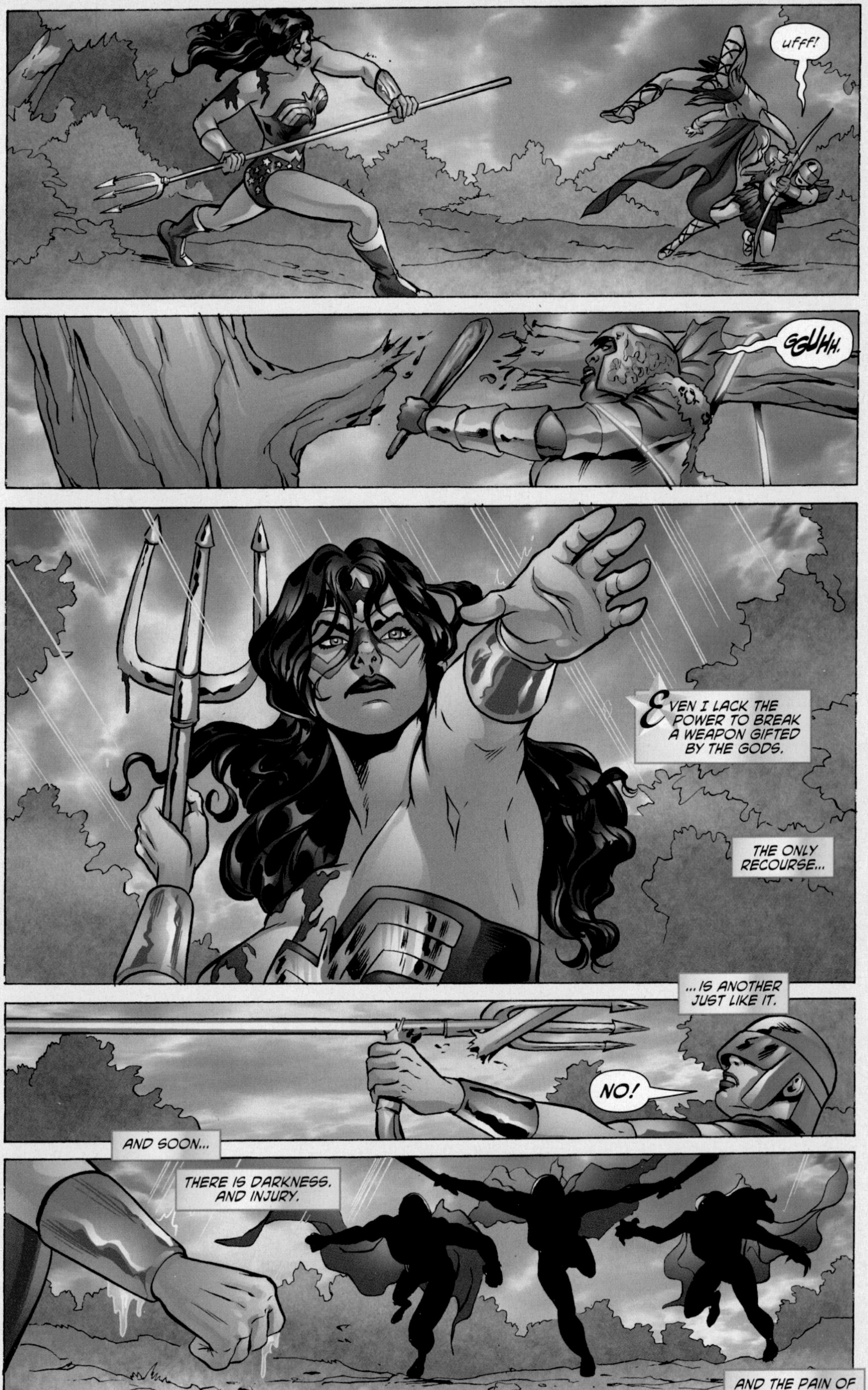

ufff!
GGUHH.
EVEN I LACK THE POWER TO BREAK A WEAPON GIFTED BY THE GODS.
THE ONLY RECOURSE...
...IS ANOTHER JUST LIKE IT.
NO!
AND SOON...
THERE IS DARKNESS. AND INJURY.
AND THE PAIN OF TEN LIFETIMES.

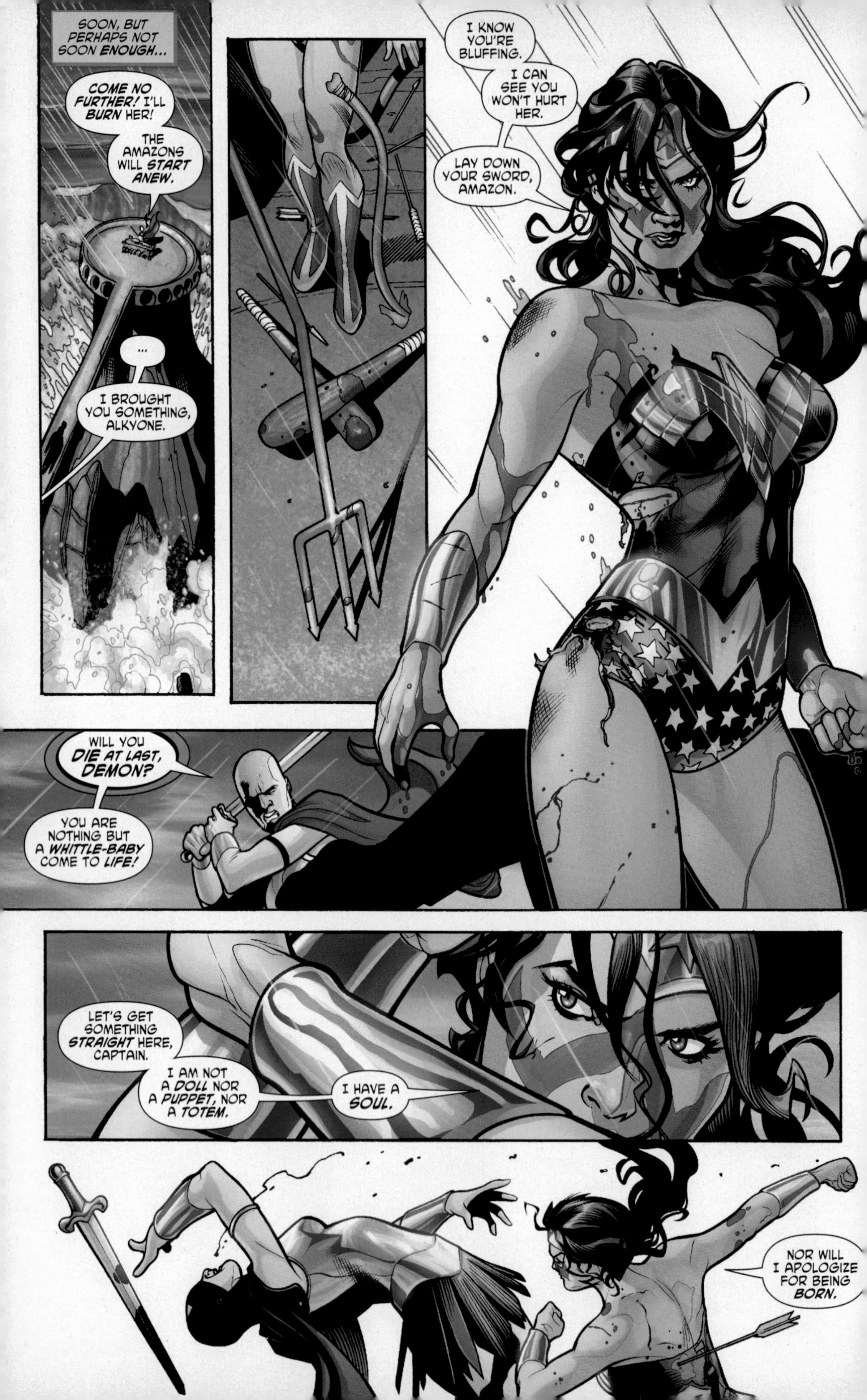
SOON, BUT PERHAPS NOT SOON ENOUGH...
COME NO FURTHER! I'LL BURN HER!
THE AMAZONS WILL START ANEW.
...
I BROUGHT YOU SOMETHING, ALKYONE.
I KNOW YOU'RE BLUFFING.
I CAN SEE YOU WON'T HURT HER.
LAY DOWN YOUR SWORD, AMAZON.
WILL YOU DIE AT LAST, DEMON?
YOU ARE NOTHING BUT A WHITTLE-BABY COME TO LIFE!
LET'S GET SOMETHING STRAIGHT HERE, CAPTAIN.
I AM NOT A DOLL NOR A PUPPET, NOR A TOTEM.
I HAVE A SOUL.
NOR WILL I APOLOGIZE FOR BEING BORN.

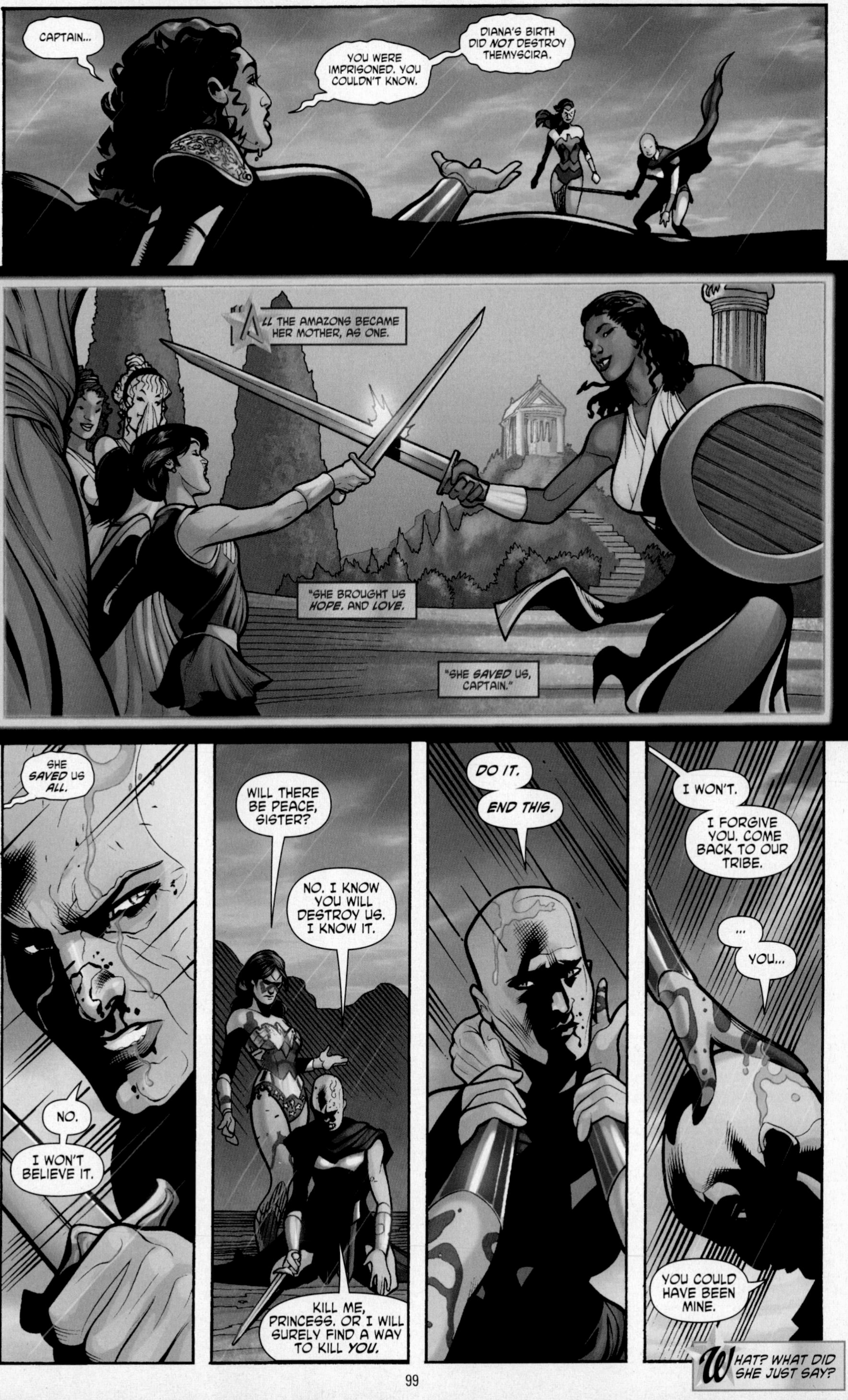
CAPTAIN...
YOU WERE IMPRISONED. YOU COULDN'T KNOW.
DIANA'S BIRTH DID NOT DESTROY THEMYSCIRA.
ALL THE AMAZONS BECAME HER MOTHER, AS ONE.
"SHE BROUGHT US HOPE. AND LOVE.
"SHE SAVED US, CAPTAIN."
SHE SAVED US ALL.
NO.
I WON'T BELIEVE IT.
WILL THERE BE PEACE, SISTER?
NO. I KNOW YOU WILL DESTROY US. I KNOW IT.
KILL ME, PRINCESS. OR I WILL SURELY FIND A WAY TO KILL YOU.
DO IT.
END THIS.
I WON'T.
I FORGIVE YOU. COME BACK TO OUR TRIBE.
...
YOU...
YOU COULD HAVE BEEN MINE.
WHAT? WHAT DID SHE JUST SAY?

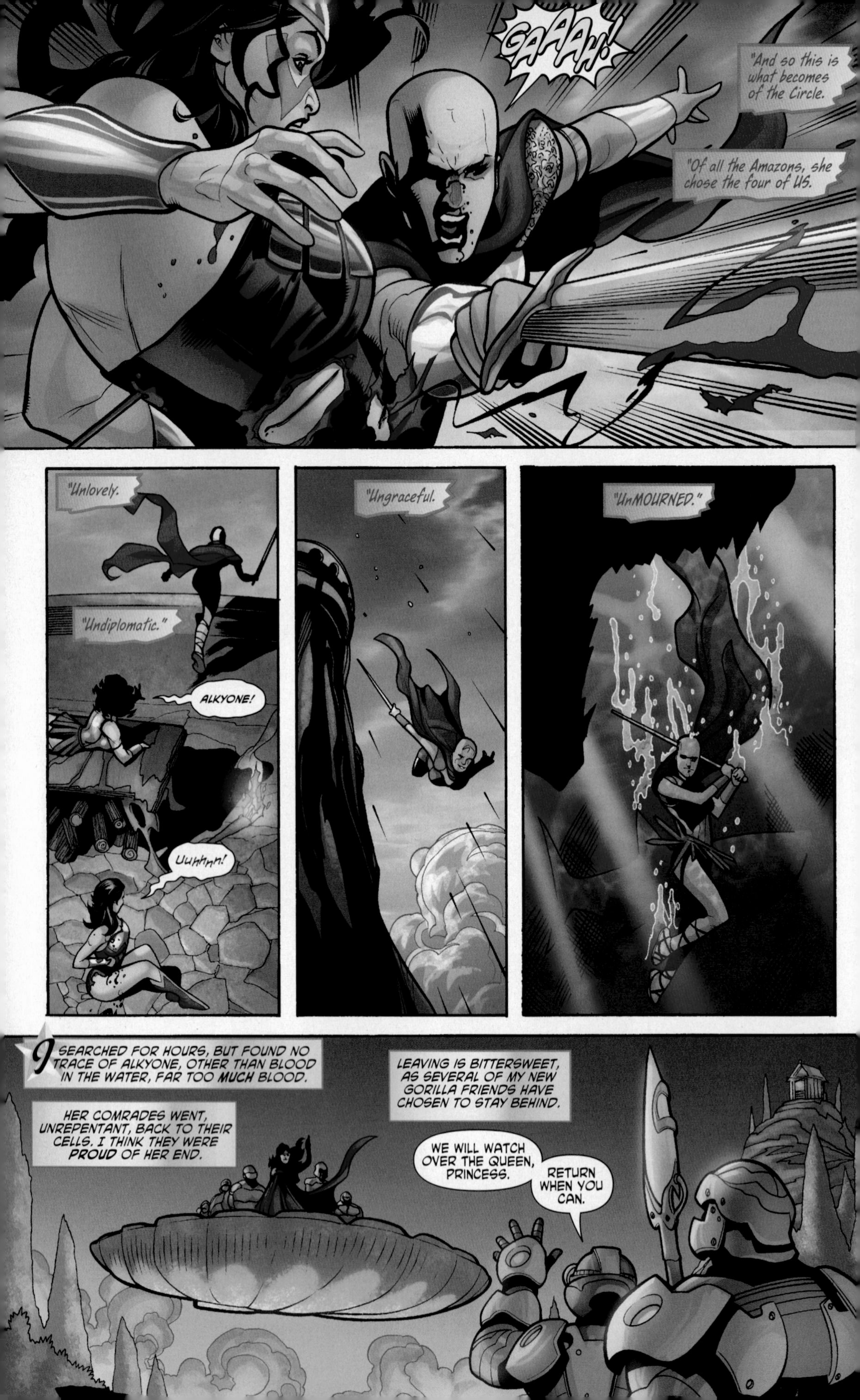
GAAAH!
"And so this is what becomes of the Circle.
"Of all the Amazons, she chose the four of US.
"Unlovely.
"Undiplomatic."
ALKYONE!
Uuhhnn!
"Ungraceful.
"UnMOURNED."
I SEARCHED FOR HOURS, BUT FOUND NO TRACE OF ALKYONE, OTHER THAN BLOOD IN THE WATER, FAR TOO MUCH BLOOD.
HER COMRADES WENT, UNREPENTANT, BACK TO THEIR CELLS. I THINK THEY WERE PROUD OF HER END.
LEAVING IS BITTERSWEET, AS SEVERAL OF MY NEW GORILLA FRIENDS HAVE CHOSEN TO STAY BEHIND.
WE WILL WATCH OVER THE QUEEN, PRINCESS.
RETURN WHEN YOU CAN.

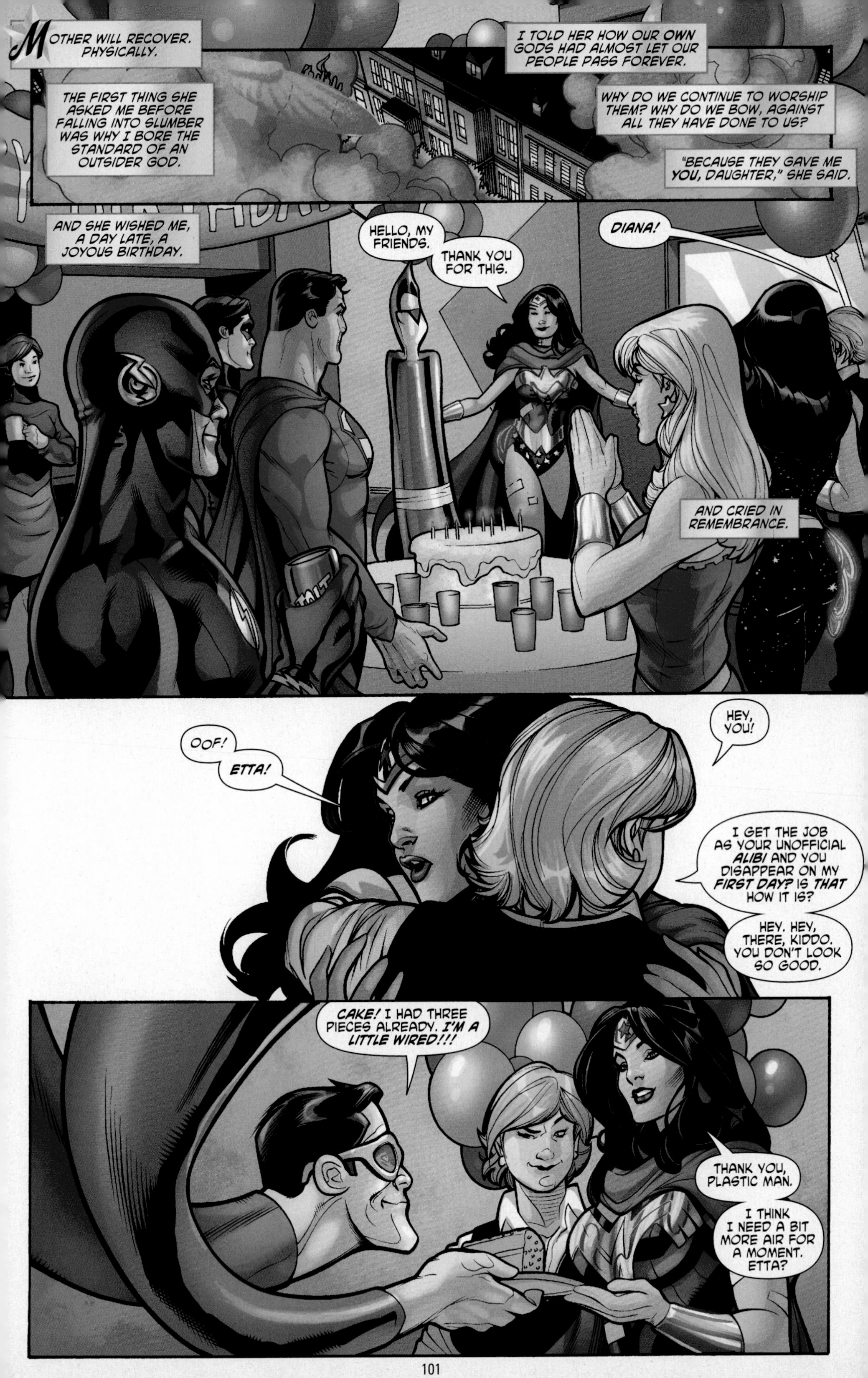
MOTHER WILL RECOVER. PHYSICALLY.
THE FIRST THING SHE ASKED ME BEFORE FALLING INTO SLUMBER WAS WHY I BORE THE STANDARD OF AN OUTSIDER GOD.
I TOLD HER HOW OUR OWN GODS HAD ALMOST LET OUR PEOPLE PASS FOREVER.
WHY DO WE CONTINUE TO WORSHIP THEM? WHY DO WE BOW, AGAINST ALL THEY HAVE DONE TO US?
"BECAUSE THEY GAVE ME YOU, DAUGHTER," SHE SAID.
AND SHE WISHED ME, A DAY LATE, A JOYOUS BIRTHDAY.
HELLO, MY FRIENDS.
THANK YOU FOR THIS.
DIANA!
AND CRIED IN REMEMBRANCE.
OOF!
ETTA!
HEY, YOU!
I GET THE JOB AS YOUR UNOFFICIAL ALIBI AND YOU DISAPPEAR ON MY FIRST DAY? IS THAT HOW IT IS?
HEY. HEY, THERE, KIDDO. YOU DON'T LOOK SO GOOD.
CAKE! I HAD THREE PIECES ALREADY. I'M A LITTLE WIRED!!!
THANK YOU, PLASTIC MAN.
I THINK I NEED A BIT MORE AIR FOR A MOMENT. ETTA?

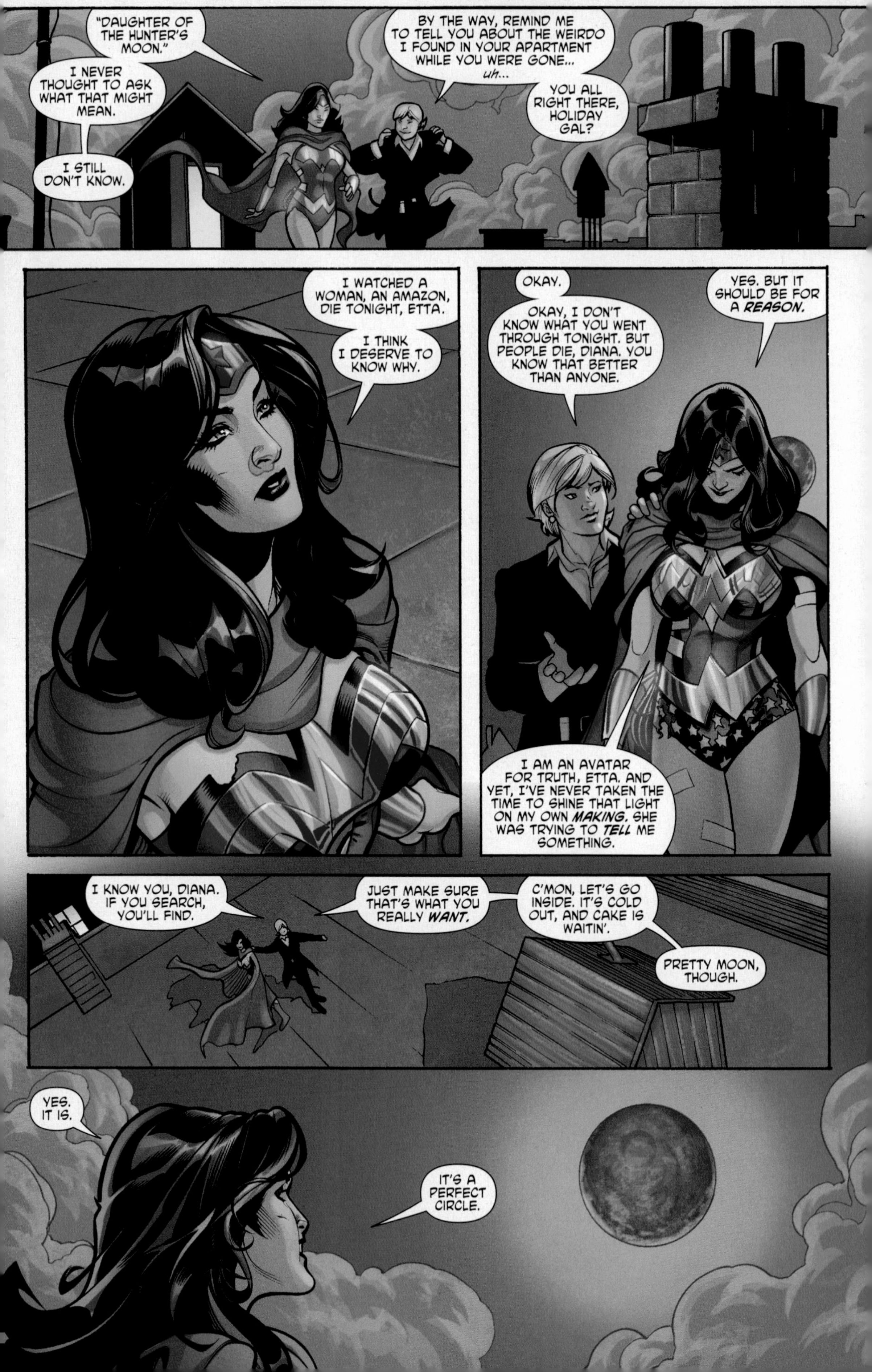
"DAUGHTER OF THE HUNTER'S MOON."
I NEVER THOUGHT TO ASK WHAT THAT MIGHT MEAN.
I STILL DON'T KNOW.
BY THE WAY, REMIND ME TO TELL YOU ABOUT THE WEIRDO I FOUND IN YOUR APARTMENT WHILE YOU WERE GONE... *uh...*
YOU ALL RIGHT THERE, HOLIDAY GAL?
I WATCHED A WOMAN, AN AMAZON, DIE TONIGHT, ETTA.
I THINK I DESERVE TO KNOW WHY.
OKAY.
OKAY, I DON'T KNOW WHAT YOU WENT THROUGH TONIGHT. BUT PEOPLE DIE, DIANA. YOU KNOW THAT BETTER THAN ANYONE.
YES. BUT IT SHOULD BE FOR A ***REASON.***
I AM AN AVATAR FOR TRUTH, ETTA. AND YET, I'VE NEVER TAKEN THE TIME TO SHINE THAT LIGHT ON MY OWN ***MAKING.*** SHE WAS TRYING TO ***TELL*** ME SOMETHING.
I KNOW YOU, DIANA. IF YOU SEARCH, YOU'LL FIND.
JUST MAKE SURE THAT'S WHAT YOU REALLY ***WANT.***
C'MON, LET'S GO INSIDE. IT'S COLD OUT, AND CAKE IS WAITIN'.
PRETTY MOON, THOUGH.
YES. IT IS.
IT'S A PERFECT CIRCLE.

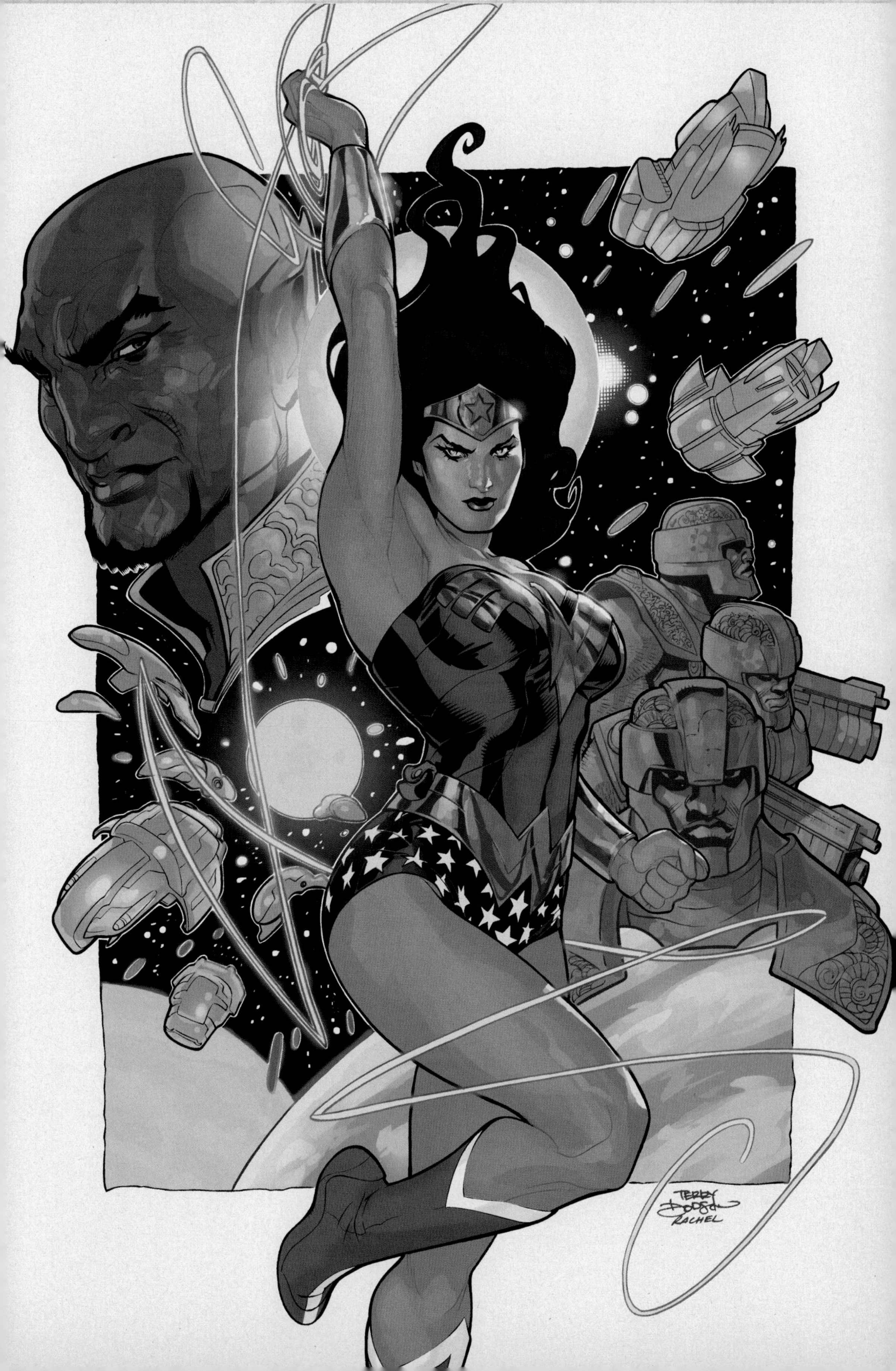
TERRY
DODSON
RACHEL

Art this issue by Bernard Chang

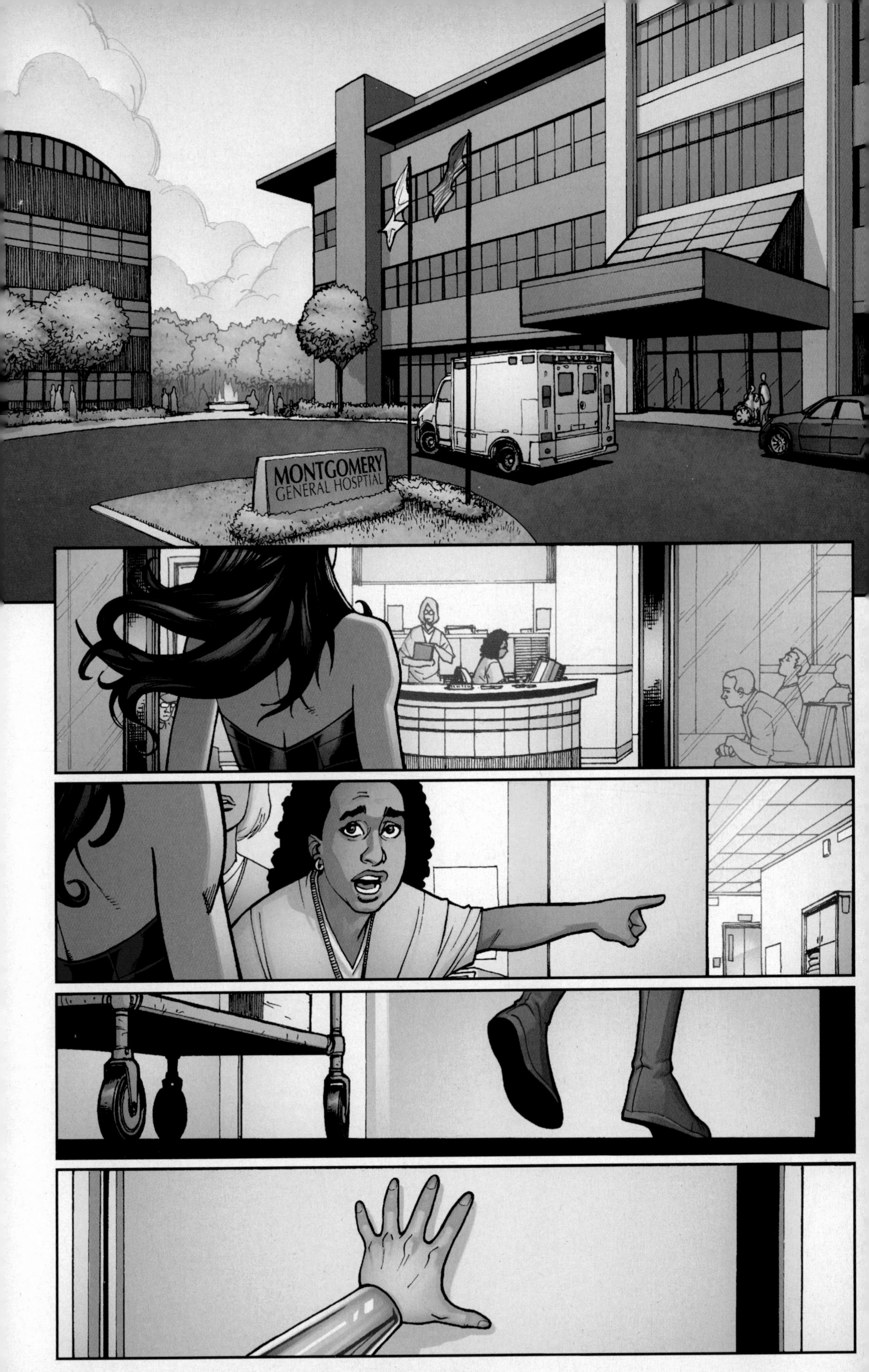
MONTGOMERY
GENERAL HOSPITAL

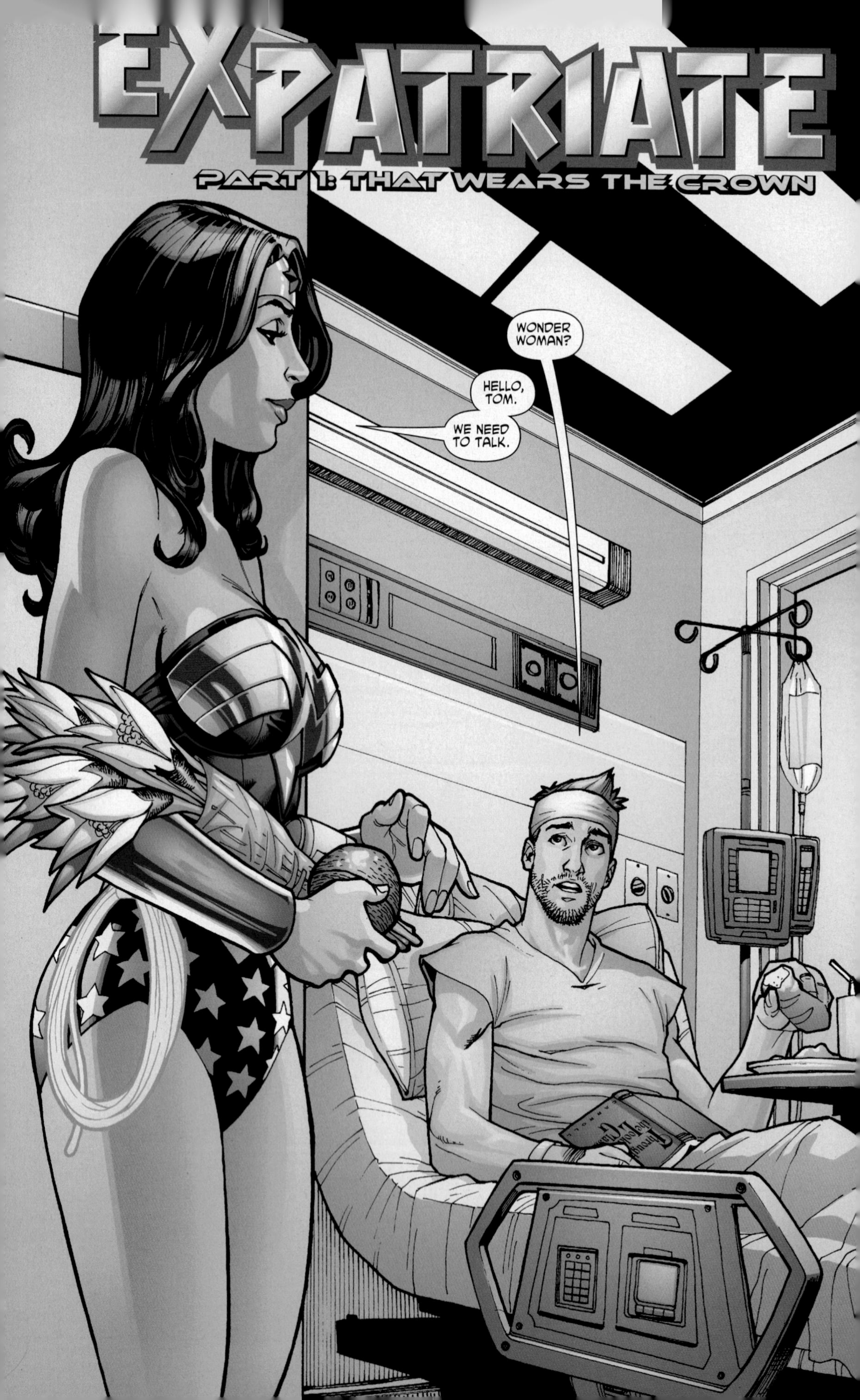
EXPATRIATE
PART 1: THAT WEARS THE CROWN
WONDER WOMAN?
HELLO, TOM.
WE NEED TO TALK.

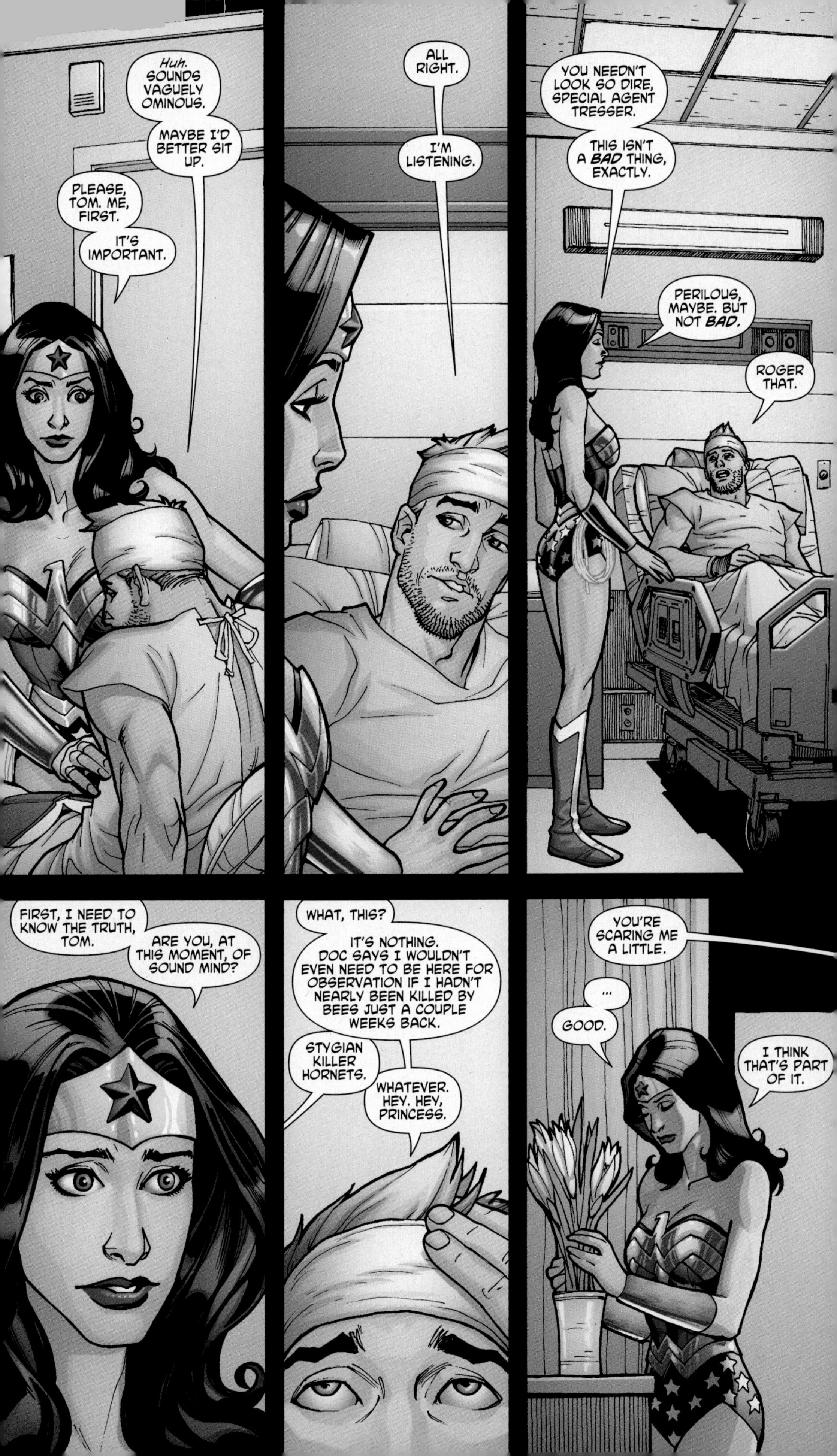
Huh. SOUNDS VAGUELY OMINOUS.
MAYBE I'D BETTER SIT UP.
PLEASE, TOM. ME, FIRST.
IT'S IMPORTANT.
ALL RIGHT.
I'M LISTENING.
YOU NEEDN'T LOOK SO DIRE, SPECIAL AGENT TRESSER.
THIS ISN'T A BAD THING, EXACTLY.
PERILOUS, MAYBE. BUT NOT BAD.
ROGER THAT.
FIRST, I NEED TO KNOW THE TRUTH, TOM.
ARE YOU, AT THIS MOMENT, OF SOUND MIND?
WHAT, THIS?
IT'S NOTHING. DOC SAYS I WOULDN'T EVEN NEED TO BE HERE FOR OBSERVATION IF I HADN'T NEARLY BEEN KILLED BY BEES JUST A COUPLE WEEKS BACK.
STYGIAN KILLER HORNETS.
WHATEVER. HEY. HEY, PRINCESS.
YOU'RE SCARING ME A LITTLE.
...
GOOD.
I THINK THAT'S PART OF IT.

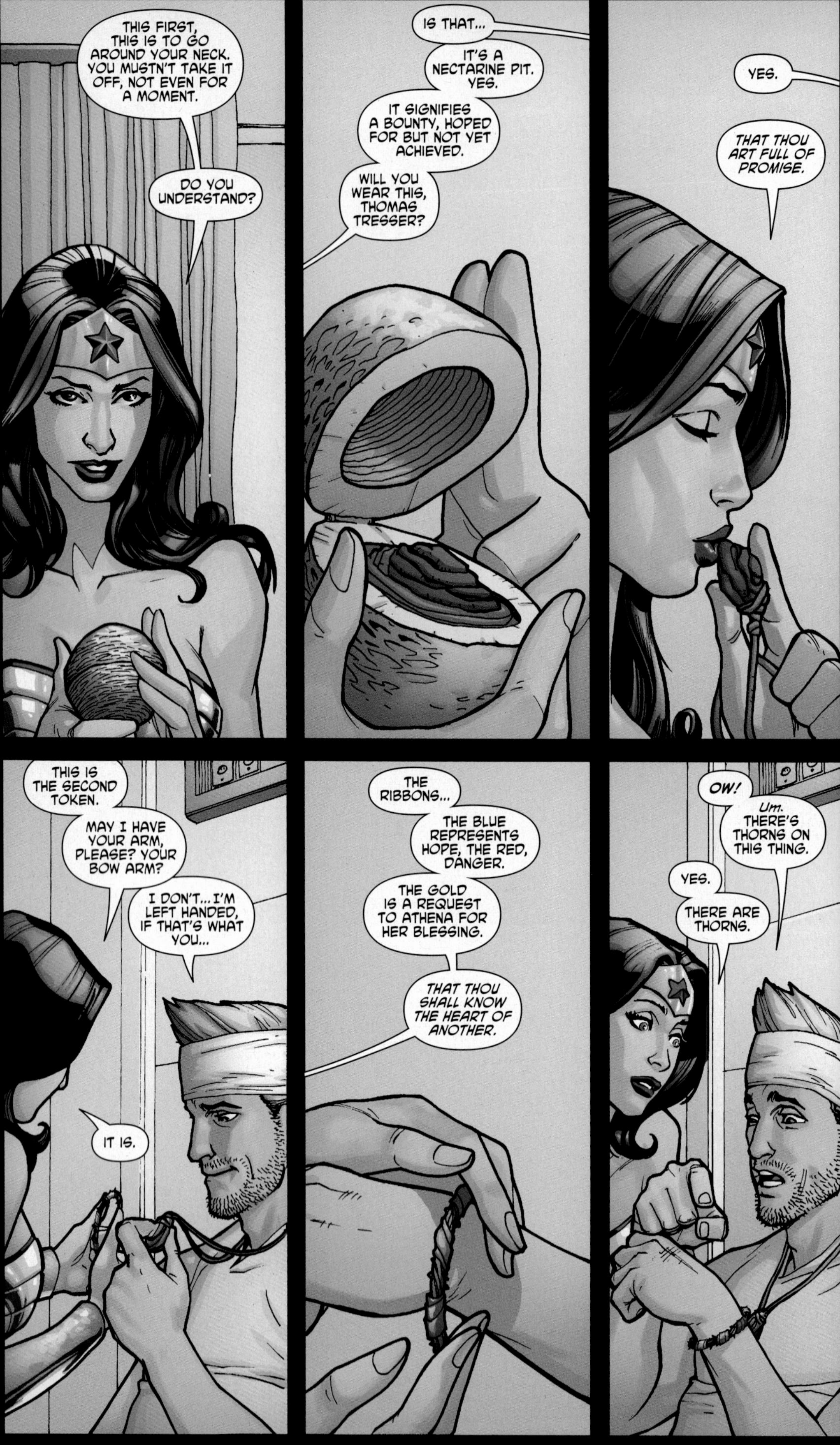

THIS FIRST, THIS IS TO GO AROUND YOUR NECK. YOU MUSTN'T TAKE IT OFF, NOT EVEN FOR A MOMENT.
DO YOU UNDERSTAND?
IS THAT...
IT'S A NECTARINE PIT. YES.
IT SIGNIFIES A BOUNTY, HOPED FOR BUT NOT YET ACHIEVED.
WILL YOU WEAR THIS, THOMAS TRESSER?
YES.
THAT THOU ART FULL OF PROMISE.
THIS IS THE SECOND TOKEN.
MAY I HAVE YOUR ARM, PLEASE? YOUR BOW ARM?
I DON'T... I'M LEFT HANDED, IF THAT'S WHAT YOU...
IT IS.
THE RIBBONS...
THE BLUE REPRESENTS HOPE, THE RED, DANGER.
THE GOLD IS A REQUEST TO ATHENA FOR HER BLESSING.
THAT THOU SHALL KNOW THE HEART OF ANOTHER.
OW!
Um. THERE'S THORNS ON THIS THING.
YES.
THERE ARE THORNS.

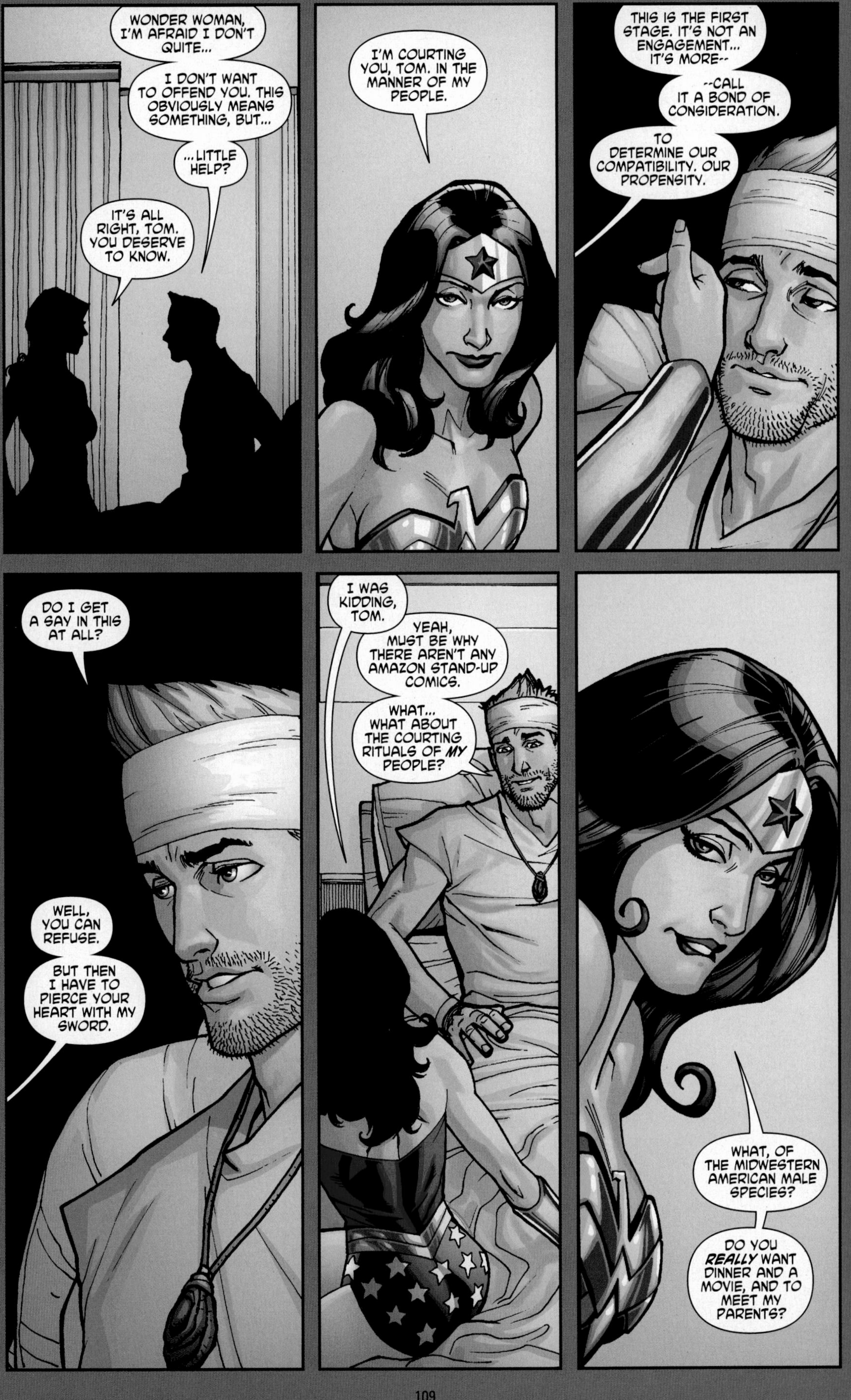
WONDER WOMAN, I'M AFRAID I DON'T QUITE...
I DON'T WANT TO OFFEND YOU. THIS OBVIOUSLY MEANS SOMETHING, BUT...
...LITTLE HELP?
IT'S ALL RIGHT, TOM. YOU DESERVE TO KNOW.
I'M COURTING YOU, TOM. IN THE MANNER OF MY PEOPLE.
THIS IS THE FIRST STAGE. IT'S NOT AN ENGAGEMENT... IT'S MORE--
--CALL IT A BOND OF CONSIDERATION.
TO DETERMINE OUR COMPATIBILITY. OUR PROPENSITY.
DO I GET A SAY IN THIS AT ALL?
WELL, YOU CAN REFUSE.
BUT THEN I HAVE TO PIERCE YOUR HEART WITH MY SWORD.
I WAS KIDDING, TOM.
YEAH, MUST BE WHY THERE AREN'T ANY AMAZON STAND-UP COMICS.
WHAT... WHAT ABOUT THE COURTING RITUALS OF *MY* PEOPLE?
WHAT, OF THE MIDWESTERN AMERICAN MALE SPECIES?
DO YOU *REALLY* WANT DINNER AND A MOVIE, AND TO MEET MY PARENTS?

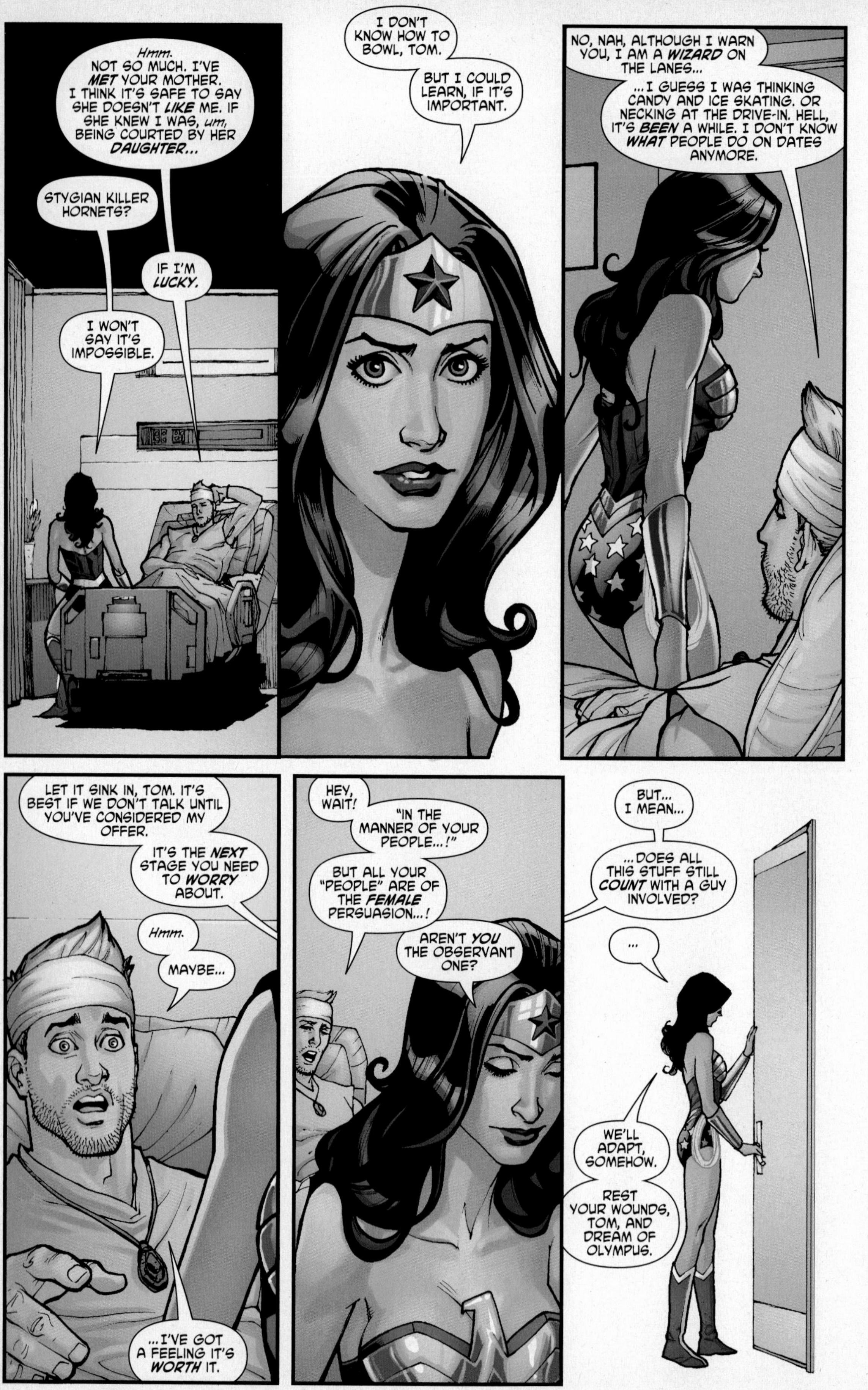
Hmm. NOT SO MUCH. I'VE MET YOUR MOTHER. I THINK IT'S SAFE TO SAY SHE DOESN'T LIKE ME. IF SHE KNEW I WAS, um, BEING COURTED BY HER DAUGHTER...
STYGIAN KILLER HORNETS?
IF I'M LUCKY.
I WON'T SAY IT'S IMPOSSIBLE.
I DON'T KNOW HOW TO BOWL, TOM.
BUT I COULD LEARN, IF IT'S IMPORTANT.
NO, NAH, ALTHOUGH I WARN YOU, I AM A WIZARD ON THE LANES...
...I GUESS I WAS THINKING CANDY AND ICE SKATING. OR NECKING AT THE DRIVE-IN. HELL, IT'S BEEN A WHILE. I DON'T KNOW WHAT PEOPLE DO ON DATES ANYMORE.
LET IT SINK IN, TOM. IT'S BEST IF WE DON'T TALK UNTIL YOU'VE CONSIDERED MY OFFER.
IT'S THE NEXT STAGE YOU NEED TO WORRY ABOUT.
Hmm.
MAYBE...
...I'VE GOT A FEELING IT'S WORTH IT.
HEY, WAIT!
"IN THE MANNER OF YOUR PEOPLE...!"
BUT ALL YOUR "PEOPLE" ARE OF THE FEMALE PERSUASION...!
AREN'T YOU THE OBSERVANT ONE?
BUT... I MEAN...
...DOES ALL THIS STUFF STILL COUNT WITH A GUY INVOLVED?
...
WE'LL ADAPT, SOMEHOW.
REST YOUR WOUNDS, TOM, AND DREAM OF OLYMPUS.

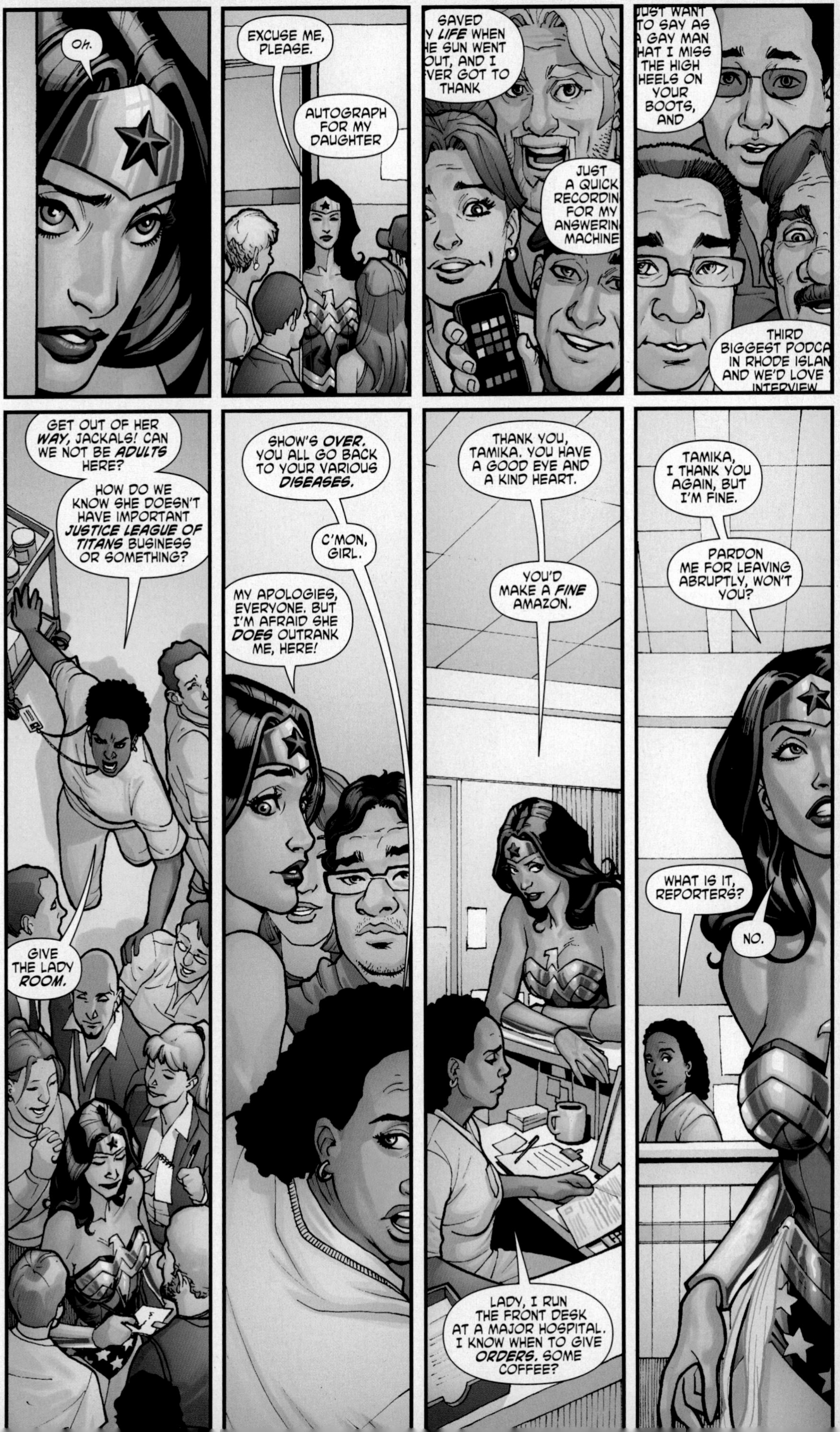

Oh.
EXCUSE ME, PLEASE.
AUTOGRAPH FOR MY DAUGHTER
SAVED Y LIFE WHEN HE SUN WENT OUT, AND I EVER GOT TO THANK
JUST A QUICK RECORDIN FOR MY ANSWERIN MACHINE
JUST WANT TO SAY AS A GAY MAN HAT I MISS THE HIGH HEELS ON YOUR BOOTS, AND
THIRD BIGGEST PODCA IN RHODE ISLAN AND WE'D LOVE INTERVIEW
GET OUT OF HER WAY, JACKALS! CAN WE NOT BE ADULTS HERE?
HOW DO WE KNOW SHE DOESN'T HAVE IMPORTANT JUSTICE LEAGUE OF TITANS BUSINESS OR SOMETHING?
GIVE THE LADY ROOM.
SHOW'S OVER. YOU ALL GO BACK TO YOUR VARIOUS DISEASES.
C'MON, GIRL.
MY APOLOGIES, EVERYONE. BUT I'M AFRAID SHE DOES OUTRANK ME, HERE!
THANK YOU, TAMIKA. YOU HAVE A GOOD EYE AND A KIND HEART.
YOU'D MAKE A FINE AMAZON.
LADY, I RUN THE FRONT DESK AT A MAJOR HOSPITAL. I KNOW WHEN TO GIVE ORDERS. SOME COFFEE?
TAMIKA, I THANK YOU AGAIN, BUT I'M FINE.
PARDON ME FOR LEAVING ABRUPTLY, WON'T YOU?
WHAT IS IT, REPORTERS?
NO.

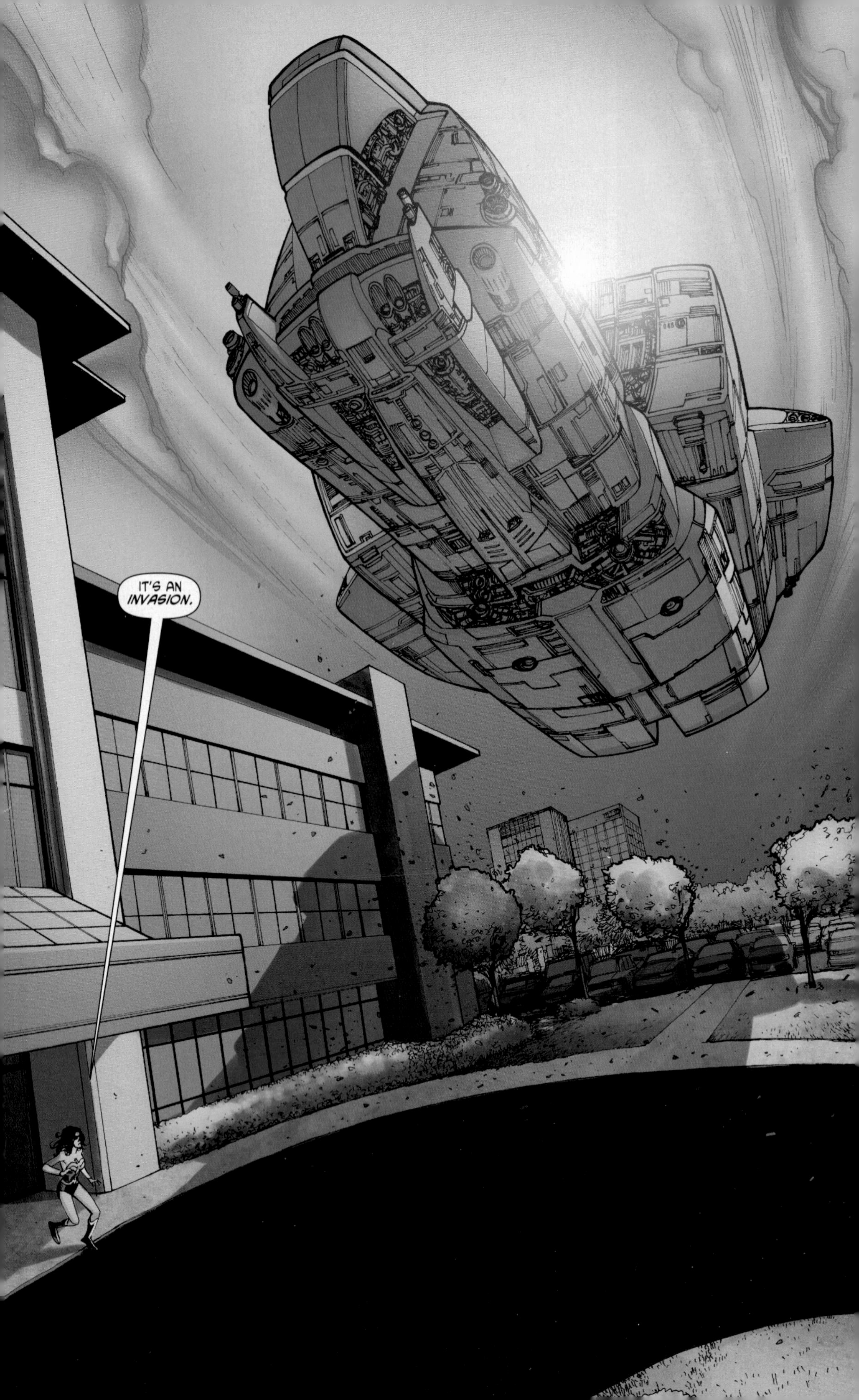
IT'S AN INVASION.

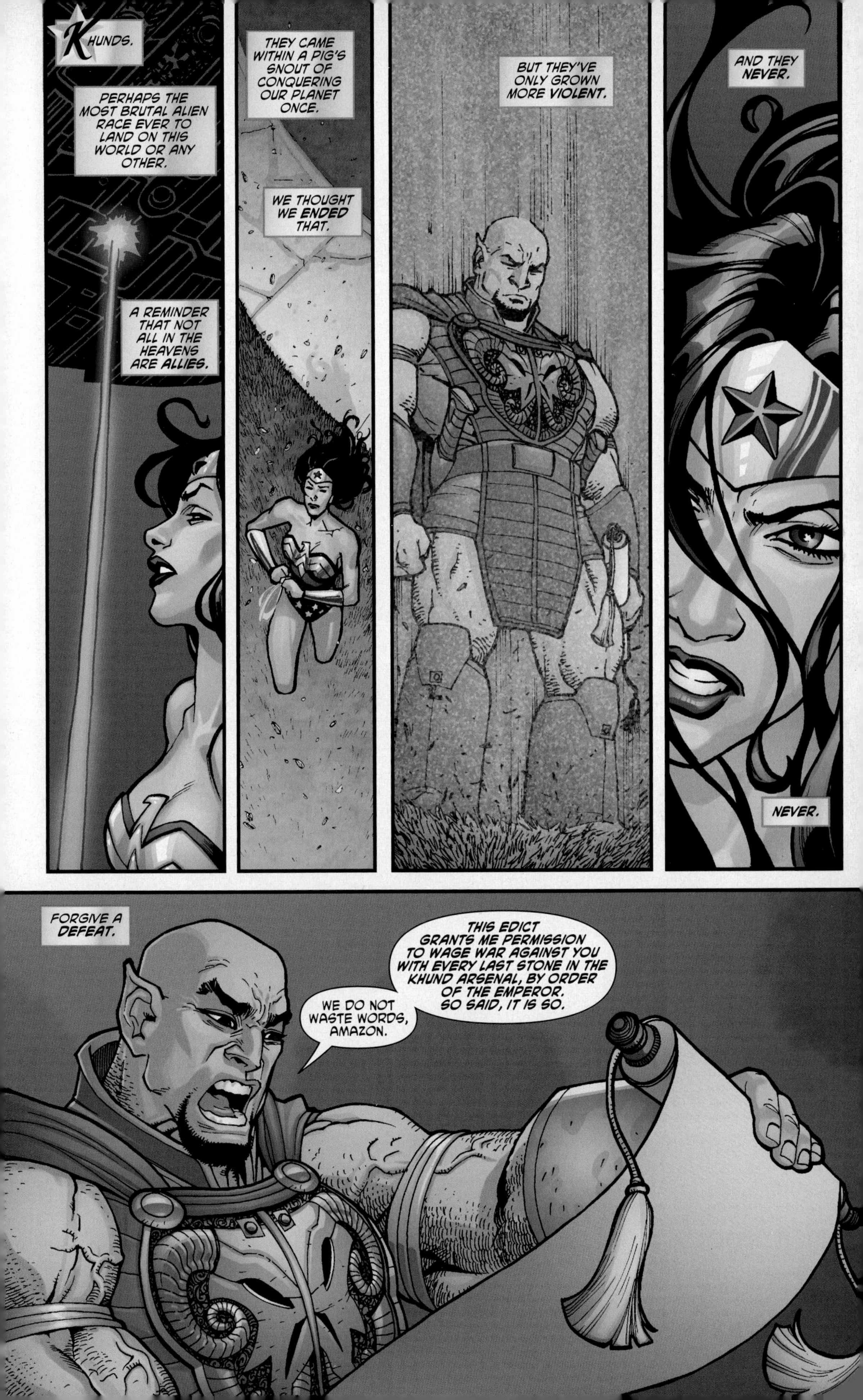
KHUNDS.
PERHAPS THE MOST BRUTAL ALIEN RACE EVER TO LAND ON THIS WORLD OR ANY OTHER.
A REMINDER THAT NOT ALL IN THE HEAVENS ARE ALLIES.
THEY CAME WITHIN A PIG'S SNOUT OF CONQUERING OUR PLANET ONCE.
WE THOUGHT WE ENDED THAT.
BUT THEY'VE ONLY GROWN MORE VIOLENT.
AND THEY NEVER.
NEVER.
FORGIVE A DEFEAT.
WE DO NOT WASTE WORDS, AMAZON.
THIS EDICT GRANTS ME PERMISSION TO WAGE WAR AGAINST YOU WITH EVERY LAST STONE IN THE KHUND ARSENAL, BY ORDER OF THE EMPEROR. SO SAID, IT IS SO.

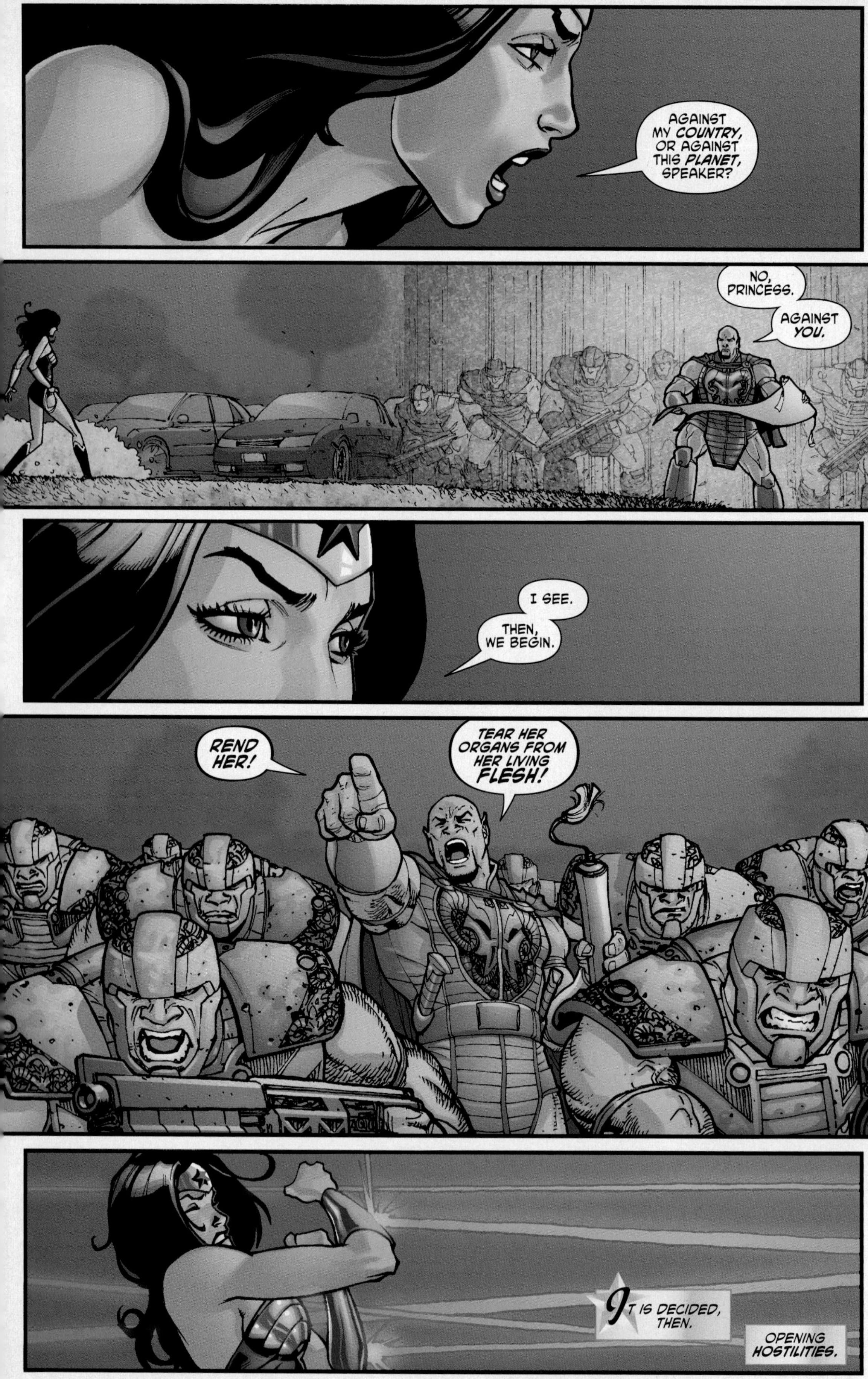
AGAINST MY COUNTRY, OR AGAINST THIS PLANET, SPEAKER?
NO, PRINCESS.
AGAINST YOU.
I SEE.
THEN, WE BEGIN.
REND HER!
TEAR HER ORGANS FROM HER LIVING FLESH!
IT IS DECIDED, THEN.
OPENING HOSTILITIES.

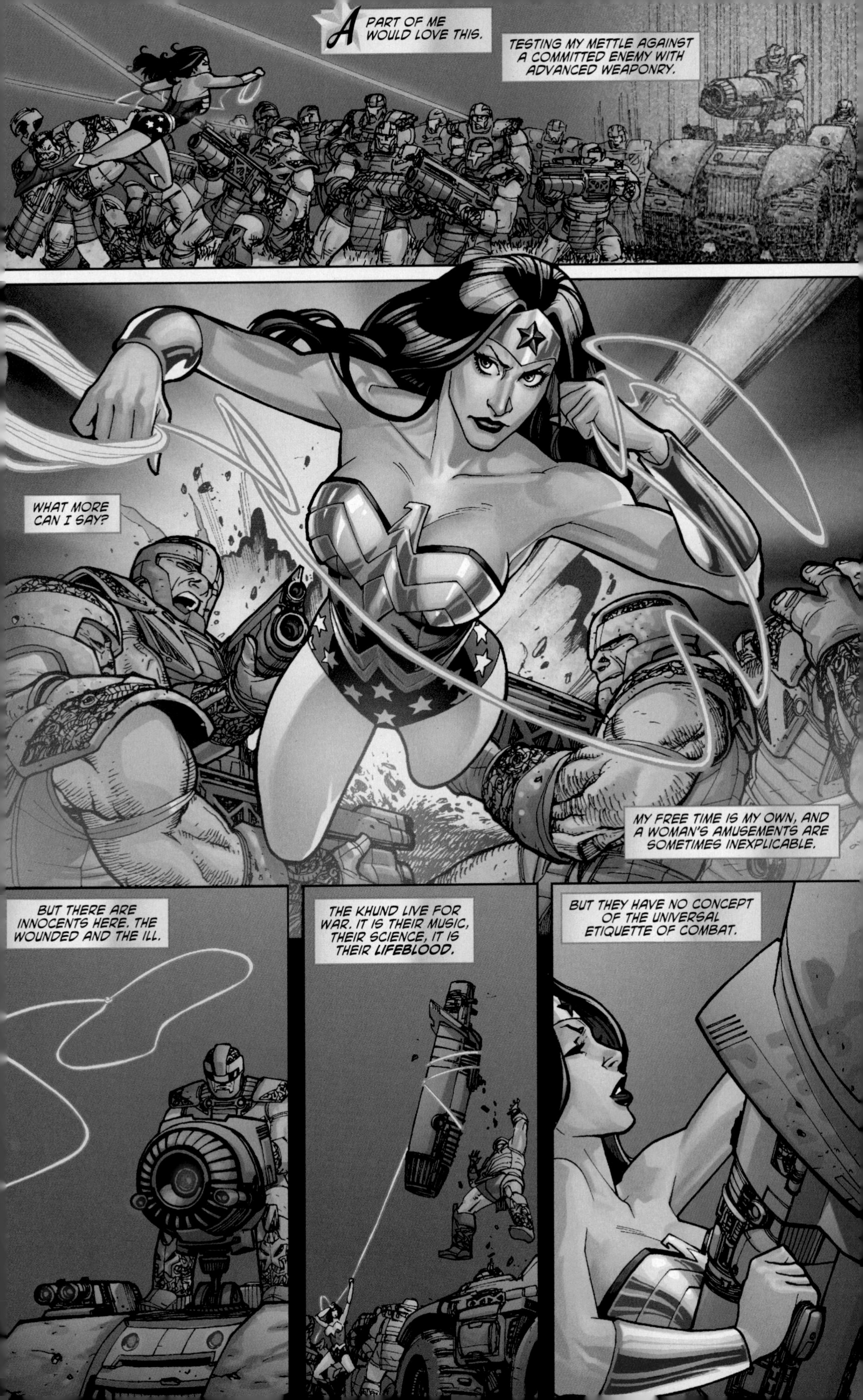
A PART OF ME WOULD LOVE THIS.
TESTING MY METTLE AGAINST A COMMITTED ENEMY WITH ADVANCED WEAPONRY.
WHAT MORE CAN I SAY?
MY FREE TIME IS MY OWN, AND A WOMAN'S AMUSEMENTS ARE SOMETIMES INEXPLICABLE.
BUT THERE ARE INNOCENTS HERE. THE WOUNDED AND THE ILL.
THE KHUND LIVE FOR WAR. IT IS THEIR MUSIC, THEIR SCIENCE, IT IS THEIR LIFEBLOOD.
BUT THEY HAVE NO CONCEPT OF THE UNIVERSAL ETIQUETTE OF COMBAT.

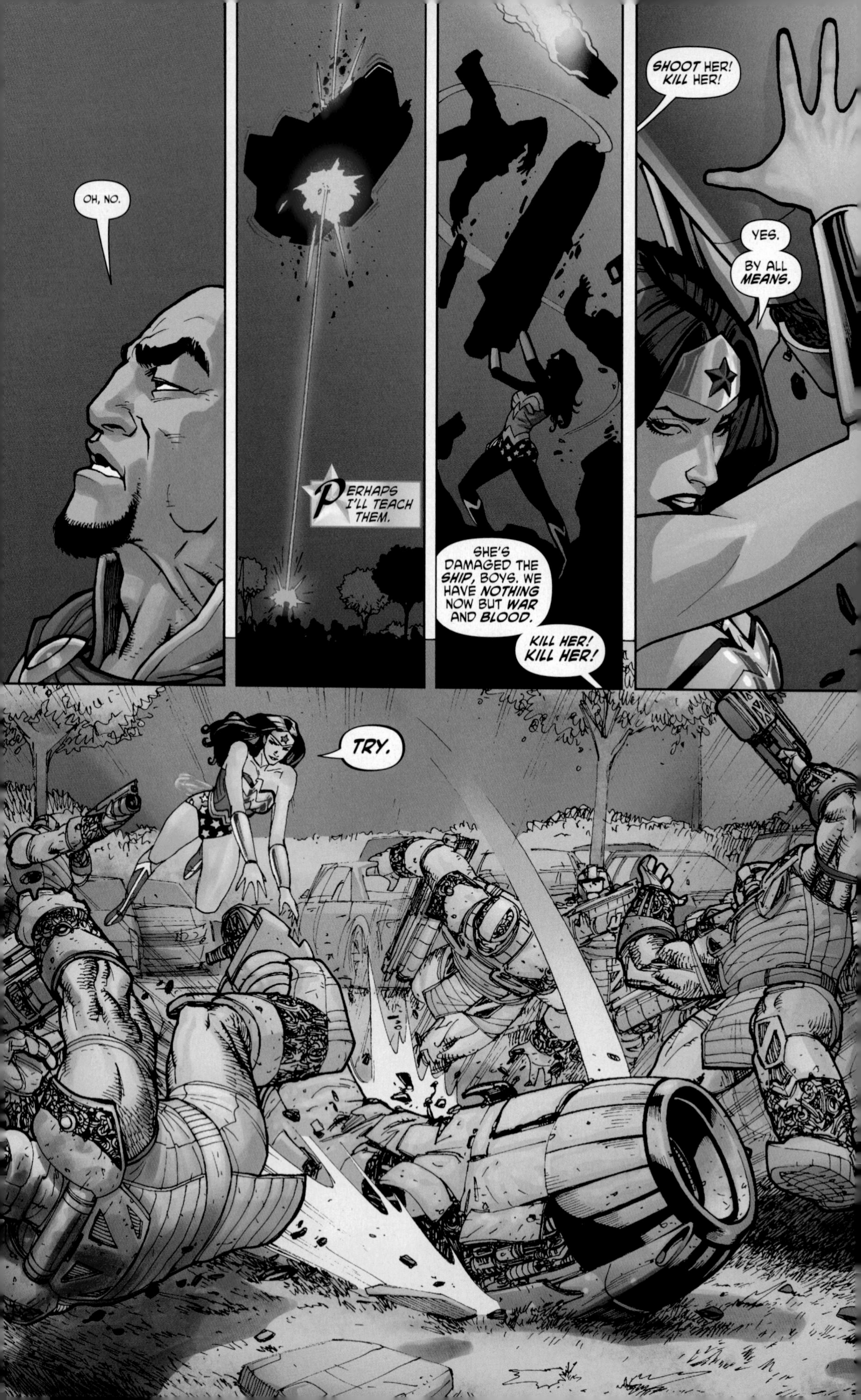
OH, NO.
PERHAPS I'LL TEACH THEM.
SHE'S DAMAGED THE SHIP, BOYS. WE HAVE NOTHING NOW BUT WAR AND BLOOD.
KILL HER! KILL HER!
SHOOT HER! KILL HER!
YES.
BY ALL MEANS.
TRY.

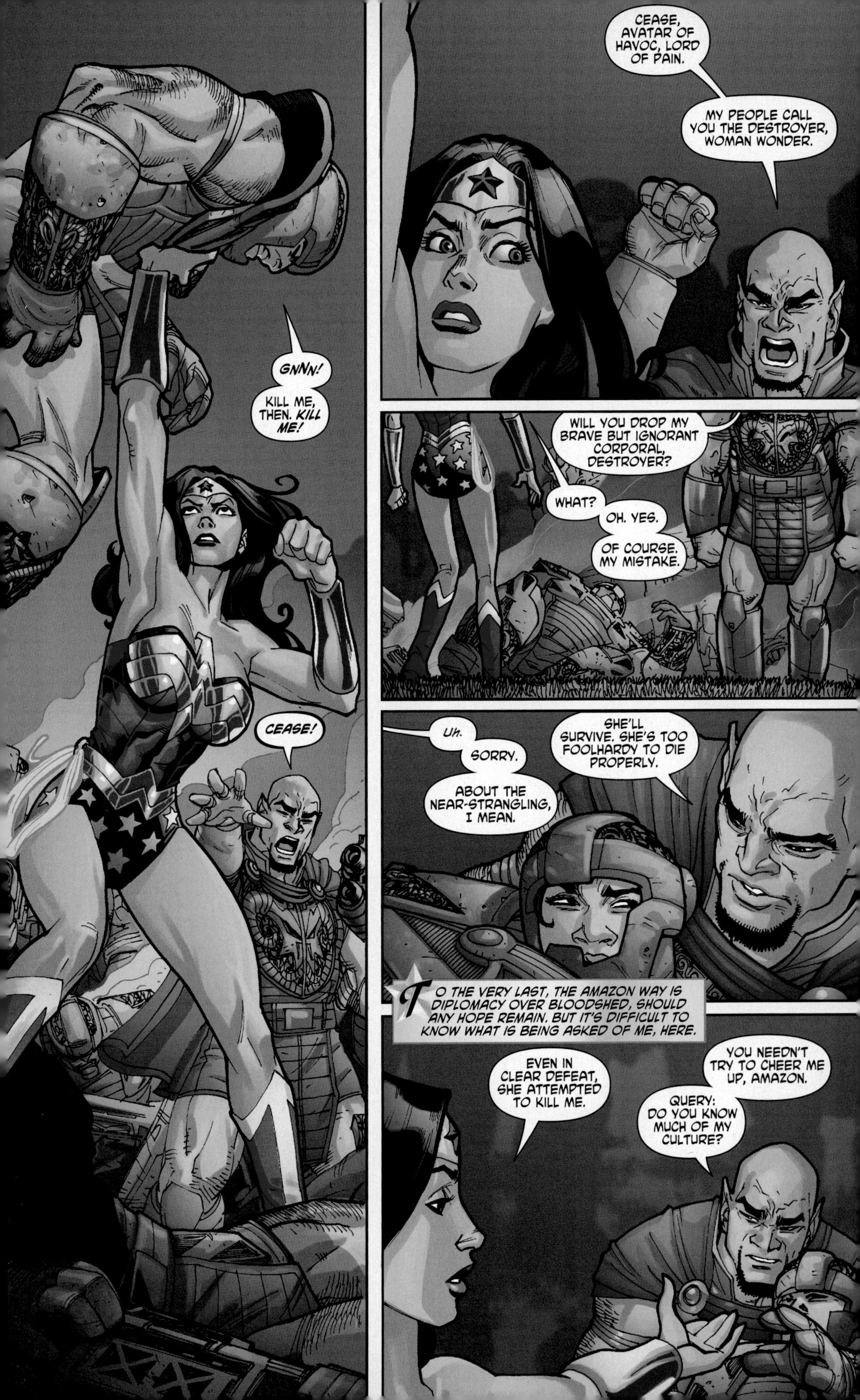
GNNN!
KILL ME, THEN. KILL ME!
CEASE!
CEASE, AVATAR OF HAVOC, LORD OF PAIN.
MY PEOPLE CALL YOU THE DESTROYER, WOMAN WONDER.
WILL YOU DROP MY BRAVE BUT IGNORANT CORPORAL, DESTROYER?
WHAT?
OH. YES.
OF COURSE. MY MISTAKE.
Uh.
SORRY.
ABOUT THE NEAR-STRANGLING, I MEAN.
SHE'LL SURVIVE. SHE'S TOO FOOLHARDY TO DIE PROPERLY.
TO THE VERY LAST, THE AMAZON WAY IS DIPLOMACY OVER BLOODSHED, SHOULD ANY HOPE REMAIN. BUT IT'S DIFFICULT TO KNOW WHAT IS BEING ASKED OF ME, HERE.
EVEN IN CLEAR DEFEAT, SHE ATTEMPTED TO KILL ME.
YOU NEEDN'T TRY TO CHEER ME UP, AMAZON.
QUERY: DO YOU KNOW MUCH OF MY CULTURE?

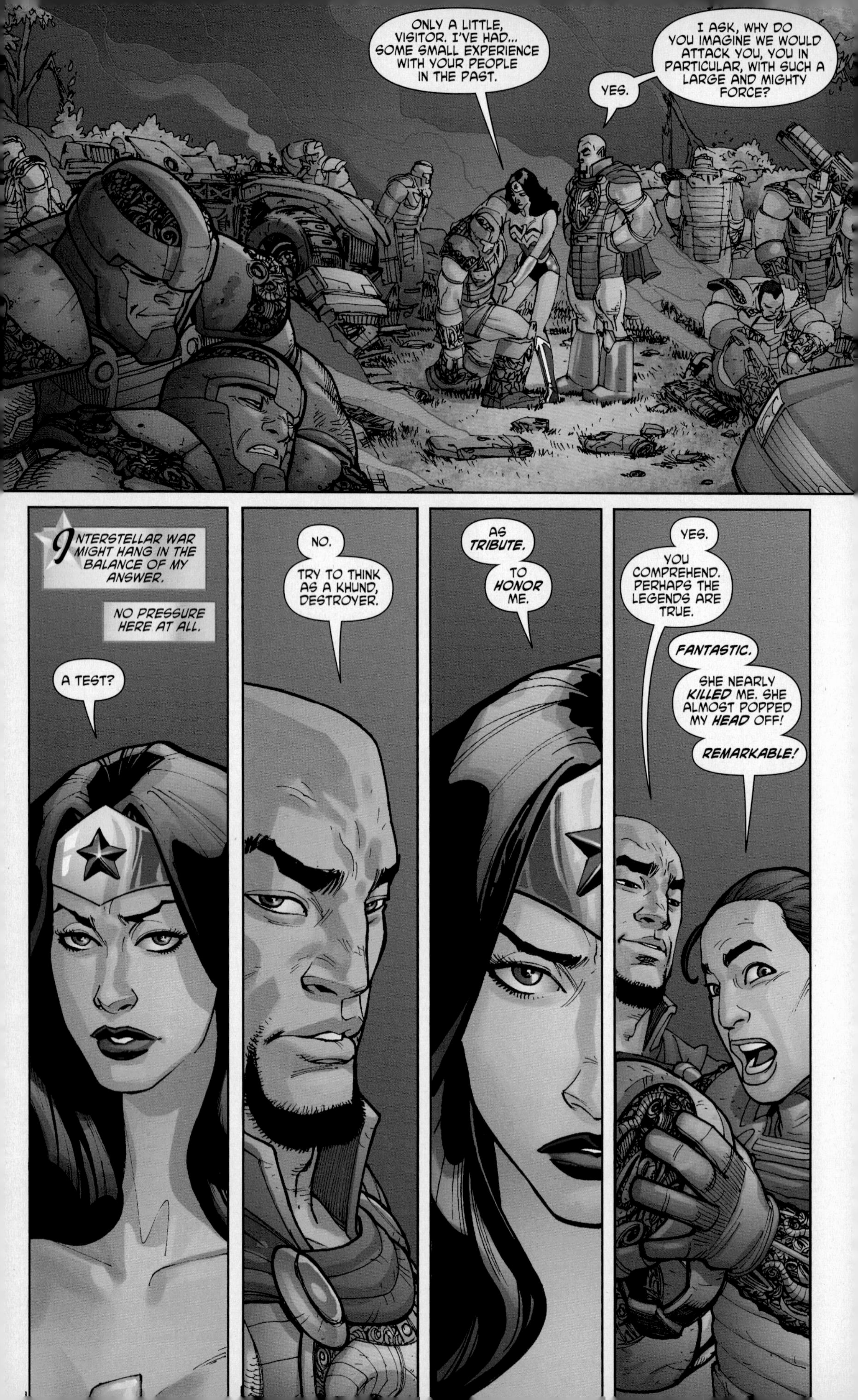
ONLY A LITTLE, VISITOR. I'VE HAD... SOME SMALL EXPERIENCE WITH YOUR PEOPLE IN THE PAST.
YES.
I ASK, WHY DO YOU IMAGINE WE WOULD ATTACK YOU, YOU IN PARTICULAR, WITH SUCH A LARGE AND MIGHTY FORCE?
INTERSTELLAR WAR MIGHT HANG IN THE BALANCE OF MY ANSWER.
NO PRESSURE HERE AT ALL.
A TEST?
NO.
TRY TO THINK AS A KHUND, DESTROYER.
AS TRIBUTE.
TO HONOR ME.
YES.
YOU COMPREHEND. PERHAPS THE LEGENDS ARE TRUE.
FANTASTIC.
SHE NEARLY KILLED ME. SHE ALMOST POPPED MY HEAD OFF!
REMARKABLE!

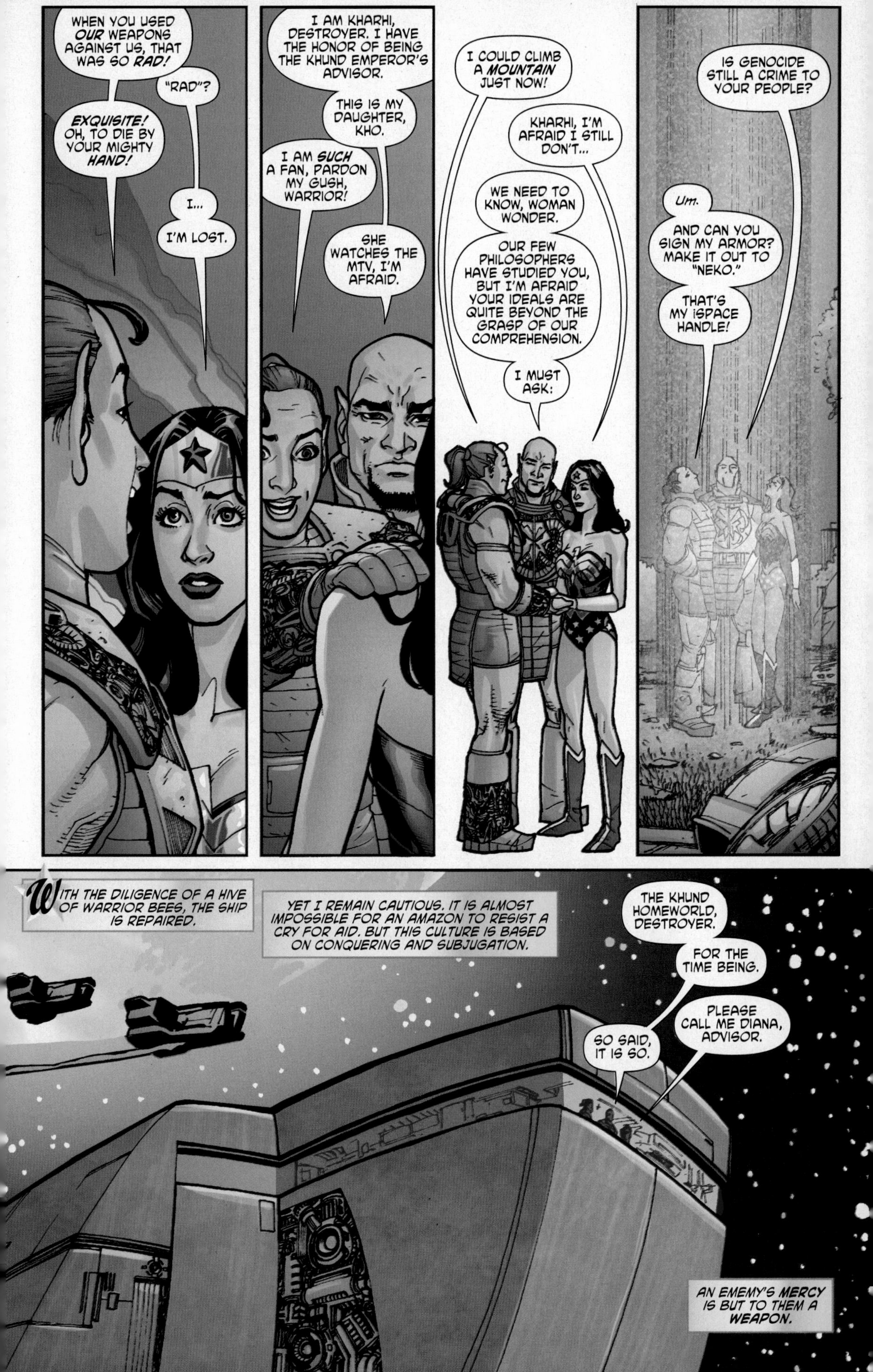
WHEN YOU USED OUR WEAPONS AGAINST US, THAT WAS SO RAD!
"RAD"?
EXQUISITE! OH, TO DIE BY YOUR MIGHTY HAND!
I...
I'M LOST.
I AM KHARHI, DESTROYER. I HAVE THE HONOR OF BEING THE KHUND EMPEROR'S ADVISOR.
THIS IS MY DAUGHTER, KHO.
I AM SUCH A FAN, PARDON MY GUSH, WARRIOR!
SHE WATCHES THE MTV, I'M AFRAID.
I COULD CLIMB A MOUNTAIN JUST NOW!
KHARHI, I'M AFRAID I STILL DON'T...
WE NEED TO KNOW, WOMAN WONDER.
OUR FEW PHILOSOPHERS HAVE STUDIED YOU, BUT I'M AFRAID YOUR IDEALS ARE QUITE BEYOND THE GRASP OF OUR COMPREHENSION.
I MUST ASK:
IS GENOCIDE STILL A CRIME TO YOUR PEOPLE?
Um.
AND CAN YOU SIGN MY ARMOR? MAKE IT OUT TO "NEKO."
THAT'S MY iSPACE HANDLE!
WITH THE DILIGENCE OF A HIVE OF WARRIOR BEES, THE SHIP IS REPAIRED.
YET I REMAIN CAUTIOUS. IT IS ALMOST IMPOSSIBLE FOR AN AMAZON TO RESIST A CRY FOR AID. BUT THIS CULTURE IS BASED ON CONQUERING AND SUBJUGATION.
THE KHUND HOMEWORLD, DESTROYER.
FOR THE TIME BEING.
PLEASE CALL ME DIANA, ADVISOR.
SO SAID, IT IS SO.
AN EMEMY'S MERCY IS BUT TO THEM A WEAPON.

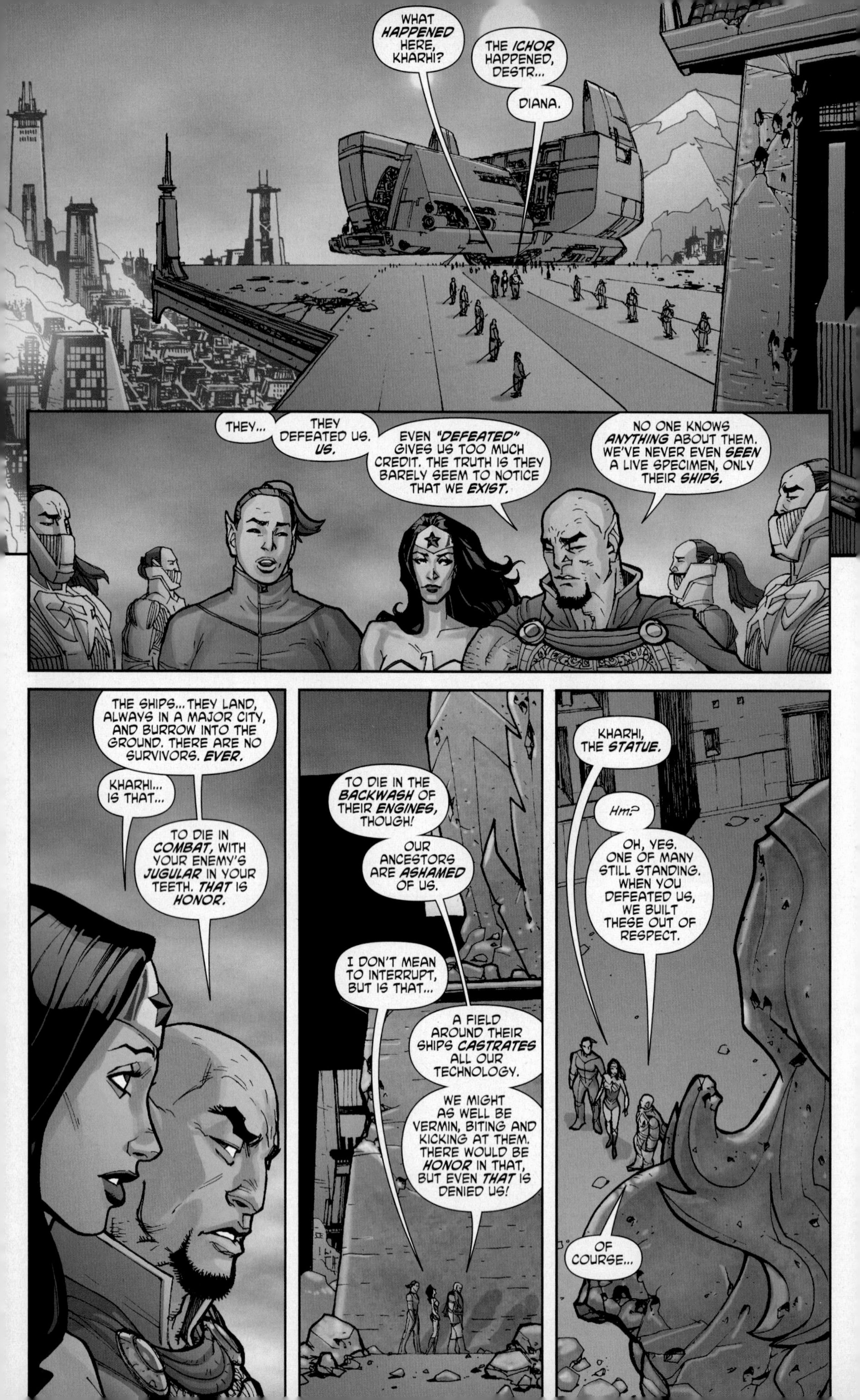
WHAT HAPPENED HERE, KHARHI?
THE ICHOR HAPPENED, DESTR...
DIANA.
THEY...
THEY DEFEATED US. US.
EVEN "DEFEATED" GIVES US TOO MUCH CREDIT. THE TRUTH IS THEY BARELY SEEM TO NOTICE THAT WE EXIST.
NO ONE KNOWS ANYTHING ABOUT THEM. WE'VE NEVER EVEN SEEN A LIVE SPECIMEN, ONLY THEIR SHIPS.
THE SHIPS... THEY LAND, ALWAYS IN A MAJOR CITY, AND BURROW INTO THE GROUND. THERE ARE NO SURVIVORS. EVER.
KHARHI... IS THAT...
TO DIE IN COMBAT, WITH YOUR ENEMY'S JUGULAR IN YOUR TEETH. THAT IS HONOR.
TO DIE IN THE BACKWASH OF THEIR ENGINES, THOUGH!
OUR ANCESTORS ARE ASHAMED OF US.
I DON'T MEAN TO INTERRUPT, BUT IS THAT...
A FIELD AROUND THEIR SHIPS CASTRATES ALL OUR TECHNOLOGY.
WE MIGHT AS WELL BE VERMIN, BITING AND KICKING AT THEM. THERE WOULD BE HONOR IN THAT, BUT EVEN THAT IS DENIED US!
KHARHI, THE STATUE.
Hm?
OH, YES. ONE OF MANY STILL STANDING. WHEN YOU DEFEATED US, WE BUILT THESE OUT OF RESPECT.
OF COURSE...

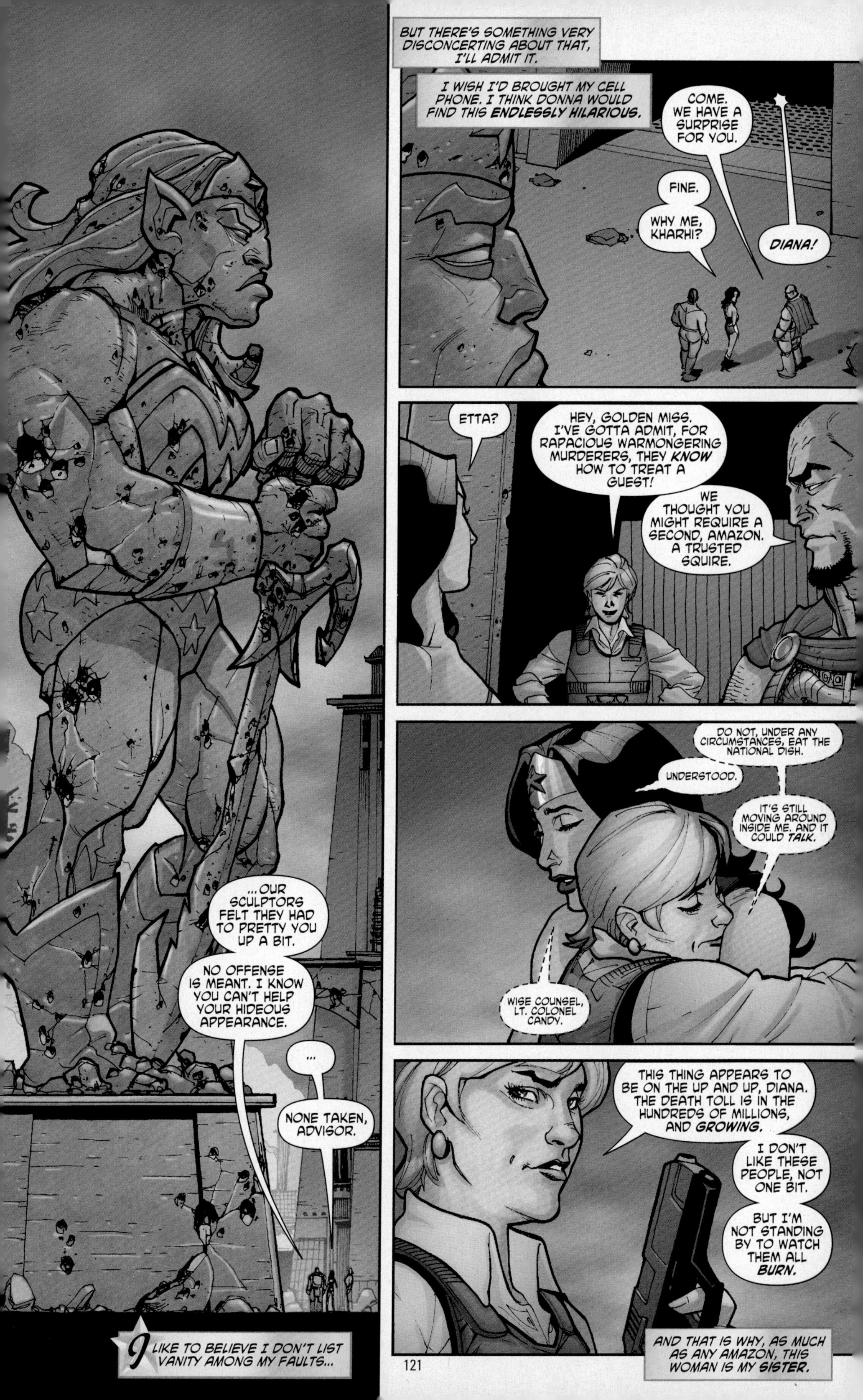

I LIKE TO BELIEVE I DON'T LIST VANITY AMONG MY FAULTS...
...OUR SCULPTORS FELT THEY HAD TO PRETTY YOU UP A BIT.
NO OFFENSE IS MEANT. I KNOW YOU CAN'T HELP YOUR HIDEOUS APPEARANCE.
...
NONE TAKEN, ADVISOR.
BUT THERE'S SOMETHING VERY DISCONCERTING ABOUT THAT, I'LL ADMIT IT.
I WISH I'D BROUGHT MY CELL PHONE. I THINK DONNA WOULD FIND THIS ENDLESSLY HILARIOUS.
COME. WE HAVE A SURPRISE FOR YOU.
FINE.
WHY ME, KHARHI?
DIANA!
ETTA?
HEY, GOLDEN MISS. I'VE GOTTA ADMIT, FOR RAPACIOUS WARMONGERING MURDERERS, THEY KNOW HOW TO TREAT A GUEST!
WE THOUGHT YOU MIGHT REQUIRE A SECOND, AMAZON. A TRUSTED SQUIRE.
DO NOT, UNDER ANY CIRCUMSTANCES, EAT THE NATIONAL DISH.
UNDERSTOOD.
IT'S STILL MOVING AROUND INSIDE ME. AND IT COULD TALK.
WISE COUNSEL, LT. COLONEL CANDY.
THIS THING APPEARS TO BE ON THE UP AND UP, DIANA. THE DEATH TOLL IS IN THE HUNDREDS OF MILLIONS, AND GROWING.
I DON'T LIKE THESE PEOPLE, NOT ONE BIT.
BUT I'M NOT STANDING BY TO WATCH THEM ALL BURN.
AND THAT IS WHY, AS MUCH AS ANY AMAZON, THIS WOMAN IS MY SISTER.

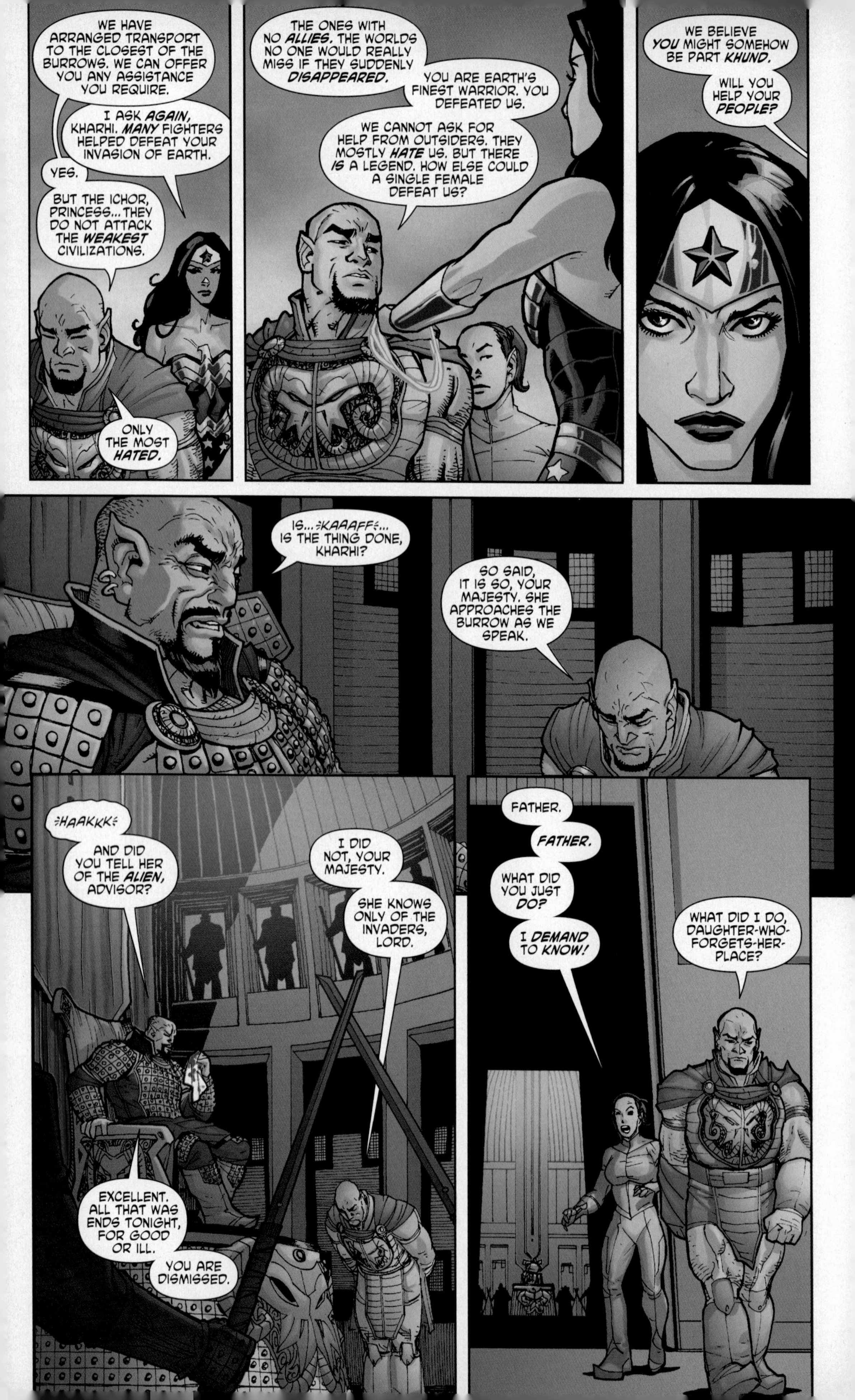

WE HAVE ARRANGED TRANSPORT TO THE CLOSEST OF THE BURROWS. WE CAN OFFER YOU ANY ASSISTANCE YOU REQUIRE.
I ASK AGAIN, KHARHI. MANY FIGHTERS HELPED DEFEAT YOUR INVASION OF EARTH.
YES.
BUT THE ICHOR, PRINCESS... THEY DO NOT ATTACK THE WEAKEST CIVILIZATIONS.
ONLY THE MOST HATED.
THE ONES WITH NO ALLIES. THE WORLDS NO ONE WOULD REALLY MISS IF THEY SUDDENLY DISAPPEARED.
YOU ARE EARTH'S FINEST WARRIOR. YOU DEFEATED US.
WE CANNOT ASK FOR HELP FROM OUTSIDERS. THEY MOSTLY HATE US. BUT THERE IS A LEGEND. HOW ELSE COULD A SINGLE FEMALE DEFEAT US?
WE BELIEVE YOU MIGHT SOMEHOW BE PART KHUND.
WILL YOU HELP YOUR PEOPLE?
IS... KAAAFF... IS THE THING DONE, KHARHI?
SO SAID, IT IS SO, YOUR MAJESTY. SHE APPROACHES THE BURROW AS WE SPEAK.
HAAKKK
AND DID YOU TELL HER OF THE ALIEN, ADVISOR?
I DID NOT, YOUR MAJESTY.
SHE KNOWS ONLY OF THE INVADERS, LORD.
EXCELLENT. ALL THAT WAS ENDS TONIGHT, FOR GOOD OR ILL.
YOU ARE DISMISSED.
FATHER.
FATHER.
WHAT DID YOU JUST DO?
I DEMAND TO KNOW!
WHAT DID I DO, DAUGHTER-WHO-FORGETS-HER-PLACE?

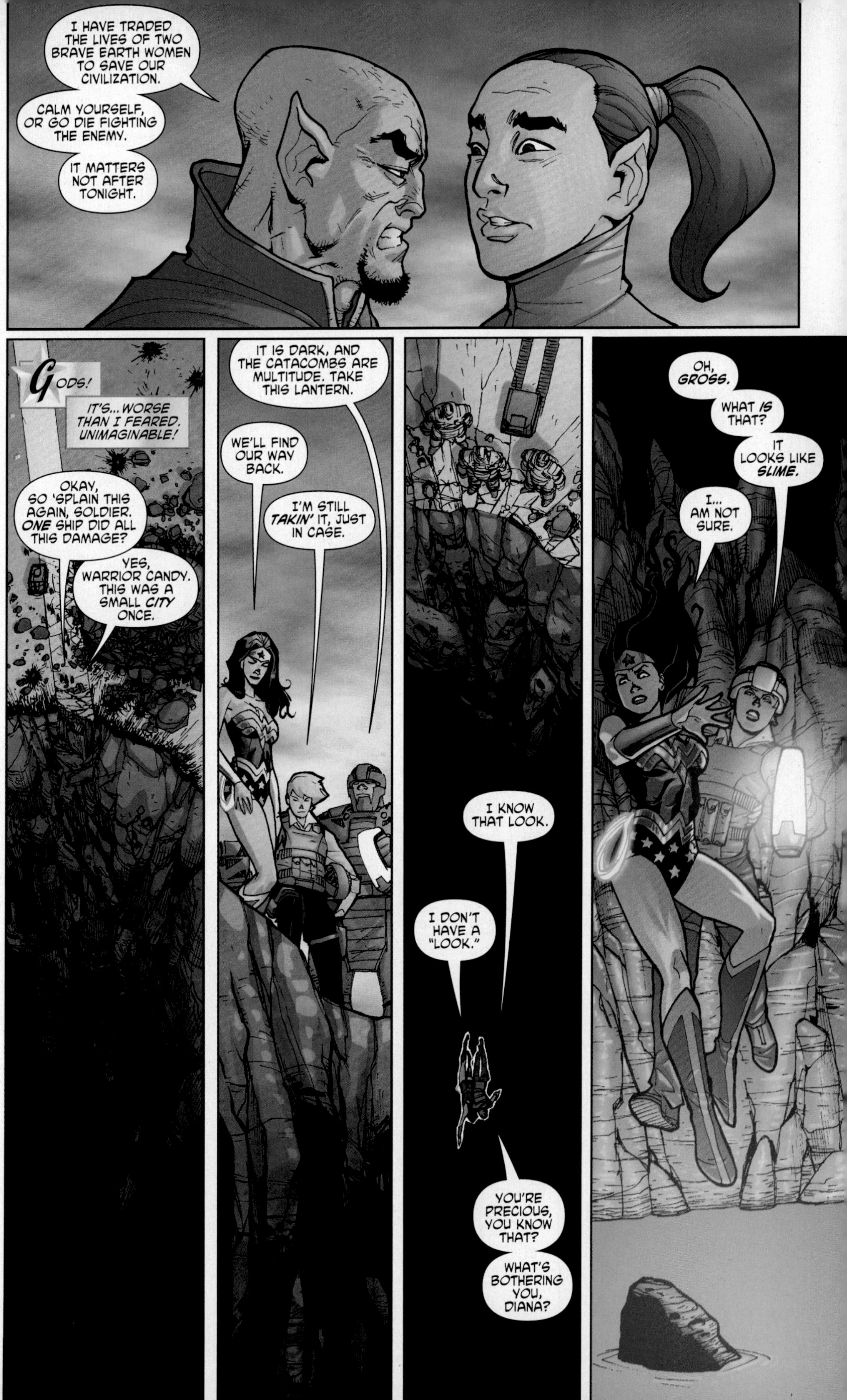

I HAVE TRADED THE LIVES OF TWO BRAVE EARTH WOMEN TO SAVE OUR CIVILIZATION.
CALM YOURSELF, OR GO DIE FIGHTING THE ENEMY.
IT MATTERS NOT AFTER TONIGHT.
GODS!
IT'S...WORSE THAN I FEARED. UNIMAGINABLE!
OKAY, SO 'SPLAIN THIS AGAIN, SOLDIER. ONE SHIP DID ALL THIS DAMAGE?
YES, WARRIOR CANDY. THIS WAS A SMALL CITY ONCE.
IT IS DARK, AND THE CATACOMBS ARE MULTITUDE. TAKE THIS LANTERN.
WE'LL FIND OUR WAY BACK.
I'M STILL TAKIN' IT, JUST IN CASE.
I KNOW THAT LOOK.
I DON'T HAVE A "LOOK."
YOU'RE PRECIOUS, YOU KNOW THAT?
WHAT'S BOTHERING YOU, DIANA?
OH, GROSS.
WHAT IS THAT?
IT LOOKS LIKE SLIME.
I... AM NOT SURE.

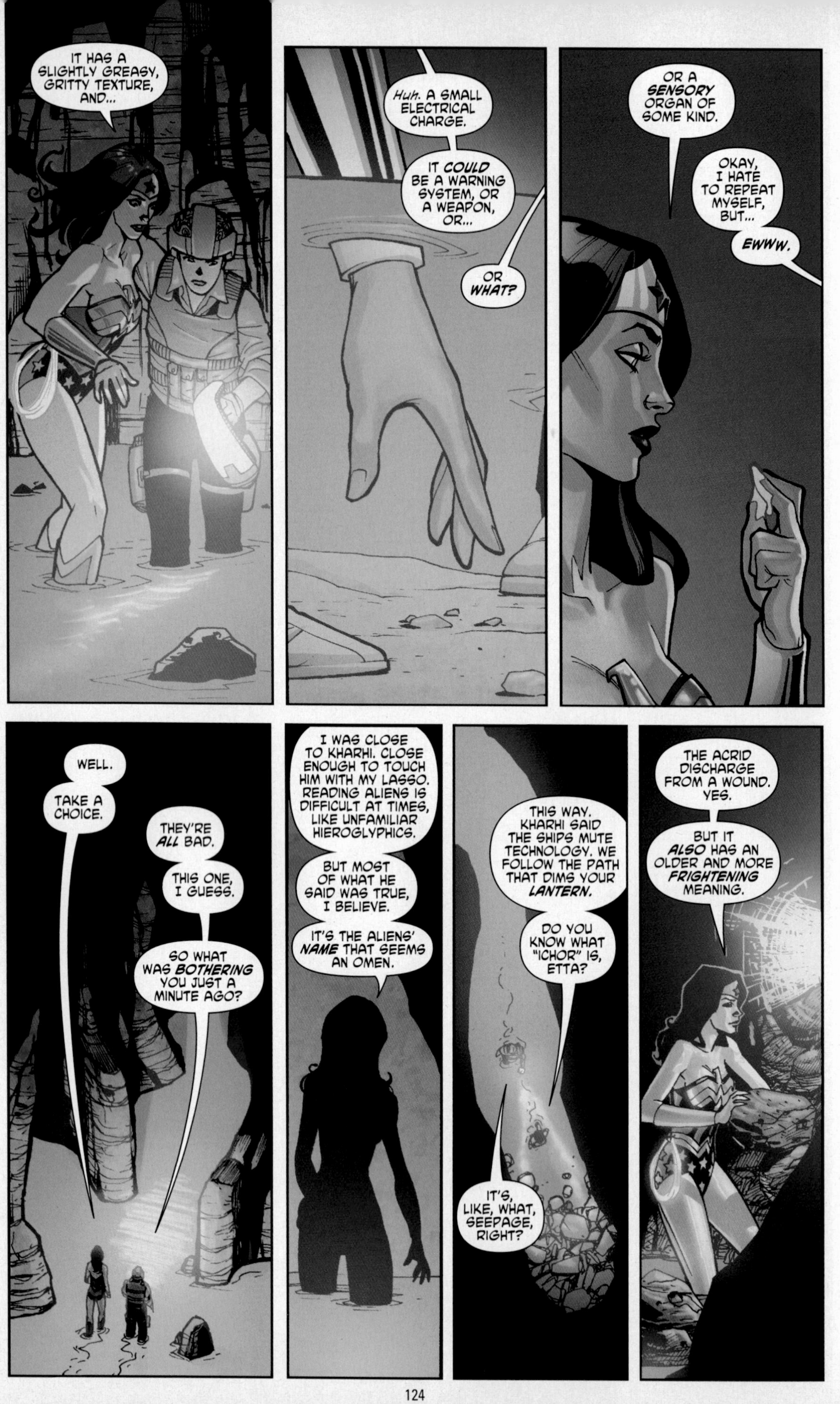
IT HAS A SLIGHTLY GREASY, GRITTY TEXTURE, AND...
Huh. A SMALL ELECTRICAL CHARGE.
IT COULD BE A WARNING SYSTEM, OR A WEAPON, OR...
OR WHAT?
OR A SENSORY ORGAN OF SOME KIND.
OKAY, I HATE TO REPEAT MYSELF, BUT...
EWWW.
WELL.
TAKE A CHOICE.
THEY'RE ALL BAD.
THIS ONE, I GUESS.
SO WHAT WAS BOTHERING YOU JUST A MINUTE AGO?
I WAS CLOSE TO KHARHI. CLOSE ENOUGH TO TOUCH HIM WITH MY LASSO. READING ALIENS IS DIFFICULT AT TIMES, LIKE UNFAMILIAR HIEROGLYPHICS.
BUT MOST OF WHAT HE SAID WAS TRUE, I BELIEVE.
IT'S THE ALIENS' NAME THAT SEEMS AN OMEN.
THIS WAY. KHARHI SAID THE SHIPS MUTE TECHNOLOGY. WE FOLLOW THE PATH THAT DIMS YOUR LANTERN.
DO YOU KNOW WHAT "ICHOR" IS, ETTA?
IT'S, LIKE, WHAT, SEEPAGE, RIGHT?
THE ACRID DISCHARGE FROM A WOUND. YES.
BUT IT ALSO HAS AN OLDER AND MORE FRIGHTENING MEANING.

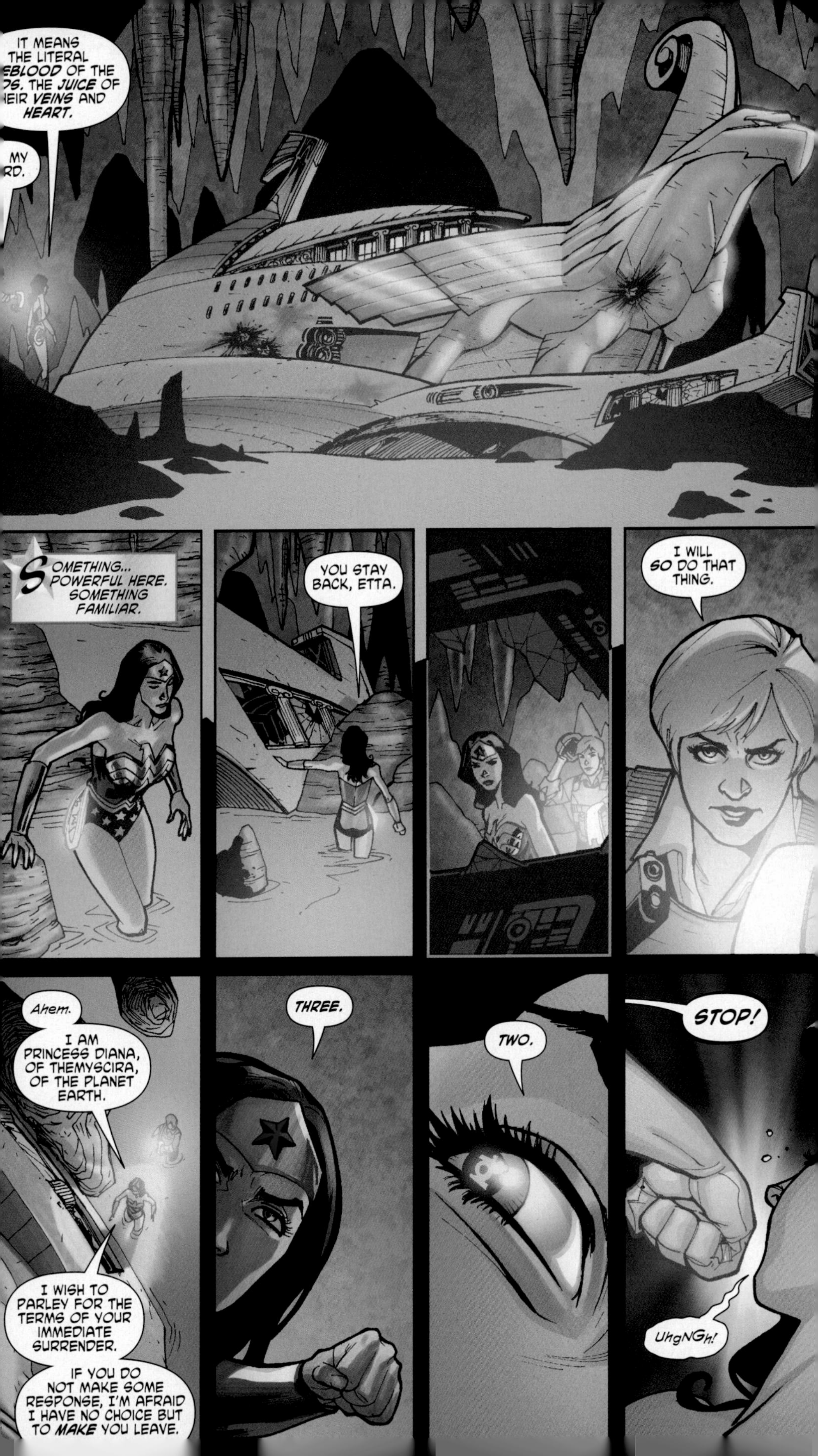
IT MEANS THE LITERAL EBLOOD OF THE DS. THE JUICE OF HEIR VEINS AND HEART.
MY RD.
SOMETHING... POWERFUL HERE. SOMETHING FAMILIAR.
YOU STAY BACK, ETTA.
I WILL SO DO THAT THING.
Ahem.
I AM PRINCESS DIANA, OF THEMYSCIRA, OF THE PLANET EARTH.
I WISH TO PARLEY FOR THE TERMS OF YOUR IMMEDIATE SURRENDER.
IF YOU DO NOT MAKE SOME RESPONSE, I'M AFRAID I HAVE NO CHOICE BUT TO MAKE YOU LEAVE.
THREE.
TWO.
STOP!
UhgNGh!

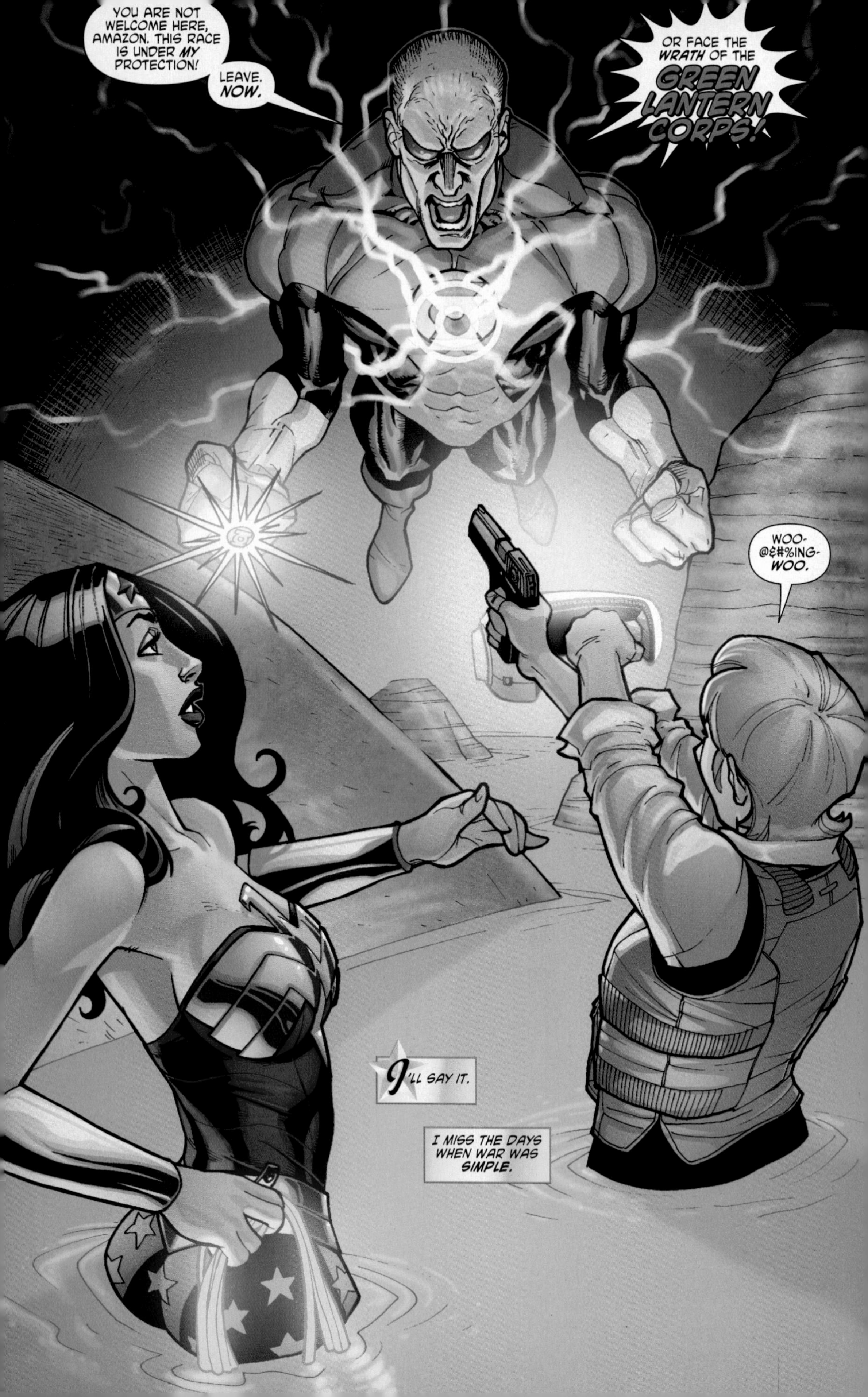
YOU ARE NOT WELCOME HERE, AMAZON. THIS RACE IS UNDER MY PROTECTION!
LEAVE. NOW.
OR FACE THE WRATH OF THE GREEN LANTERN CORPS!
WOO-@&#%ING-WOO.
I'LL SAY IT.
I MISS THE DAYS WHEN WAR WAS SIMPLE.

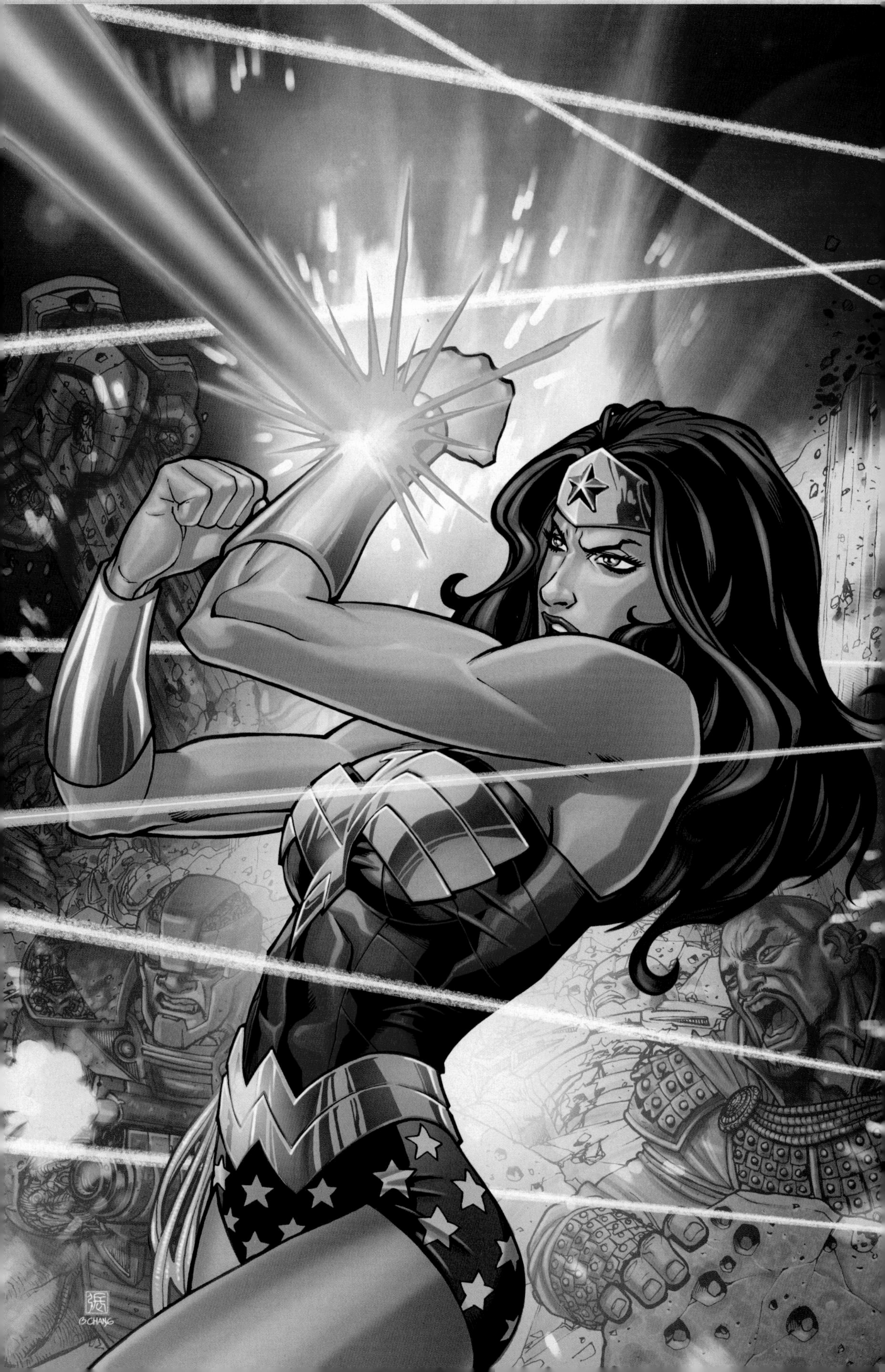

Art this issue by Bernard Chang & Jon Holdridge

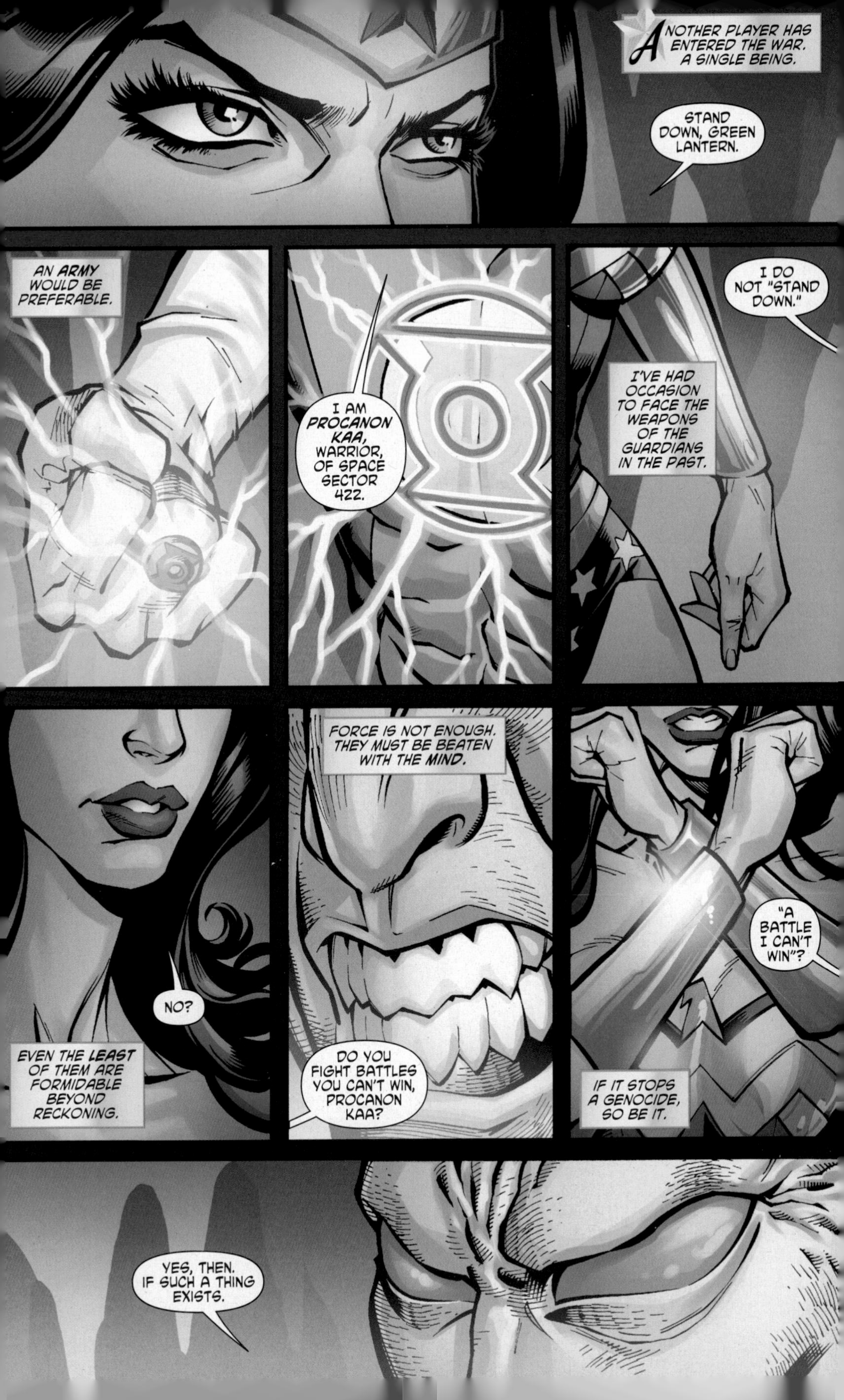
ANOTHER PLAYER HAS ENTERED THE WAR. A SINGLE BEING.
STAND DOWN, GREEN LANTERN.
AN ARMY WOULD BE PREFERABLE.
I AM PROCANON KAA, WARRIOR, OF SPACE SECTOR 422.
I DO NOT "STAND DOWN."
I'VE HAD OCCASION TO FACE THE WEAPONS OF THE GUARDIANS IN THE PAST.
NO?
EVEN THE LEAST OF THEM ARE FORMIDABLE BEYOND RECKONING.
FORCE IS NOT ENOUGH. THEY MUST BE BEATEN WITH THE MIND.
DO YOU FIGHT BATTLES YOU CAN'T WIN, PROCANON KAA?
"A BATTLE I CAN'T WIN"?
IF IT STOPS A GENOCIDE, SO BE IT.
YES, THEN. IF SUCH A THING EXISTS.

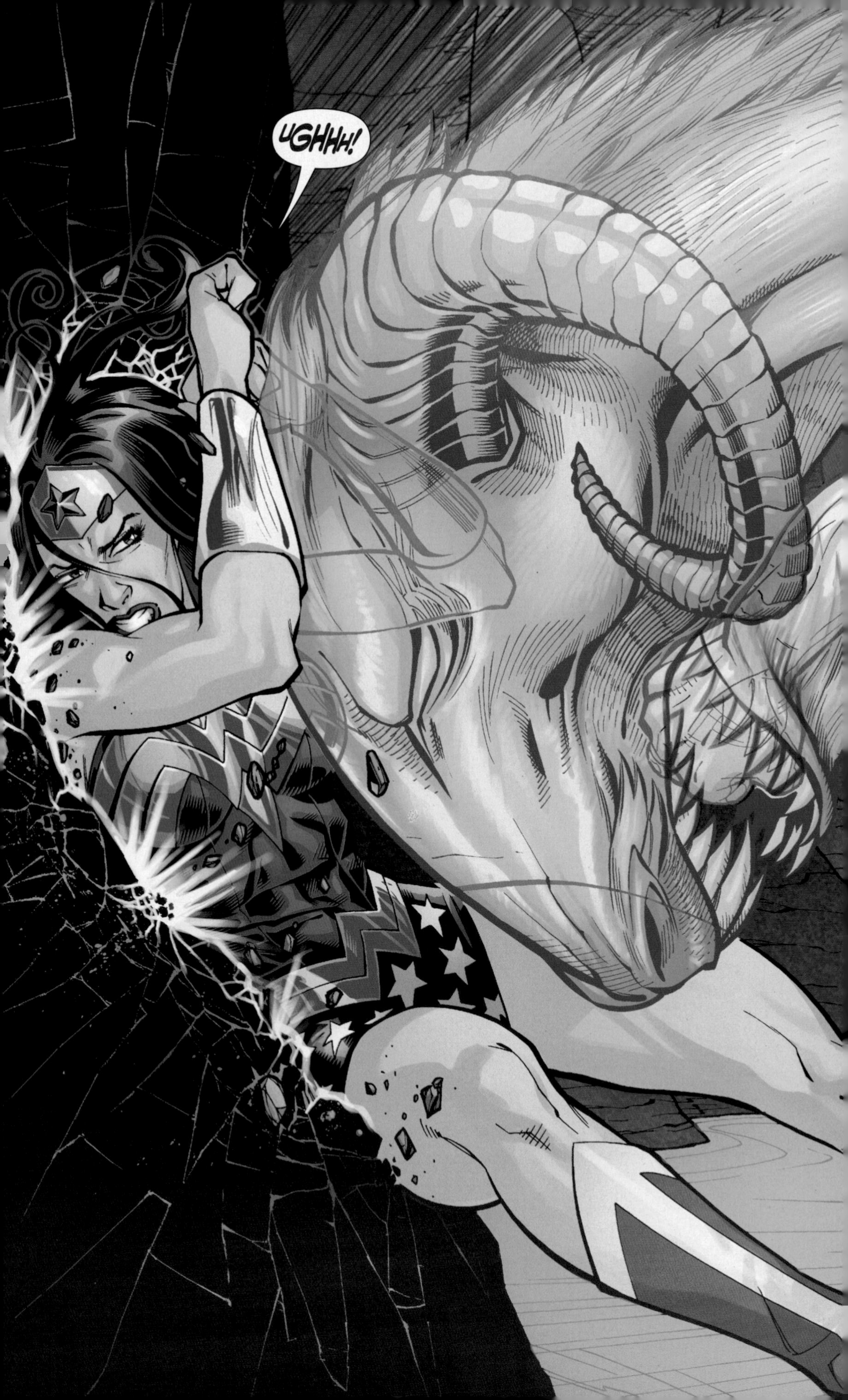
UGHHH!

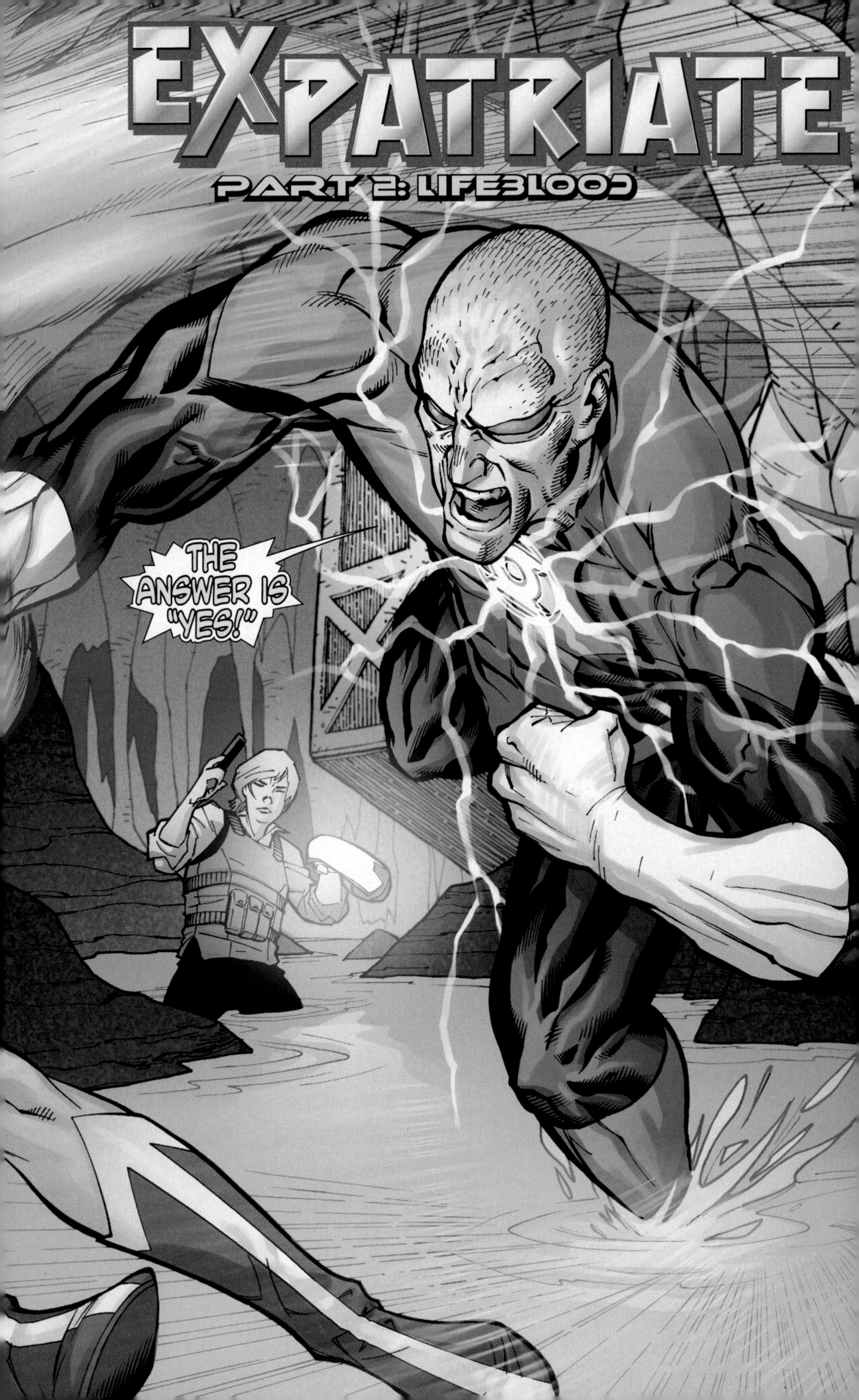
EXPATRIATE
PART 2: LIFEBLOOD
THE ANSWER IS "YES!"

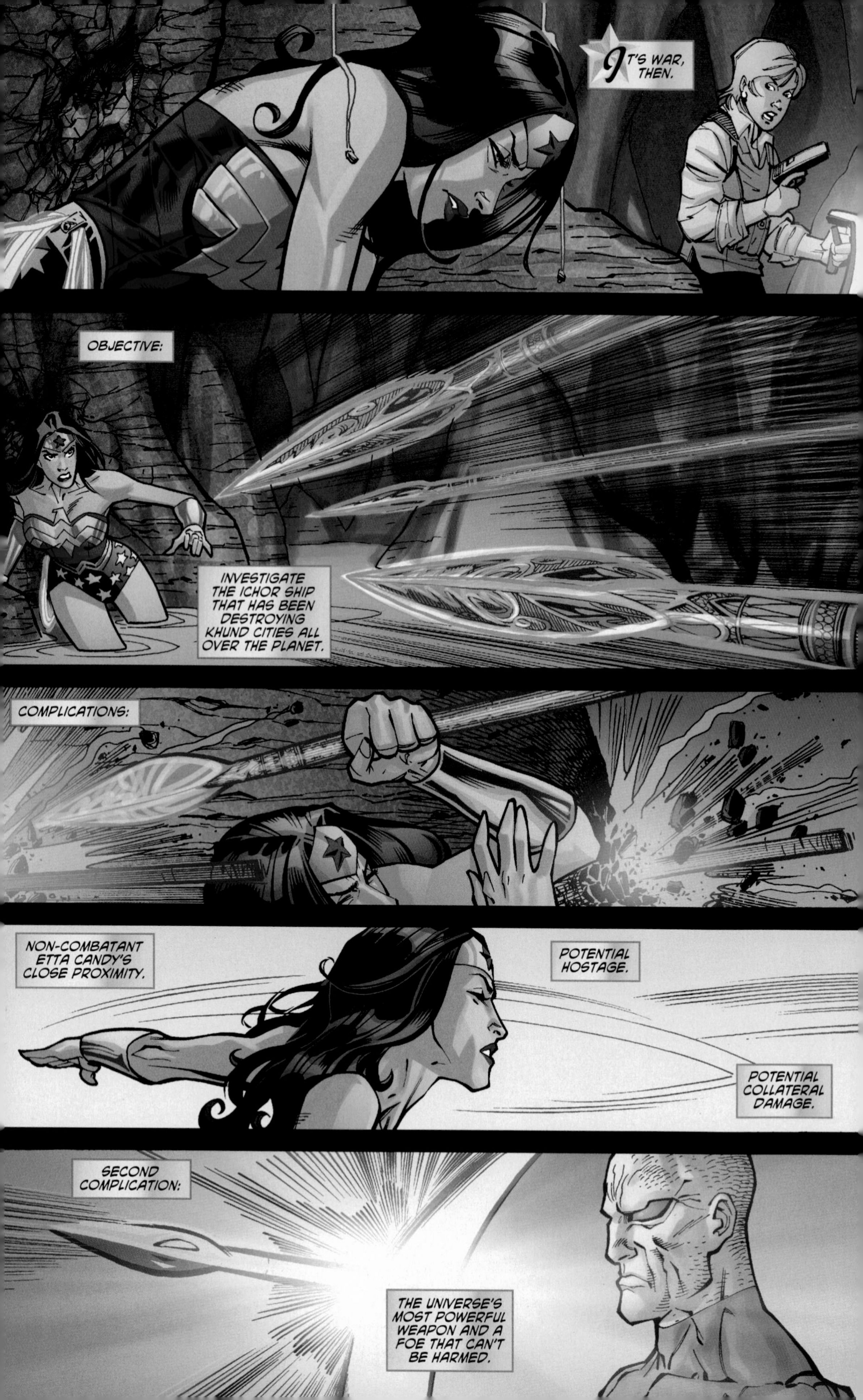
IT'S WAR, THEN.
OBJECTIVE:
INVESTIGATE THE ICHOR SHIP THAT HAS BEEN DESTROYING KHUND CITIES ALL OVER THE PLANET.
COMPLICATIONS:
NON-COMBATANT ETTA CANDY'S CLOSE PROXIMITY.
POTENTIAL HOSTAGE.
POTENTIAL COLLATERAL DAMAGE.
SECOND COMPLICATION:
THE UNIVERSE'S MOST POWERFUL WEAPON AND A FOE THAT CAN'T BE HARMED.

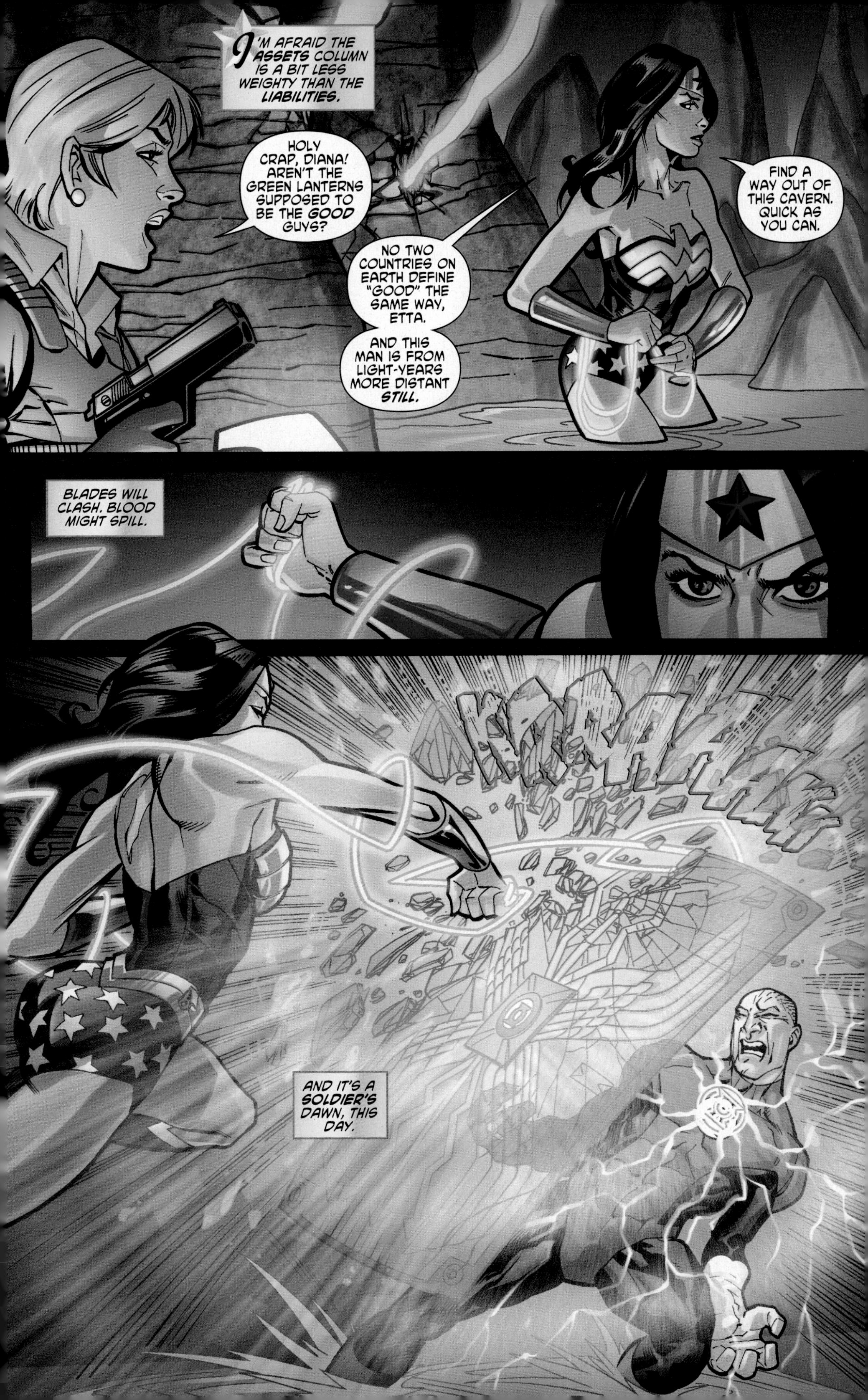
I'M AFRAID THE ASSETS COLUMN IS A BIT LESS WEIGHTY THAN THE LIABILITIES.
HOLY CRAP, DIANA! AREN'T THE GREEN LANTERNS SUPPOSED TO BE THE GOOD GUYS?
NO TWO COUNTRIES ON EARTH DEFINE "GOOD" THE SAME WAY, ETTA.
AND THIS MAN IS FROM LIGHT-YEARS MORE DISTANT STILL.
FIND A WAY OUT OF THIS CAVERN. QUICK AS YOU CAN.
BLADES WILL CLASH. BLOOD MIGHT SPILL.
AND IT'S A SOLDIER'S DAWN, THIS DAY.

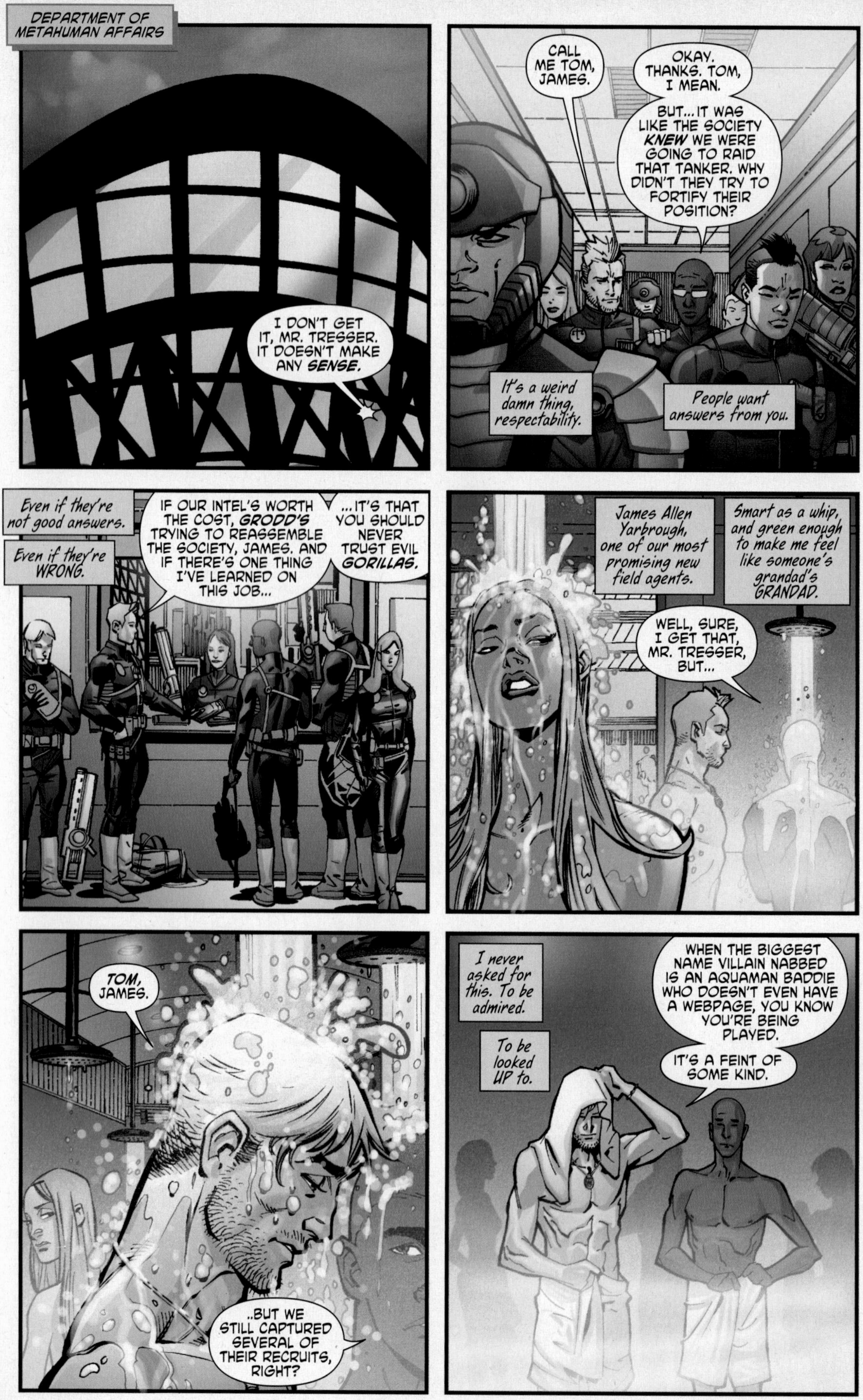

DEPARTMENT OF METAHUMAN AFFAIRS
I DON'T GET IT, MR. TRESSER. IT DOESN'T MAKE ANY SENSE.
CALL ME TOM, JAMES.
OKAY. THANKS. TOM, I MEAN.
BUT... IT WAS LIKE THE SOCIETY KNEW WE WERE GOING TO RAID THAT TANKER. WHY DIDN'T THEY TRY TO FORTIFY THEIR POSITION?
It's a weird damn thing, respectability.
People want answers from you.
Even if they're not good answers.
Even if they're WRONG.
IF OUR INTEL'S WORTH THE COST, GRODD'S TRYING TO REASSEMBLE THE SOCIETY, JAMES. AND IF THERE'S ONE THING I'VE LEARNED ON THIS JOB...
...IT'S THAT YOU SHOULD NEVER TRUST EVIL GORILLAS.
James Allen Yarbrough, one of our most promising new field agents.
Smart as a whip, and green enough to make me feel like someone's grandad's GRANDAD.
WELL, SURE, I GET THAT, MR. TRESSER, BUT...
TOM, JAMES.
..BUT WE STILL CAPTURED SEVERAL OF THEIR RECRUITS, RIGHT?
I never asked for this. To be admired.
To be looked UP to.
WHEN THE BIGGEST NAME VILLAIN NABBED IS AN AQUAMAN BADDIE WHO DOESN'T EVEN HAVE A WEBPAGE, YOU KNOW YOU'RE BEING PLAYED.
IT'S A FEINT OF SOME KIND.

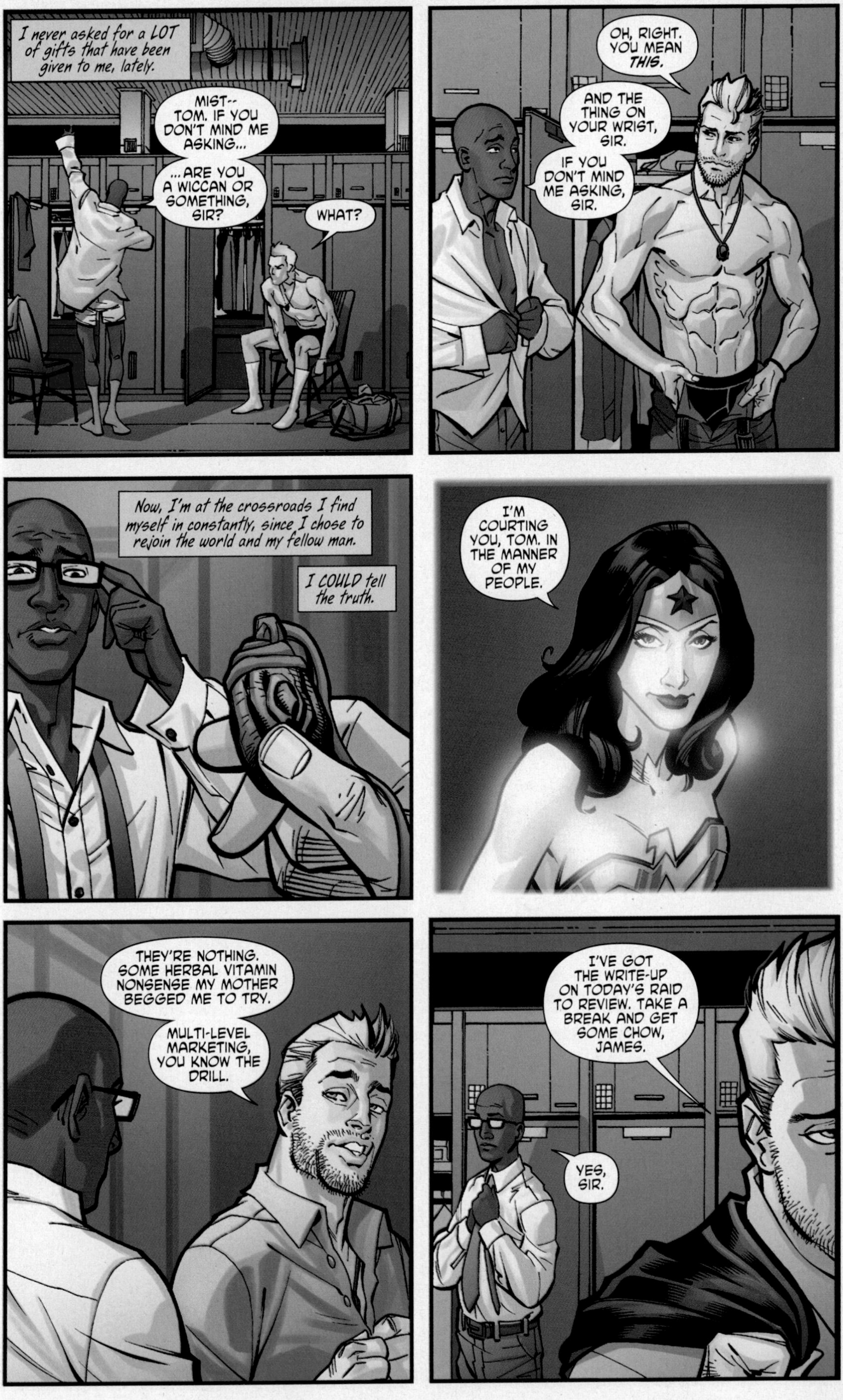
I never asked for a LOT of gifts that have been given to me, lately.
MIST-- TOM. IF YOU DON'T MIND ME ASKING...
...ARE YOU A WICCAN OR SOMETHING, SIR?
WHAT?
OH, RIGHT. YOU MEAN THIS.
AND THE THING ON YOUR WRIST, SIR.
IF YOU DON'T MIND ME ASKING, SIR.
Now, I'm at the crossroads I find myself in constantly, since I chose to rejoin the world and my fellow man.
I COULD tell the truth.
I'M COURTING YOU, TOM. IN THE MANNER OF MY PEOPLE.
THEY'RE NOTHING. SOME HERBAL VITAMIN NONSENSE MY MOTHER BEGGED ME TO TRY.
MULTI-LEVEL MARKETING, YOU KNOW THE DRILL.
I'VE GOT THE WRITE-UP ON TODAY'S RAID TO REVIEW. TAKE A BREAK AND GET SOME CHOW, JAMES.
YES, SIR.

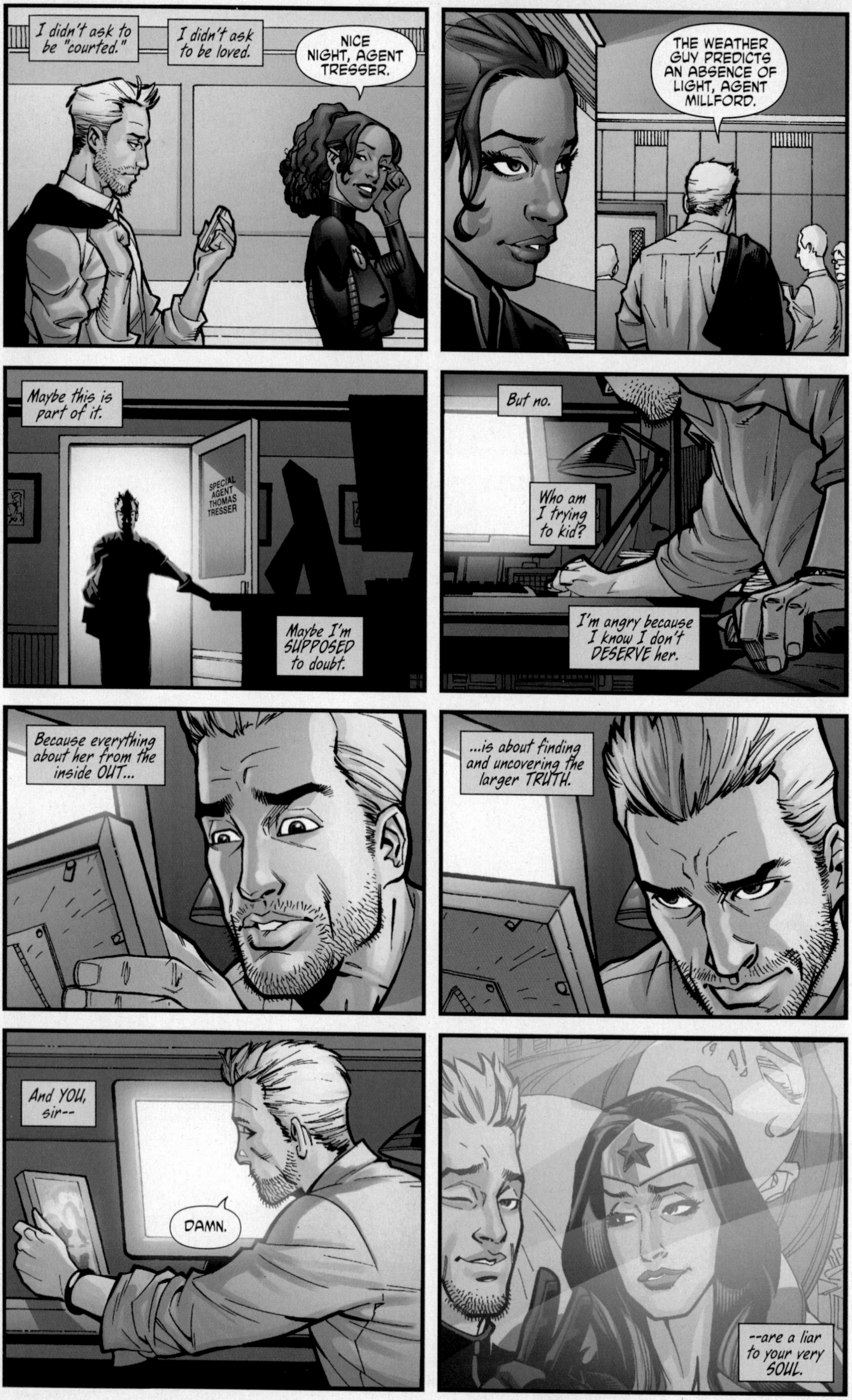
I didn't ask to be "courted."
I didn't ask to be loved.
NICE NIGHT, AGENT TRESSER.
THE WEATHER GUY PREDICTS AN ABSENCE OF LIGHT, AGENT MILLFORD.
Maybe this is part of it.
SPECIAL AGENT THOMAS TRESSER
Maybe I'm SUPPOSED to doubt.
But no.
Who am I trying to kid?
I'm angry because I know I don't DESERVE her.
Because everything about her from the inside OUT...
...is about finding and uncovering the larger TRUTH.
And YOU, sir--
DAMN.
--are a liar to your very SOUL.

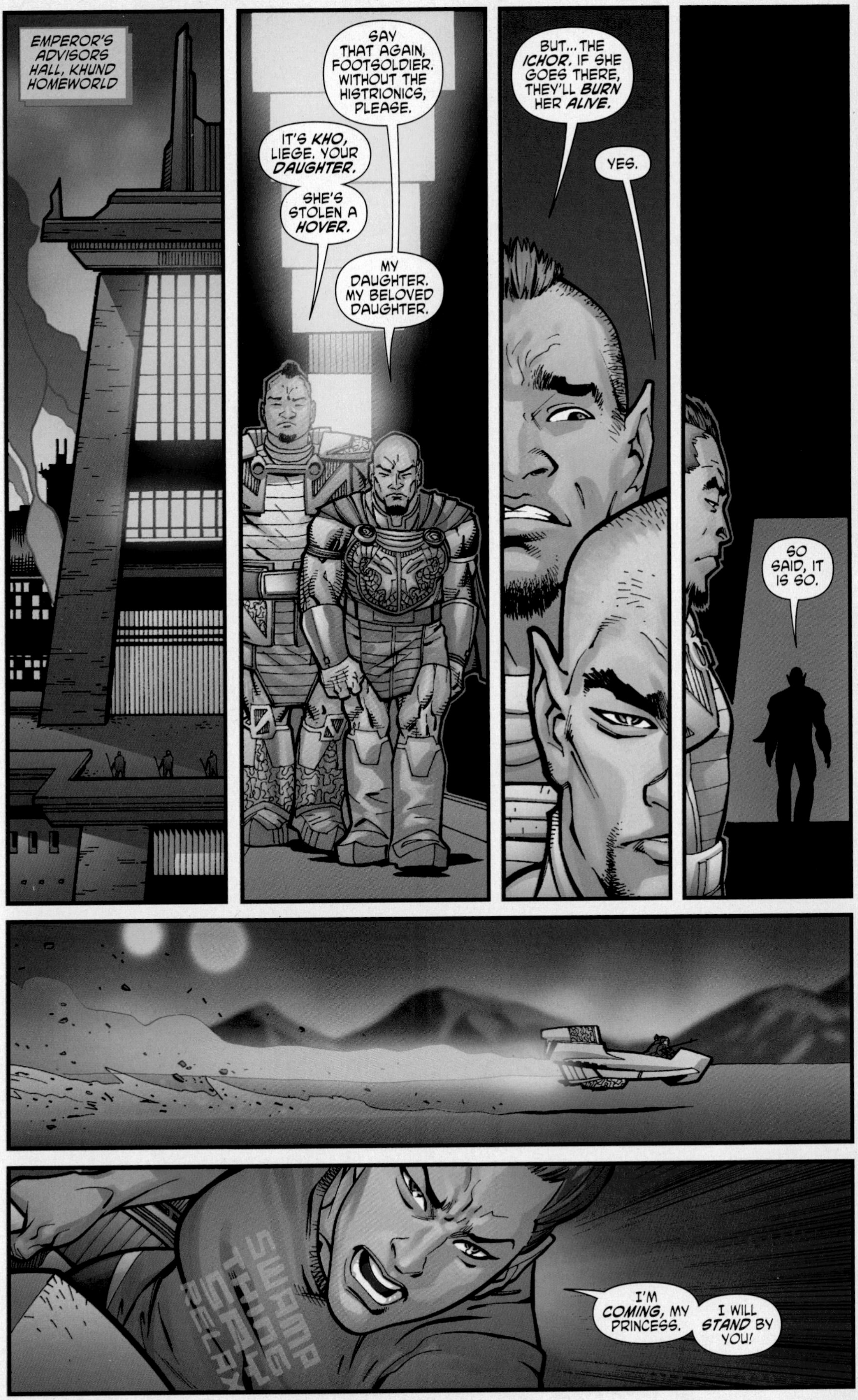
EMPEROR'S ADVISORS HALL, KHUND HOMEWORLD
SAY THAT AGAIN, FOOTSOLDIER. WITHOUT THE HISTRIONICS, PLEASE.
IT'S KHO, LIEGE. YOUR DAUGHTER.
SHE'S STOLEN A HOVER.
MY DAUGHTER. MY BELOVED DAUGHTER.
BUT... THE ICHOR. IF SHE GOES THERE, THEY'LL BURN HER ALIVE.
YES.
SO SAID, IT IS SO.
I'M COMING, MY PRINCESS.
I WILL STAND BY YOU!

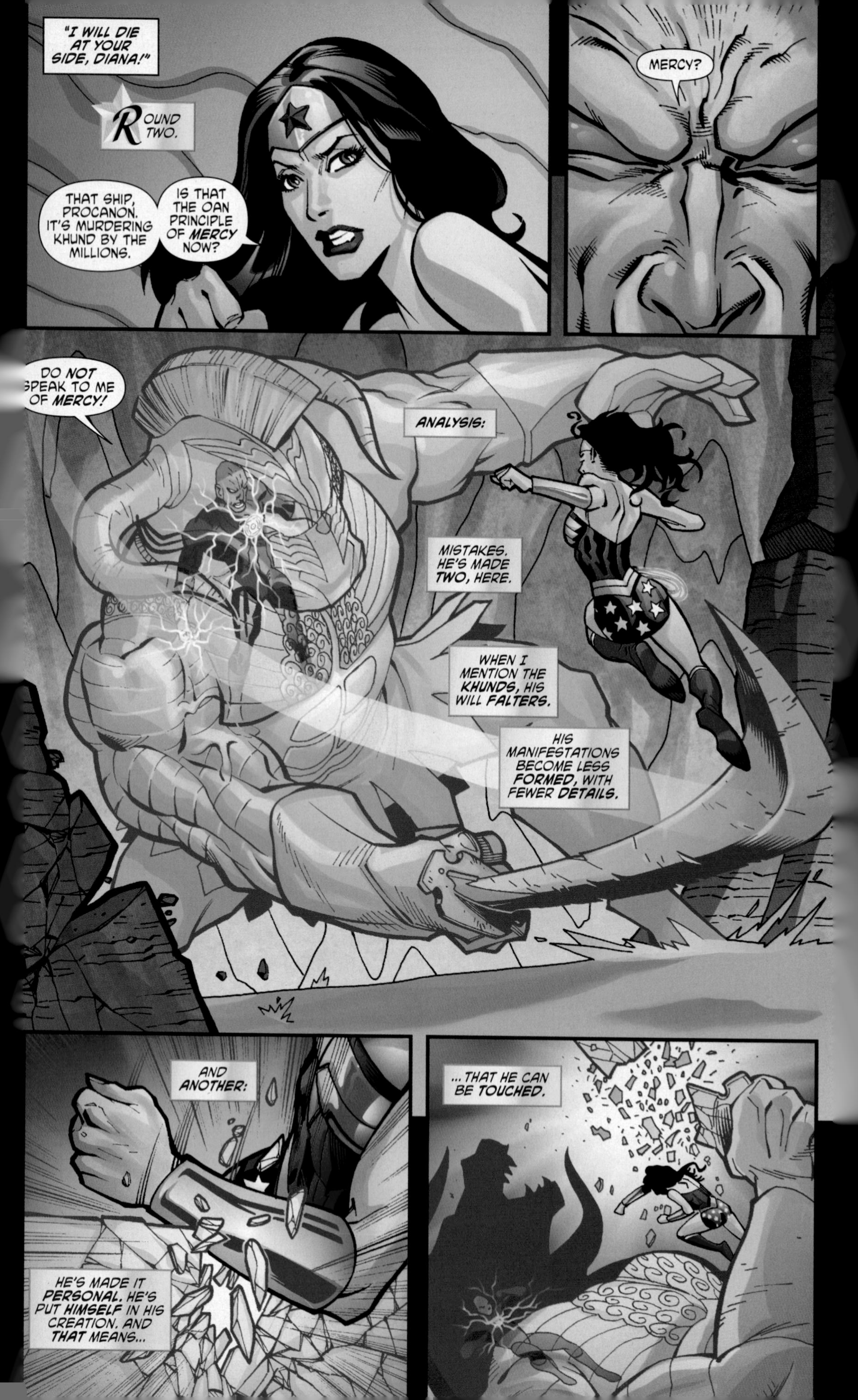
"I WILL DIE AT YOUR SIDE, DIANA!"
ROUND TWO.
THAT SHIP, PROCANON. IT'S MURDERING KHUND BY THE MILLIONS.
IS THAT THE OAN PRINCIPLE OF MERCY NOW?
MERCY?
DO NOT SPEAK TO ME OF MERCY!
ANALYSIS:
MISTAKES. HE'S MADE TWO, HERE.
WHEN I MENTION THE KHUNDS, HIS WILL FALTERS.
HIS MANIFESTATIONS BECOME LESS FORMED, WITH FEWER DETAILS.
AND ANOTHER:
HE'S MADE IT PERSONAL. HE'S PUT HIMSELF IN HIS CREATION. AND THAT MEANS...
...THAT HE CAN BE TOUCHED.

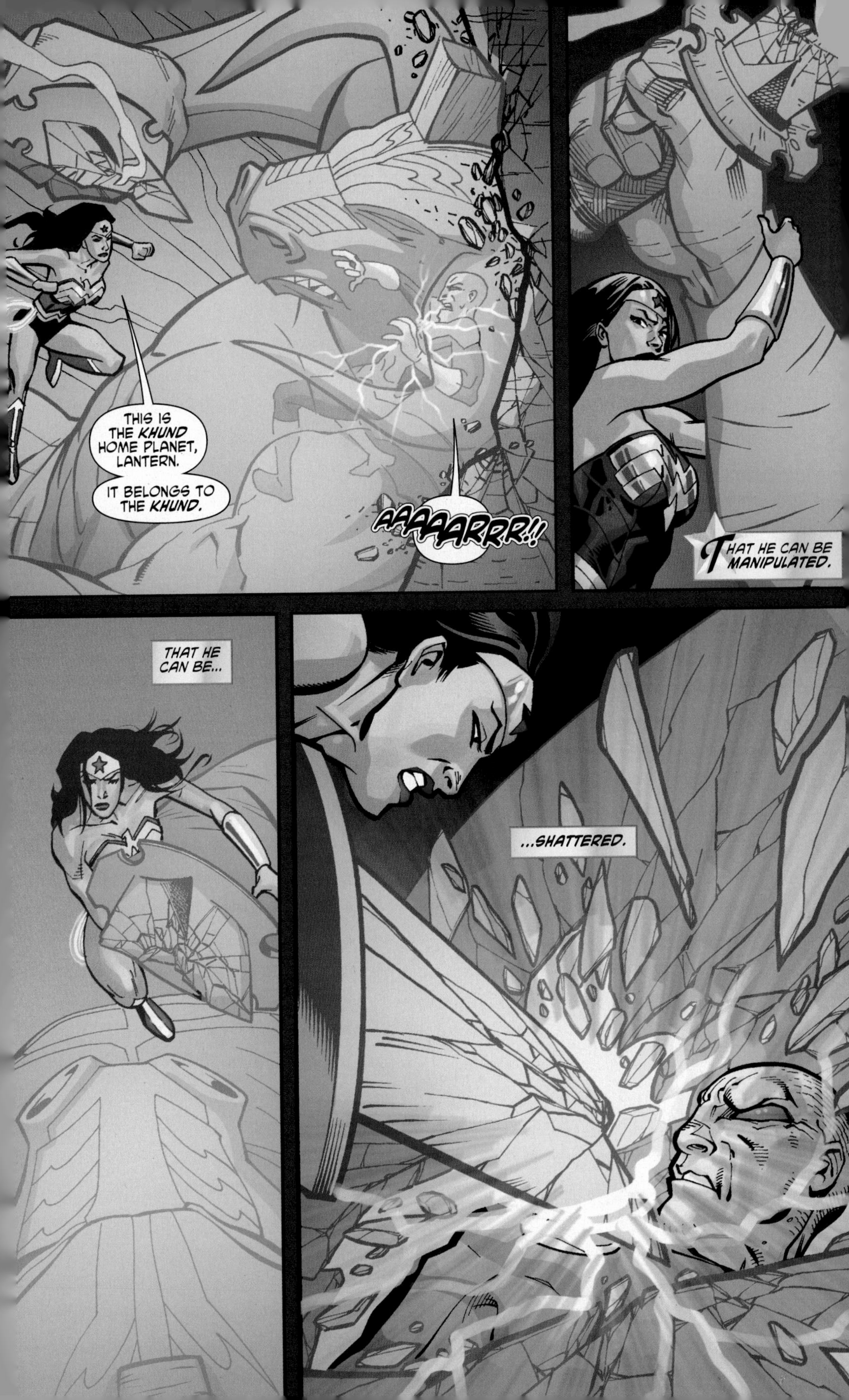

THIS IS THE KHUND HOME PLANET, LANTERN.
IT BELONGS TO THE KHUND.
AAAAARRR!!
THAT HE CAN BE MANIPULATED.
THAT HE CAN BE...
...SHATTERED.

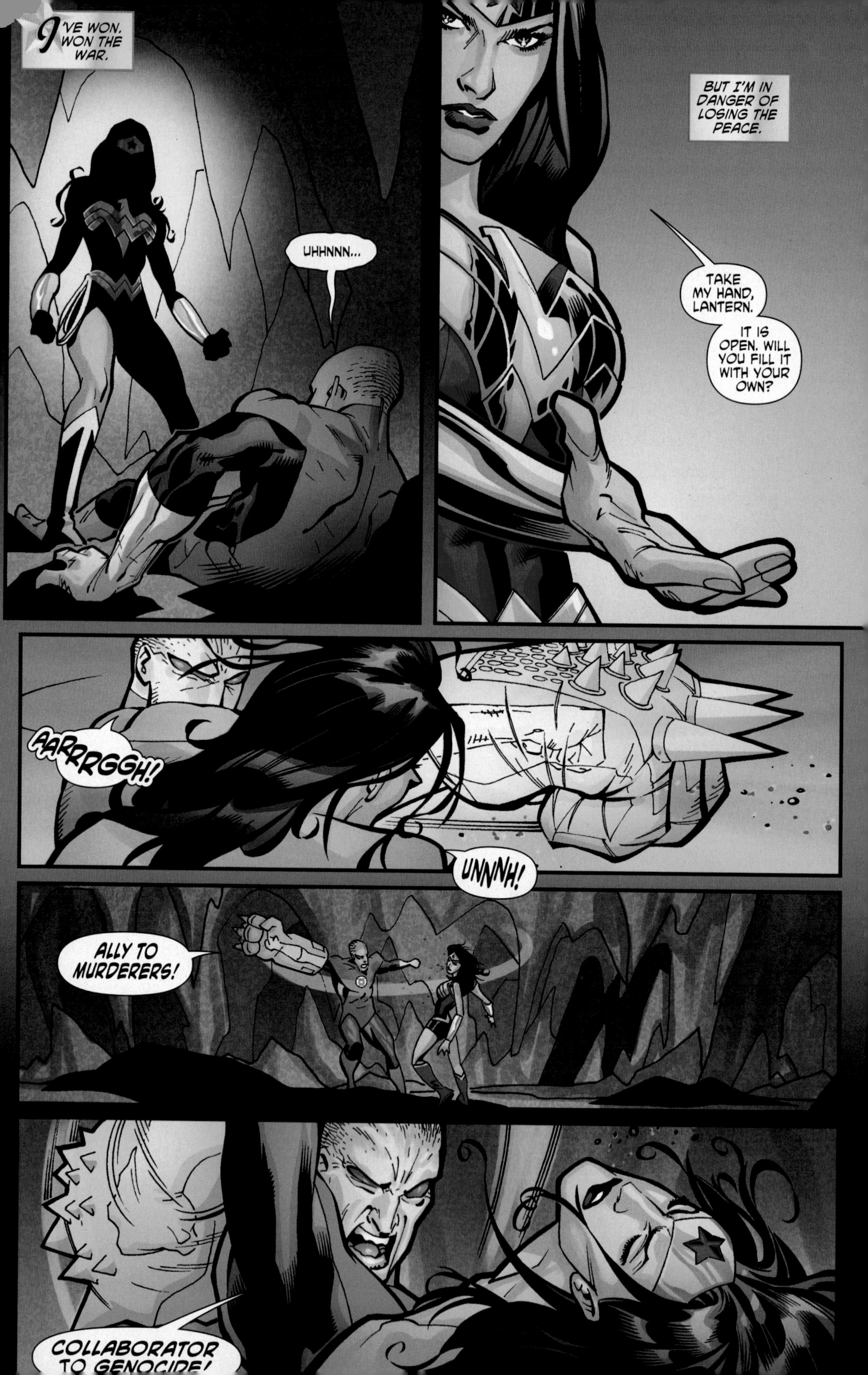
I'VE WON. WON THE WAR.
UHHNNN...
BUT I'M IN DANGER OF LOSING THE PEACE.
TAKE MY HAND, LANTERN.
IT IS OPEN. WILL YOU FILL IT WITH YOUR OWN?
AARRRGGH!
UNNNH!
ALLY TO MURDERERS!
COLLABORATOR TO GENOCIDE!

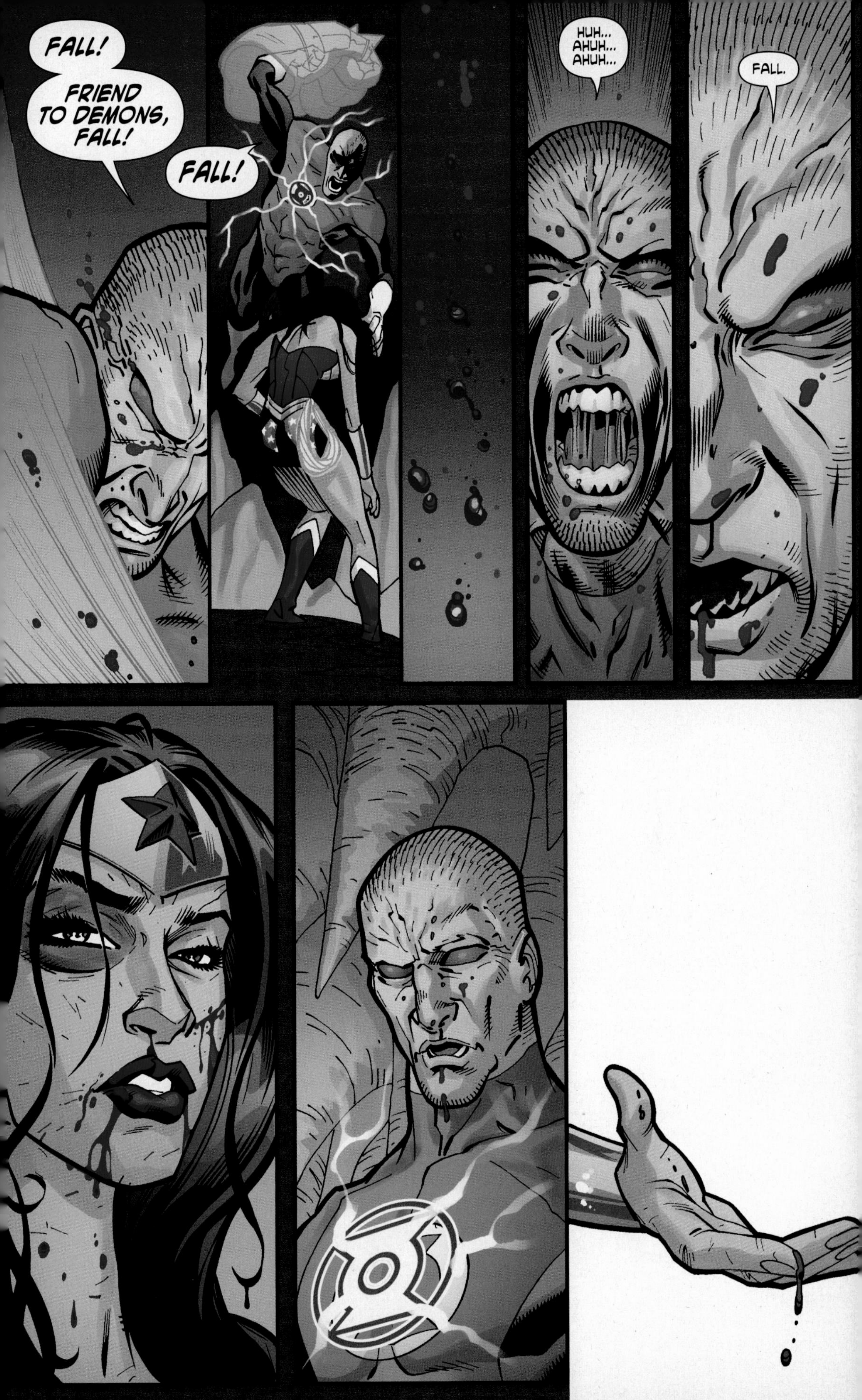
FALL!
FRIEND TO DEMONS, FALL!
FALL!
HUH... AHUH... AHUH...
FALL.

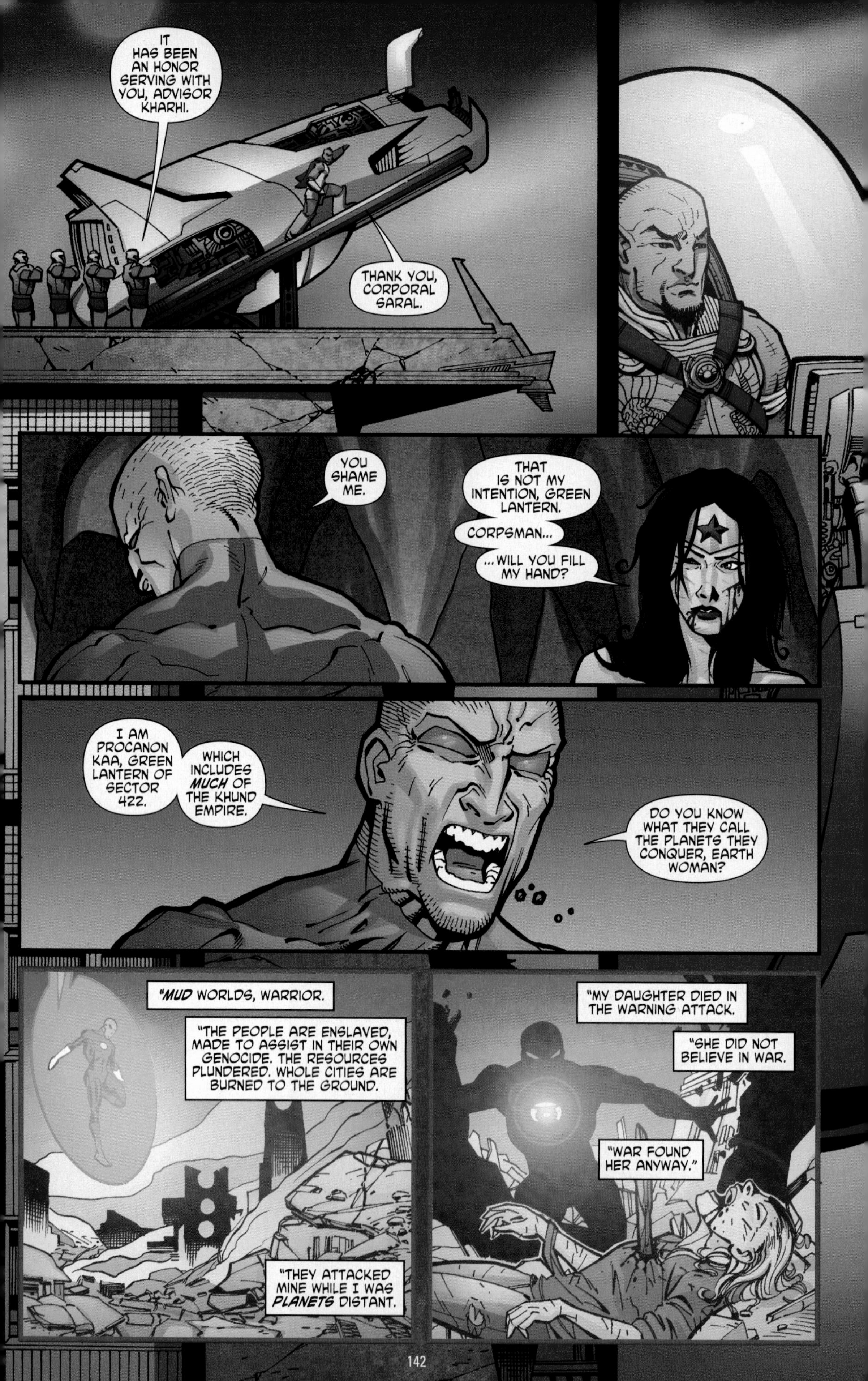

IT HAS BEEN AN HONOR SERVING WITH YOU, ADVISOR KHARHI.
THANK YOU, CORPORAL SARAL.
YOU SHAME ME.
THAT IS NOT MY INTENTION, GREEN LANTERN.
CORPSMAN...
...WILL YOU FILL MY HAND?
I AM PROCANON KAA, GREEN LANTERN OF SECTOR 422.
WHICH INCLUDES *MUCH* OF THE KHUND EMPIRE.
DO YOU KNOW WHAT THEY CALL THE PLANETS THEY CONQUER, EARTH WOMAN?
"*MUD* WORLDS, WARRIOR.
"THE PEOPLE ARE ENSLAVED, MADE TO ASSIST IN THEIR OWN GENOCIDE. THE RESOURCES PLUNDERED. WHOLE CITIES ARE BURNED TO THE GROUND.
"THEY ATTACKED MINE WHILE I WAS *PLANETS* DISTANT.
"MY DAUGHTER DIED IN THE WARNING ATTACK.
"SHE DID NOT BELIEVE IN WAR.
"WAR FOUND HER ANYWAY."

"THE GREEN LANTERNS BELIEVE IN JUSTICE."

"BUT I AM UNCERTAIN IF *I* SHARE THAT BELIEF, STILL."

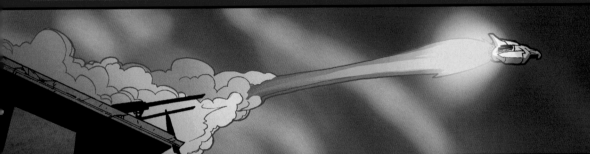

I'M SORRY FOR YOUR LOSS, MY FRIEND.

BUT IF LOSS MAKES YOU DOUBT YOUR BELIEF IN JUSTICE...

...THEN YOU NEVER *TRULY* BELIEVED IN JUSTICE AT ALL.

THE ICHOR. I'M NOT CERTAIN THAT ALL THE GREEN LANTERNS COMBINED CAN CHANGE THEIR MINDS. THEIR POWER IS UNIMAGINABLE.

IT'S SAID THAT THEY ARE BLOOD RELATIVES OF THE GODS OF A HUNDRED DIFFERENT WORLDS.

IF THEY JUDGE THE KHUND RACE DESERVING OF EXTINCTION--

--THEN THEY ARE WRONG. AND I WILL FIGHT THEM.

YOU'D LOSE, WARRIOR. YOU'D DIE IN AN INSTANT.

THAT IS NOT GERMANE TO THIS DISCUSSION.

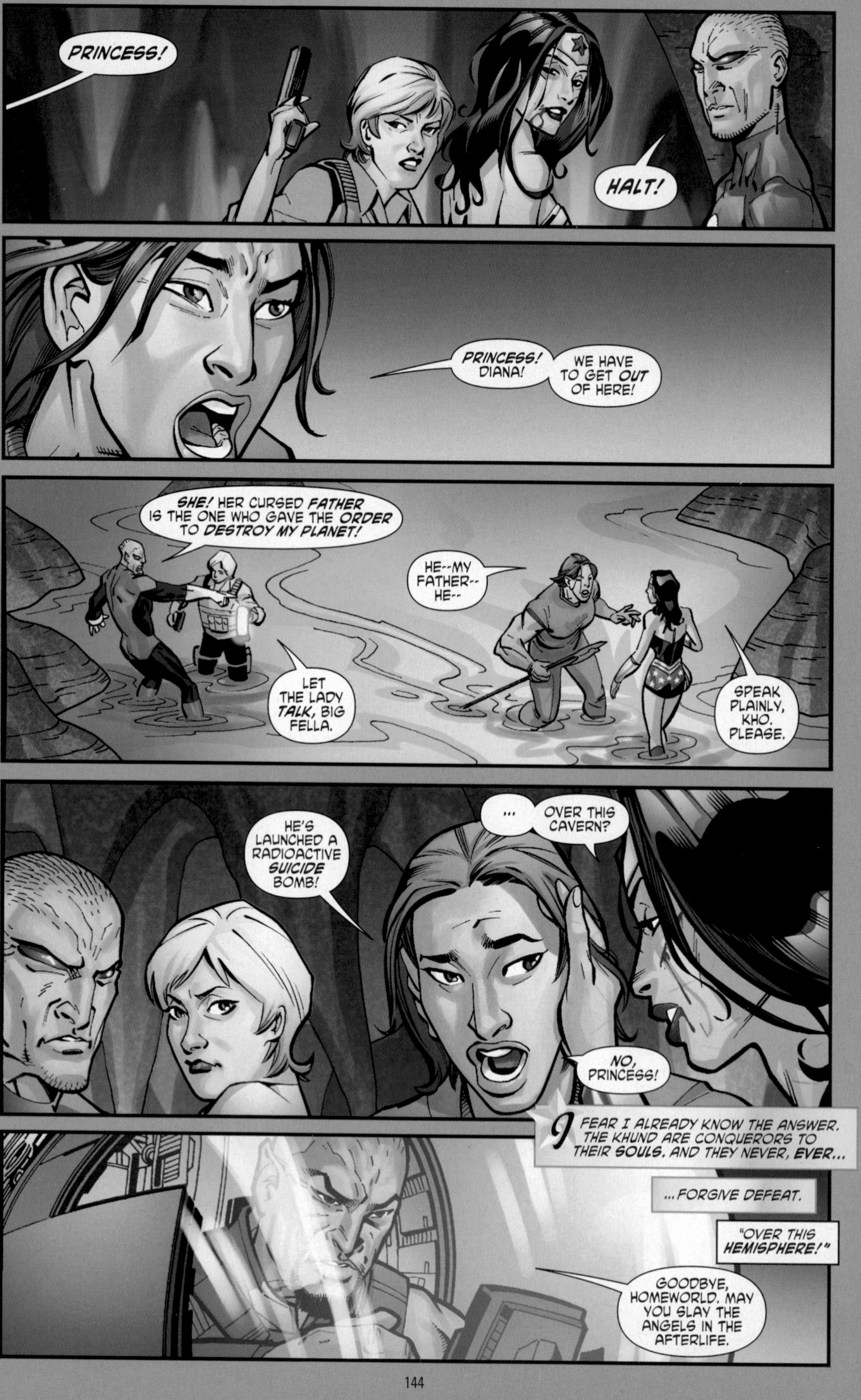
PRINCESS!
HALT!
PRINCESS! DIANA!
WE HAVE TO GET OUT OF HERE!
SHE! HER CURSED FATHER IS THE ONE WHO GAVE THE ORDER TO DESTROY MY PLANET!
LET THE LADY TALK, BIG FELLA.
HE--MY FATHER-- HE--
SPEAK PLAINLY, KHO. PLEASE.
HE'S LAUNCHED A RADIOACTIVE SUICIDE BOMB!
...
OVER THIS CAVERN?
NO, PRINCESS!
I FEAR I ALREADY KNOW THE ANSWER. THE KHUND ARE CONQUERORS TO THEIR SOULS. AND THEY NEVER, EVER...
...FORGIVE DEFEAT.
"OVER THIS HEMISPHERE!"
GOODBYE, HOMEWORLD. MAY YOU SLAY THE ANGELS IN THE AFTERLIFE.

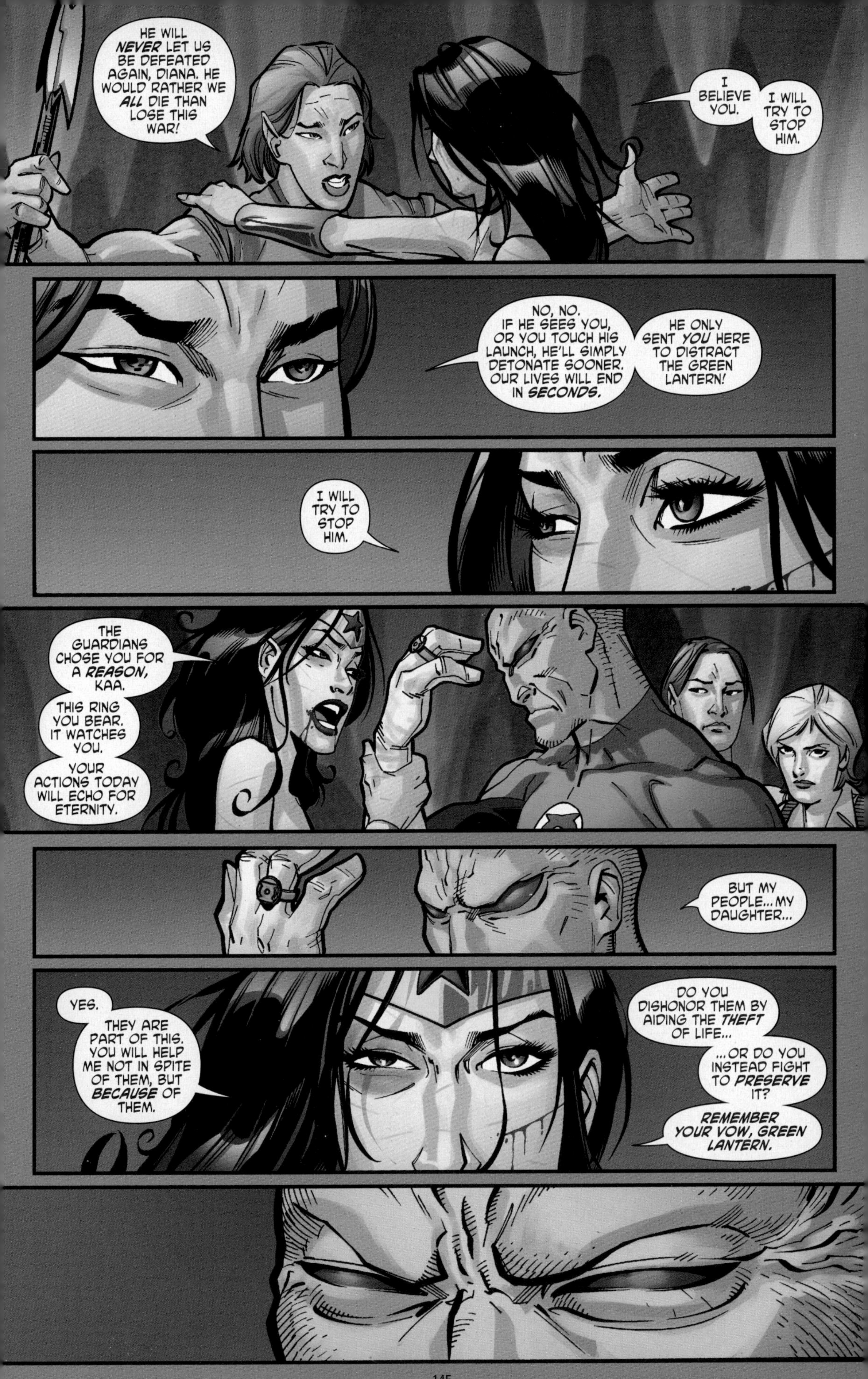

HE WILL NEVER LET US BE DEFEATED AGAIN, DIANA. HE WOULD RATHER WE ALL DIE THAN LOSE THIS WAR!
I BELIEVE YOU.
I WILL TRY TO STOP HIM.
NO, NO. IF HE SEES YOU, OR YOU TOUCH HIS LAUNCH, HE'LL SIMPLY DETONATE SOONER. OUR LIVES WILL END IN SECONDS.
HE ONLY SENT YOU HERE TO DISTRACT THE GREEN LANTERN!
I WILL TRY TO STOP HIM.
THE GUARDIANS CHOSE YOU FOR A REASON, KAA.
THIS RING YOU BEAR. IT WATCHES YOU.
YOUR ACTIONS TODAY WILL ECHO FOR ETERNITY.
BUT MY PEOPLE...MY DAUGHTER...
YES.
THEY ARE PART OF THIS. YOU WILL HELP ME NOT IN SPITE OF THEM, BUT BECAUSE OF THEM.
DO YOU DISHONOR THEM BY AIDING THE THEFT OF LIFE...
...OR DO YOU INSTEAD FIGHT TO PRESERVE IT?
REMEMBER YOUR VOW, GREEN LANTERN.

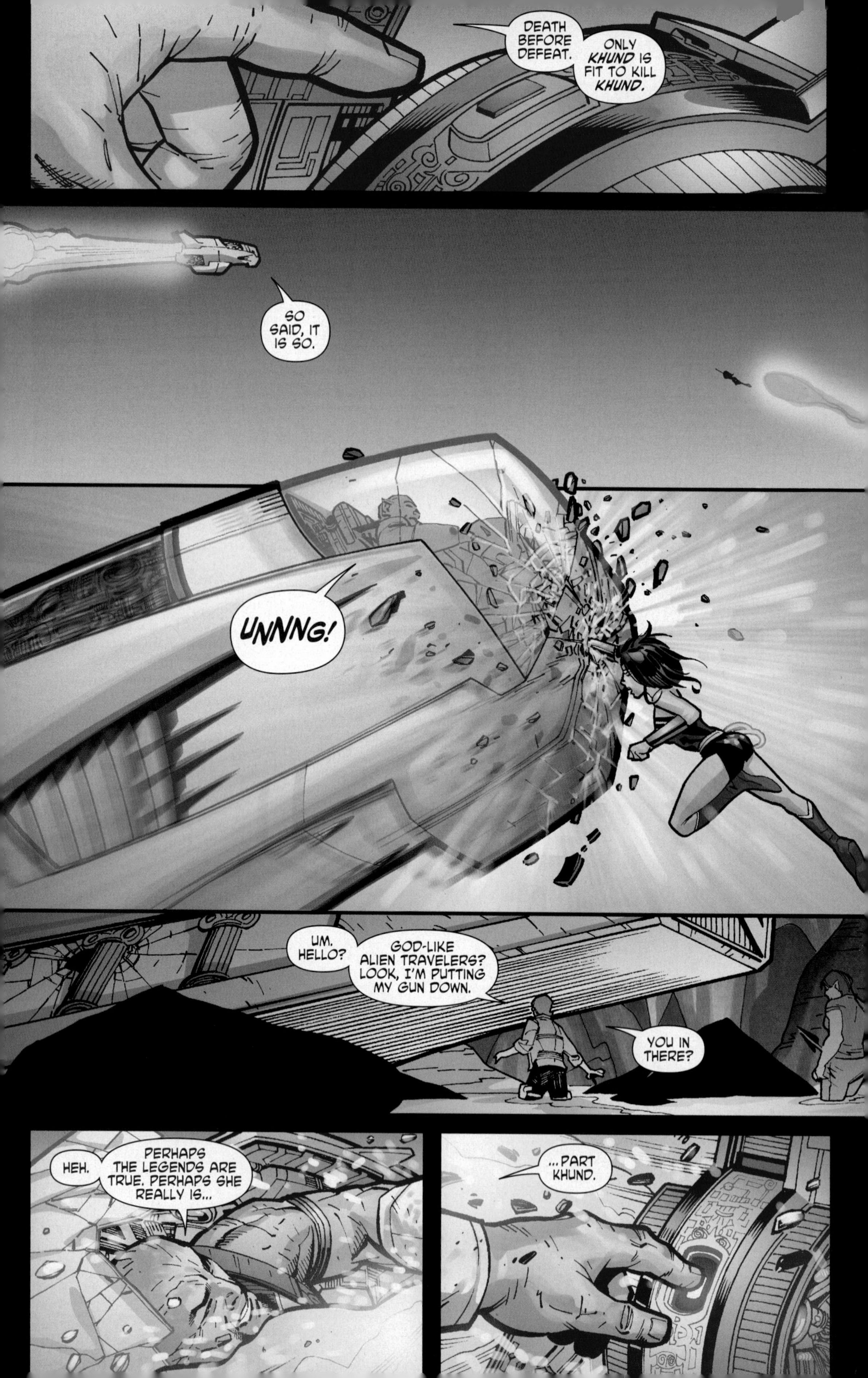
DEATH BEFORE DEFEAT.
ONLY KHUND IS FIT TO KILL KHUND.
SO SAID, IT IS SO.
UNNNG!
UM. HELLO?
GOD-LIKE ALIEN TRAVELERS? LOOK, I'M PUTTING MY GUN DOWN.
YOU IN THERE?
HEH.
PERHAPS THE LEGENDS ARE TRUE. PERHAPS SHE REALLY IS...
...PART KHUND.

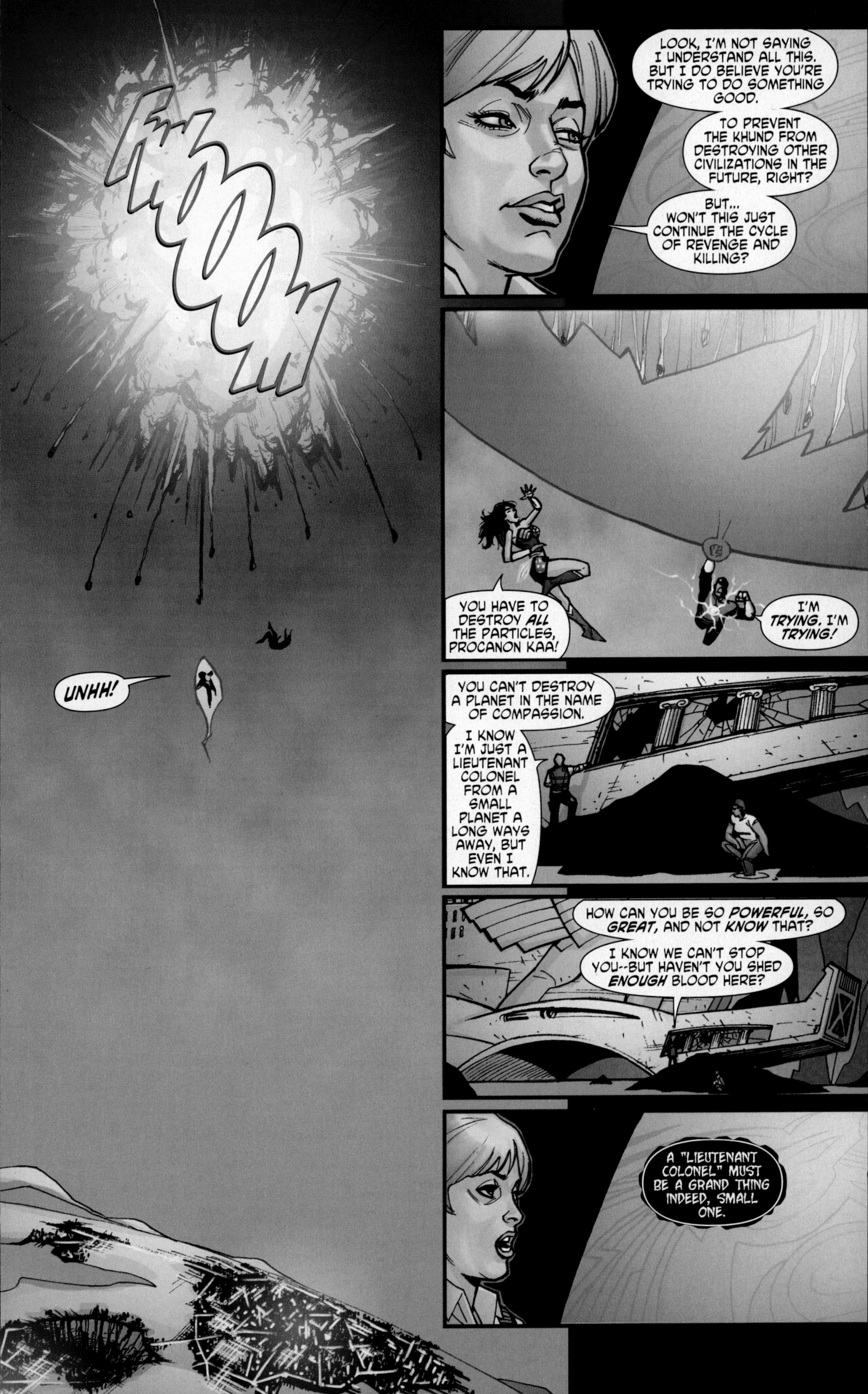
FZOOOM
UNHH!
LOOK, I'M NOT SAYING I UNDERSTAND ALL THIS. BUT I DO BELIEVE YOU'RE TRYING TO DO SOMETHING GOOD.
TO PREVENT THE KHUND FROM DESTROYING OTHER CIVILIZATIONS IN THE FUTURE, RIGHT?
BUT... WON'T THIS JUST CONTINUE THE CYCLE OF REVENGE AND KILLING?
YOU HAVE TO DESTROY *ALL* THE PARTICLES, PROCANON KAA!
I'M *TRYING*. I'M *TRYING!*
YOU CAN'T DESTROY A PLANET IN THE NAME OF COMPASSION.
I KNOW I'M JUST A LIEUTENANT COLONEL FROM A SMALL PLANET A LONG WAYS AWAY, BUT EVEN I KNOW THAT.
HOW CAN YOU BE SO *POWERFUL*, SO *GREAT*, AND NOT *KNOW* THAT?
I KNOW WE CAN'T STOP YOU--BUT HAVEN'T YOU SHED *ENOUGH* BLOOD HERE?
A "LIEUTENANT COLONEL" MUST BE A GRAND THING INDEED, SMALL ONE.

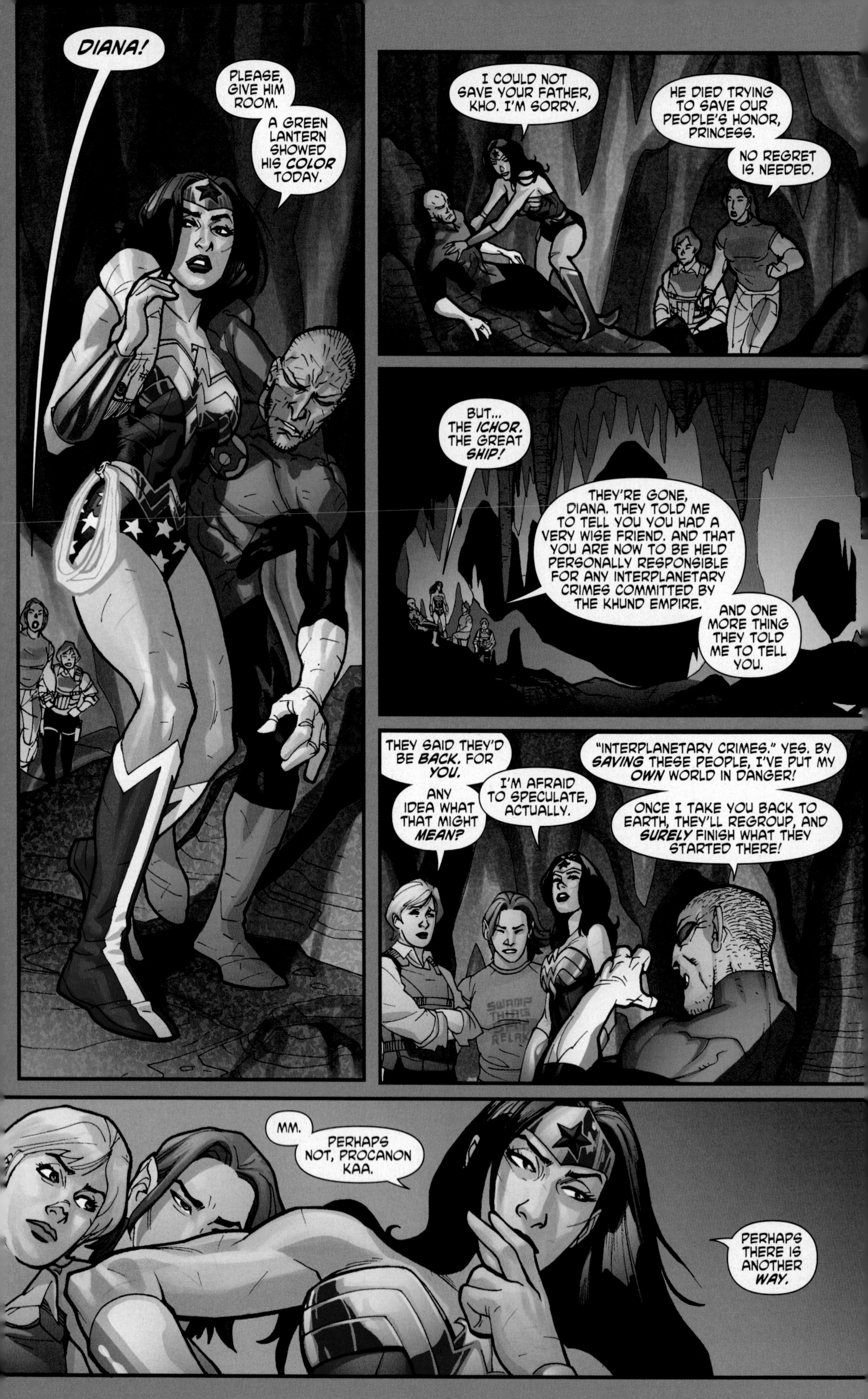
DIANA!
PLEASE, GIVE HIM ROOM.
A GREEN LANTERN SHOWED HIS COLOR TODAY.
I COULD NOT SAVE YOUR FATHER, KHO. I'M SORRY.
HE DIED TRYING TO SAVE OUR PEOPLE'S HONOR, PRINCESS.
NO REGRET IS NEEDED.
BUT... THE ICHOR. THE GREAT SHIP!
THEY'RE GONE, DIANA. THEY TOLD ME TO TELL YOU YOU HAD A VERY WISE FRIEND. AND THAT YOU ARE NOW TO BE HELD PERSONALLY RESPONSIBLE FOR ANY INTERPLANETARY CRIMES COMMITTED BY THE KHUND EMPIRE.
AND ONE MORE THING THEY TOLD ME TO TELL YOU.
THEY SAID THEY'D BE BACK. FOR YOU.
ANY IDEA WHAT THAT MIGHT MEAN?
I'M AFRAID TO SPECULATE, ACTUALLY.
"INTERPLANETARY CRIMES." YES. BY SAVING THESE PEOPLE, I'VE PUT MY OWN WORLD IN DANGER!
ONCE I TAKE YOU BACK TO EARTH, THEY'LL REGROUP, AND SURELY FINISH WHAT THEY STARTED THERE!
SWAMP THING RELAX
MM.
PERHAPS NOT, PROCANON KAA.
PERHAPS THERE IS ANOTHER WAY.

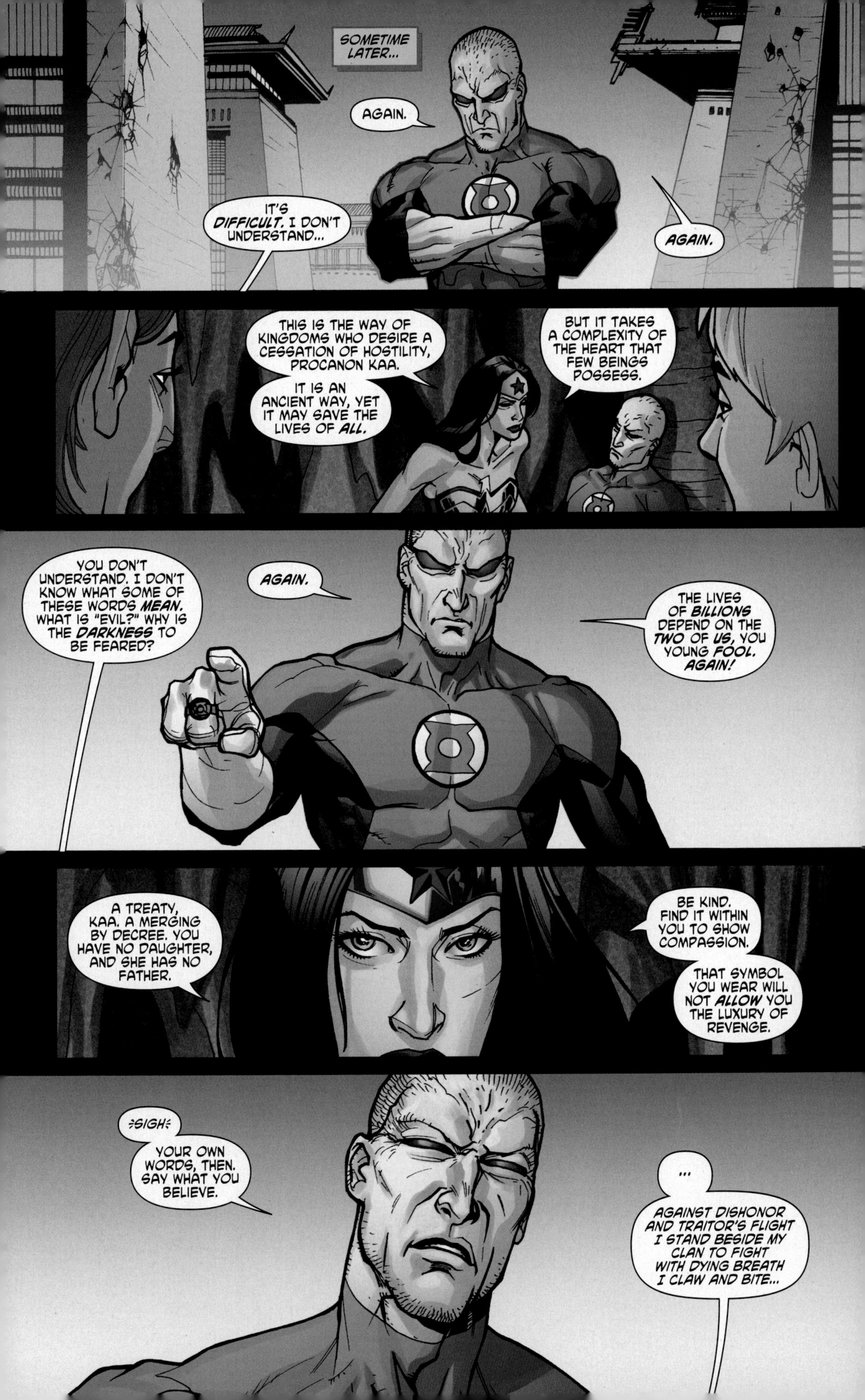

SOMETIME LATER...
AGAIN.
IT'S DIFFICULT. I DON'T UNDERSTAND...
AGAIN.
THIS IS THE WAY OF KINGDOMS WHO DESIRE A CESSATION OF HOSTILITY, PROCANON KAA.
IT IS AN ANCIENT WAY, YET IT MAY SAVE THE LIVES OF ALL.
BUT IT TAKES A COMPLEXITY OF THE HEART THAT FEW BEINGS POSSESS.
YOU DON'T UNDERSTAND. I DON'T KNOW WHAT SOME OF THESE WORDS MEAN. WHAT IS "EVIL?" WHY IS THE DARKNESS TO BE FEARED?
AGAIN.
THE LIVES OF BILLIONS DEPEND ON THE TWO OF US, YOU YOUNG FOOL. AGAIN!
A TREATY, KAA. A MERGING BY DECREE. YOU HAVE NO DAUGHTER, AND SHE HAS NO FATHER.
BE KIND. FIND IT WITHIN YOU TO SHOW COMPASSION.
THAT SYMBOL YOU WEAR WILL NOT ALLOW YOU THE LUXURY OF REVENGE.
SIGH
YOUR OWN WORDS, THEN. SAY WHAT YOU BELIEVE.
...
AGAINST DISHONOR AND TRAITOR'S FLIGHT I STAND BESIDE MY CLAN TO FIGHT WITH DYING BREATH I CLAW AND BITE...

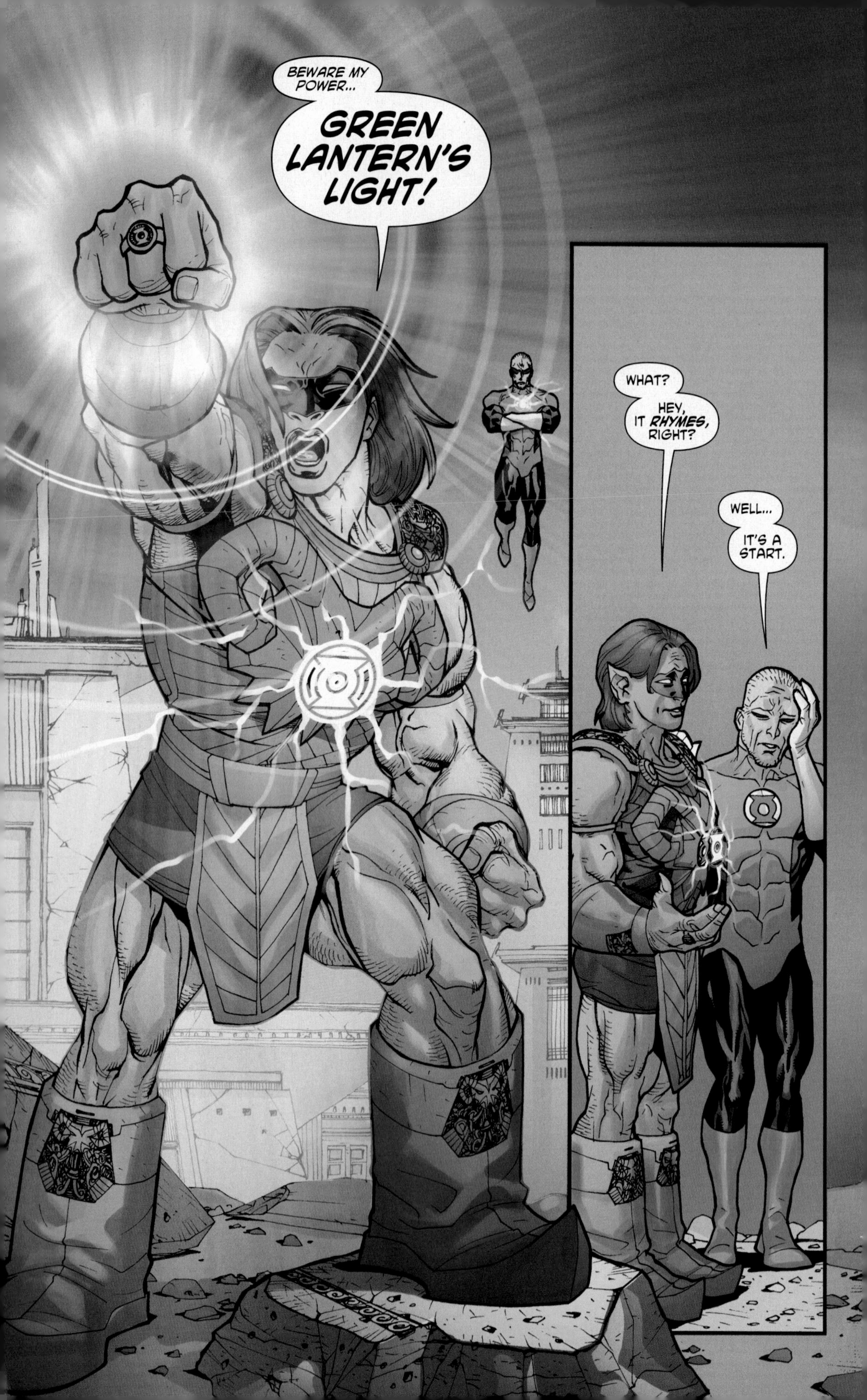
BEWARE MY POWER...
GREEN LANTERN'S LIGHT!
WHAT?
HEY, IT RHYMES, RIGHT?
WELL...
IT'S A START.